Fannie Barrier Williams

THE NEW BLACK STUDIES SERIES

Edited by Darlene Clark Hine and Dwight A. McBride

A list of books in the series appears at the end of this book.

Fannie Barrier Williams

Crossing the Borders of Region and Race

WANDA A. HENDRICKS

University of Illinois Press

URBANA, CHICAGO, AND SPRINGFIELD

Library of Congress Control Number: 2013953993

Contents

Illustrations

Acknowledgments

I had no idea who Fannie Barrier Williams was until I began the research for my dissertation on black women in Illinois in the late nineteenth and early twentieth centuries at Purdue University more than two decades ago. Of all the women that I examined she intrigued me the most, in part because she was so unlike any other black woman in the state or, for that matter, the nation. Born at a time when the debate about slavery and race had grown more contentious and acrimonious, she was a northerner who grew up living an unencumbered insulated life, sharing both public and private spaces with whites. Fully integrated into her community of the small upstate village of Brockport, New York, she had never known the horrors of racism and discrimination that many of her southern female contemporaries endured. By the time that she was thirty-two years old, she had become a national traveler and a resident of multiple regions. Crossing regional borders helped her develop a keen insight into the distinctive differences and similarities between the North, South, and West/Midwest. As a mixed-race educated elitist she engaged in both a sophisticated black aristocratic community and a cross-racial black and white world that often blurred the entrenched segregated lines of Jim Crow. Activism in the budding women's club movement and religious affiliation with the Unitarians provided her segues to a prolific career as a reform activist and writer. She penned more than fifty articles and essays in many of the major periodicals of the period, delivered as many speeches to both black and white audiences, and was a major architect shaping black life during the Progressive Era. Yet for all of her success, scholars and the general public know little about her. To be sure, she has been recognized as one of the stalwarts of the women's club movement and has been quoted in all the major works on club women and black women, but in spite of her public celebrity Barrier Williams left few personal papers. The brief autobiographical sketch of her life that she wrote for the *Independent* in 1904 remains to date her only personal narrative. But the essay was broad and vague, omitting names and specific dates and providing few clues about how significant she was to the social, political, and economic transformation of the country.

It has taken me more than a decade to complete the research and writing of this book. Life experiences intervened, and it took some time for me to figure out that the process of writing biography was much different than working on a historical monograph. Barrier Williams's presence became my constant companion, living in my head and eventually taking up residence in my home. She was there while I taught my classes and deliberated with graduate students. She was there as I assumed the role of national director for the Association of Black Women Historians and when I initiated the creation of and raised the endowment funds for the Darlene Clark Hine Award for the best book on African American women's and gender history in the Organization of American Historians. She wouldn't let me forget her even as my responsibilities as a long-distance primary caregiver exhausted me.

The collegial spirit and generosity of supportive scholars made this difficult and oftentimes daunting task possible. Darlene Clark Hine introduced me to the amazing community of black women in the Midwest while I was her graduate student at Purdue University. She always had the unwavering belief that I would complete this book. Her kind words and inspiring letters of encouragement arrived when I needed them most. Deborah Gray White, whose own work on club women set the bar high, forced me to articulate why Barrier Williams needed to have a biography in the first place. In the process of our deliberations she became both a staunch ally and one of my biggest champions. Kenneth Hamilton has such a kind spirit. Our weekly philosophical discussions and debates made me think about the ways in which Barrier Williams's interaction with Booker T. Washington, the most powerful black figure at the time, changes the gendered and intellectual narrative of the black experience during the nadir of race relations. My colleagues Eva Baham, Jacqueline McLeod, Carolyn Powell, and Dorothy "Dottie" Pratt listened to me talk about Barrier Williams as if she was alive and didn't call me crazy. They read parts or all of the manuscript and held my hand when times got really tough both personally and professionally. I am most thankful to the MV Reading Group, Carolyn Brown, Natalie Byfield, Donna Murch, and Deborah Gray White for welcoming me into their circle, pushing me when I wanted to quit writing, and critiquing my ideas and the chapters of the manuscript. I thank Nancy Hewitt for giving the manuscript such a close reading, seeing the merit in it, and for making me remember why it is cool to do this work.

Barrier Williams witnessed the agonies and triumphs of American life through the Civil War, Reconstruction, the rise of Jim Crow, industrialization, the beginning and maturation of the club women's movement, and the Great Migration. She participated in and wrote about much of it, but she didn't leave a diary, and the records detailing her life are so scattered throughout the country that it has been very difficult to harness it all. That is why the projects to digitize national newspapers initiated by the Library of Congress, states, and universities have been so valuable to the research for this biography. Those databases released me from the process of requesting individual newspapers through Interlibrary Loan and being chained to a microfilm reader searching each page of multiple newspapers for any mention of Barrier Williams and her contemporaries, as I had to do for the many years prior to the debut of these enterprises.

In my travels to numerous archives and through phone calls and e-mails to scholars, archivists, librarians, and administrative staff, I encountered a community that wanted Barrier Williams's story told as much as I wanted to write it. I am deeply indebted to the wonderful residents of Brockport. Mary J. Gigliotti and Charles Cowan at SUNY Brockport were invaluable resources. The village historian William Andrews, who had been working on and writing about Barrier Williams and her family long before I knew who she was, generously shared his files with me and introduced me to others who could tell me something about her. Minister Kenneth McCathy and the secretary Frances Fuller of First Baptist Church trusted me with their reports and minutes, and Scott Rightmyer and the staff in the administrative offices in Brockport gave me free rein to rummage through village records.

Numerous others called attention to materials that I undoubtedly would have overlooked. Christopher Reed, who has written a great deal about blacks in Chicago, shared his voluminous notes on Barrier Williams with me. Mary Jo Deegan collected many of Barrier Williams's writings and published them in 2002. Kimberly Springle at the Charles Sumner School in Washington welcomed me into the archives and shared her expertise on black education in the late nineteenth century. The staffs at the Library of Congress; the Women's History and Resource Center at the General Federation of Women's Clubs; the Moorland-Spingarn Research Center at Howard University, especially Ida Jones and Lela Sewell-Williams; the Hannibal Free Public Library in Hannibal Missouri, especially Claire Ewersmann; the State Historical Society in Columbia, Missouri; and the Archives and Museums at Tuskegee University, most notably Cynthia Wilson, led me to some surprising and undiscovered collections. Because religion was such an integral part of Barrier Williams's life, the Unitarian Universalist records from Andover-Harvard Theological Library at Harvard Divinity School and the Unitarian Universalist Association of Congregations in Boston were invaluable. G. David Anderson and Lyle Slovick at George Washington University; Alton Hart of the Lapeer County Genealogical Society and Laura Fromwiller at the DeAngelia Branch Library in Lapeer, Michigan; the staff at the National Archives; Walter Pratt at the University of South Carolina Law School; and Duncan Alford, director of the Law Library at the University of South Carolina, helped me develop the rather elusive Samuel Laing Williams, Barrier Williams's husband, more fully.

I began this work at Arizona State University, where I received support from the faculty and staff in the Department of History, in the Women's Studies Program, and at the library. But the bulk of this work has been researched and written at the University of South Carolina. Several staff members, colleagues, and students have been generous with their assistance. Tony McLawhorn patiently provided necessary aid with the technology. Rosa Thorn Jones made travel arrangements for research trips and has been cheering for me for a decade. The time that the gracious Cooper Library staff, particularly Karen Brown, Kytt Moore, and William Sudduth, invested in my searches was invaluable. Colleagues Lewis Burke, Bobby Donaldson, and Dianne Johnson shared valuable research and time. Several graduate students assisted throughout this process, including Ramon Jackson and Candace Cunningham from the History Department and Jessica Forehand and Bethany Williams from the Women's and Gender Studies Program.

The Women's Studies Program (now Women's and Gender Studies) and the Dean of the College of Arts and Sciences provided much of the funding for this book. During the four years that I was the Graduate Director of the program I was given generous travel and research funding as well as student assistance to ensure that my goal of finishing the biography did not suffer because of my administrative responsibilities. The Associate Professor Development Award from the College of Arts and Sciences assisted me with the final stages of the manuscript.

I am very grateful to the University of Illinois Press staff. Former editor Joan Catapano always believed that this was a story worth writing. Larin McLaughlin, Dawn Durante, Jennifer Reichlin, and Kate Babbitt have guided me with steady hands and kept me on task.

My family, friends and neighbors have sustained me for the duration of the project. I can never repay them for their generosity, support, and faith. Beverly Glover Logan and Larry Logan opened their home and hearts to me and filled my soul when I needed it most. My sister Anita Lucinda Hendricks has taught me what it really means to persevere in the face of adversity. My aunt Joyce Ford Stewart nurtured me after the death of my mother when I was thirteen and continues to encourage my aspirations. My dearest friends Laura Adair Johnson and Nancy Davis Spencer have been steady, stable, and consistent champions. Annie Lawrence Holmes and Renee Brown reminded me that I had community outside the academy. Daisy Block, Walter Prince, Sampson Hammett, Fred Easley, Mary Gilmore, and Joseph Gilmore kept watch when I couldn't. My early-rising neighbors in Melrose Heights who know me as the lady walker with the stick inspired me because they kept asking about the book and when it would be finished. Now it finally is.

Fannie Barrier Williams

Introduction

Dressed in "beautiful blue silk," Fannie Barrier attended the "fashionable colored wedding" of Josephine A. Stewart and George W. Ball in April 1881, which was held at Berean Baptist Church in Washington, D.C. She joined an illustrious group of what one of the leading white newspapers, the *National Republican*, called "the youth and beauty of our colored citizens." A major social event of the season, the wedding illuminated the prominence of black elite culture and highlighted the aristocratic stature of the bride's family. Her father, Carter A. Stewart, held key positions in numerous social and political organizations and was one of the first fire department commissioner appointees in the city. The invited guests were part of his inner circle and some of the most influential members of the community. In addition to Barrier, they included Francis Grimké, the minister of the Fifteenth Street Presbyterian Church, and his wife Charlotte Forten Grimké, a writer, teacher and activist; Anna Thompson Wormley, the wife of hotel owner James Wormley; William Syphax, the first chair of the Board of Trustees for the black school system; and physician Samuel LeCount Cook.[1]

Barrier's pedigree, professional status, and physical appearance linked her to the distinguished group. As a member of a prominent mixed-race family from Brockport, New York, she was part of a privileged class. None of her family had ever been enslaved, and like many other upper-class northern blacks, she could trace her lineage to white Europeans. Her father, Anthony J. Barrier, owned a profitable business, had built a substantial real estate portfolio, and was regarded as a leading citizen. Her mother, Harriet Prince Barrier, led the same female-gender-centered life as elite white women in the early nineteenth century. She never worked outside the home, spent most of her time raising three children, and engaged in church activities. Fannie Barrier was an educated professional. She had earned a teaching certificate from Brockport Normal School in 1870 and had taught in the Washington, D.C., public school system since 1877. In addition, her light complexion was in keeping with the affinity of the black upper class for using color as a way to stratify the black community. She looked, one newspaper reported, like an "east Indian of the higher caste."[2]

However, a distinct difference made her unique among the black elite. None of the other wedding guests enjoyed the level of social equality that Barrier had prior to her arrival in Washington, the mecca for southern black aristocrats. The subordination of nonwhites and the racial acrimony that defined black life nationally (and in varying degrees in New York) prior to the Civil War had little effect on her. She was unencumbered by racial restraints in Brockport because she had grown up in an environment where the number of blacks remained exceptionally small and the white community embraced her and her family. It was an unsegregated society that encouraged social equality and insulated her from the political turmoil surrounding the debates about slavery and black rights. As she grew up, she had intimate contact with whites: she lived in the neighborhoods with them, attended schools with them, and worshipped together with them. Because so few blacks lived in the village, she engaged more with whites on a daily basis than she did with members of her own race. That changed when she moved south and for the first time experienced the virulent onslaught of white supremacy. In the South, she simultaneously engaged with perhaps the leading black elite society in the country and encountered a large post-slavery generation population of working-class and poor blacks.

The adjustment forced her to recognize that regional residency, historical period, and population determined the extent of racial interaction. Arriving in the border state of Missouri during the waning years of Reconstruction to assist newly freed women and men, she was caught in the vortex of white Democrats' redemption of the region, a process that pervasively usurped black rights. While some black Republican officeholders continued to retain some of their power well into the 1880s and while the circumscribed world of Jim Crow that was unleashed in the 1890s was not yet entrenched, institutionalized injustice had already begun to appear in the form of proscriptions against contact between blacks and whites. Even in its infancy, segregation imposed racial boundaries in public venues and in transportation, ushering in two separate worlds. And despite Washington's more liberal culture and the black elite's attempts to remain aloof from the black masses and challenge inequality, the black elite remained unequal to whites. Race defined their lives. They lived in racially segregated neighborhoods, sent their children to all-black schools, and found employment in racially designated jobs. The unfamiliar and unwelcome restrictions and limitations proved disconcerting to Fannie Barrier. Although she "tried to adapt" to what she called "these hateful conditions," she could not escape the onslaught.[3] She was raced as a black person and in the process came to understand the limits of a privileged class.

If her northern insulated village provided unlimited freedom and the South labeled and bound her, the Midwest proved to be a middle ground between the two both metaphorically and in reality. When she married the mixed-raced Samuel Laing Williams in 1887, the couple relocated to what was then the western outpost of Chicago, a city that had already become a center of the industrial revolution. As the North continued its process of industrialization, lucrative and efficient economic engines drove the economy and changed the nature of work. In addition, a wave of new immigrants greatly contributed to a multiethnic population in the country's major cities. The aristocratic black society of Chicago that had its roots in the early nineteenth century was resilient and progressive. Its members had been so successful in their challenge to discrimination in public spaces in the city that segregation had been legally prohibited long before Fannie Barrier Williams arrived. The racial barriers that were so prevalent in the South were not as strictly defined in Chicago. Social interaction between blacks and whites, while not pervasive, was not uncommon. This tolerance allowed her to straddle the racial divide. She joined other black elites as they created social and literary clubs, and she also interacted with a number of whites in interracial institutions and worked with them to achieve common goals. Her career as an activist developed in this progressive environment and set her on a trajectory that catapulted her to local, regional, and national celebrity. She became one of the most celebrated, recognized, and distinguished American figures of the late nineteenth and early twentieth centuries.

*   *   *

This biography examines the complexities of the life of Fannie Barrier Williams and how the intersection of privilege and race were shaped by the geographical distinctiveness of regions. It also explores how her emergence as an activist influenced the Progressive Era, the club women's movement, the social and economic impact of industrialization on the black community, and the contours of the challenges to racism and discrimination. Barrier Williams enjoyed a cross-regional mobility that determined how she lived, how she engaged with the black and white communities, and how she formulated her ideas. Beyond the legal enforcement of state and federal policies, race had little significance in the overwhelmingly white insulated northern community of Brockport. The egalitarianism of the village afforded her the ability to view race as a socially constructed entity that was formed more by class delineation than by skin complexion. Although the racial bifurcation of the South determined that despite her class status she was black, denying her access to the privileges of whiteness, she refused to bow to its restrictions. She maneuvered around them and found a space within a well-established and socially and politically connected black aristocratic culture that did not exist in Brockport. The ten years that she spent in Washington proved advantageous and provided the basis for her quick access and easy admission to the evolving aristocratic culture in the Midwest.

In Chicago, she first found success in the exclusive Prudence Crandall Literary Club that included a mixture of the old guard, who had in many instances been born in slavery, had lived in Chicago for several decades, and had fostered the legislation that had brought an end to discrimination and had attracted a new generation of educated and refined migrants like her. The two groups forged a bond that made them one of the most powerful forces in the city. In the literary club, politicians, physicians, attorneys, and businessmen and their wives held weekly and monthly meetings to discuss some of the great works of the period. Enticed by the budding club women's movement, the women's section became the public voice of the club and discussed how they wanted to influence and shape policy pertaining to the black community. That association proved profitable for Barrier Williams. It was a springboard to inclusion in an interracial alliance between elite black women and some of the most prominent white female civic-minded activists in the city. That alliance had been forged in the Illinois Woman's Alliance (IWA), which was organized in 1888 to combat the devastating effects of industrialization and to advocate for a comprehensive government program to provide for the general welfare of women and children. Barrier Williams was a vocal and active member. As a club member, she honed her skills as an activist by attending city council meetings and engaging in public discussions with elected officials, policy makers, and employers. She played such a significant role in the organization that she was elected to several key offices. By the time the alliance disbanded in 1894, Barrier Williams had helped bring attention to the needs of women in the workplace, exploitative child labor practices, and the need for free baths for the poor.

Barrier Williams parlayed her achievements in the IWA into a career as a labor activist for black women, particularly nurses and stenographers. She became a vociferous proponent of their professionalization in a number of new positions. She spearheaded the campaign to establish a nurses' training program for black women at the newly created Provident Hospital in 1891, the only interracial medical facility in the city. She recruited both black and white benefactors for this project. For two decades she challenged discrimination against black female stenographers by acting as a broker between white employers and potential candidates and drawing on the wealth and power of white friends to intercede. She found some success placing workers and even offered her own classes in stenography to counter the exclusion of black women in clerical schools in the city.

She perfected her ability to successfully navigate between black and white worlds by gaining a reputation among blacks as a champion of black rights and among whites as a resilient and cooperative leader. The perceptions proved rewarding and advantageous. With the aid of white peers such as fellow Unitarian

Celia Parker Woolley and Chicago Woman's Club member and second president of the General Federation of Women's Clubs Ellen Henrotin, she became one of the few black female presenters at the Chicago World's Fair in 1893, the only black woman to present on the main program at the Parliament of Religions in September 1893, and the first black member of the Chicago Woman's Club (CWC), one of the largest and most powerful groups of white women in the country. The appearances at the fair and the parliament and her subsequent admission to the CWC made her a national celebrity. She toured the county as a paid lecturer and began a writing career that spanned nearly three decades.[4]

The local community of black women in Chicago recognized her acumen. She joined a powerful cast that was dedicated to meeting the social welfare needs of the city's black community that included anti-lynching crusader Ida B. Wells-Barnett and reformer Elizabeth Lindsay Davis. Together these and other women created a coalition of clubs and programs that became the engines of a range of social welfare services that included caring for orphaned and abandoned children, operating nurseries, assisting with housing and employment for women, and developing health facilities for families. By 1898, Barrier Williams had taken the lead in presiding over a loosely based federation that included nearly ten black female clubs.

Her progressive accomplishments in Chicago and her personal connections in both the Northeast and the South endeared her to the national community of black women. She became a conduit through which activist women in Chicago centered themselves in the national social network of club women. A year after her successful presentation at the World's Fair, she merged her regional ties by assuming the role of Chicago correspondent for the *Woman's Era*, a first-of-its-kind Boston periodical dedicated to highlighting and reporting on the activism of black club women in every region of the country. For nearly two years she provided commentary on local activism and on the national issues that faced black women. In that time she gained a reputation as a stalwart leader, and when the call for the creation of a national organization began in 1895, many women looked to her for guidance. By 1896, they had formed the National Association of Colored Women, the largest convergence of black club women in history. The association recast the role of black women by positioning them as a dominant force in shaping the social, political, and economic progress of the black community. Barrier Williams cemented the Illinois black female club women's alliance to the national movement by spearheading the creation of the Illinois Federation of Colored Women's Clubs in 1899. At the dawn of the twentieth century she was, the *Richmond Planet* reported, "one of the most noted colored ladies in the United States."[5]

Her fame was particularly advanced by her engagement in the fight for the enfranchisement of women. When women in Illinois gained the ability to vote in school-related matters in 1891, the legislation fueled her premature declaration that a federal constitutional suffrage amendment was close at hand. Known for her committed efforts to the cause, she was invited to share the podium with the two stalwarts of the movement, Elizabeth Cady Stanton and Susan B. Anthony.[6] But Barrier Williams also formulated a raced and gendered analysis of black women's access to the ballot. Arguing that black women had unique needs that were defined as much by race as they were by gender and region, she insisted that reform-minded black women had to vote in their own best interests. Expressing weariness about the motives of white female candidates, she encouraged black female voters to make platform rather than gender or party affiliation the primary issue. She insisted that they query the candidates about their proposals concerning black women and the black community, and she opposed blacks who believed in an unwavering loyalty to the party of Lincoln.

When a universal federal amendment had not materialized by the turn of the century, she joined a citywide effort by black and white club women and labor activists to transform the gendered nature of municipal politics. Barrier Williams became a key architect of a plan to engage black women in shaping public policy, particularly as it pertained to combating police brutality and discrimination in housing, employment, and schools. The battle for the woman's vote in Illinois, as it was in many states, was long and hard. When Illinois became the first state east of the Mississippi to pass legislation enabling women to vote for city council representatives and U.S. presidents, Barrier Williams led the charge in encouraging black women to become politicized. The new law coincided with the beginnings of the Great Migration. Because of the interest and enthusiasm of black women, the powerful white Republican machine that had ruled the overwhelmingly black South Side of Chicago finally was forced to relinquish some control by endorsing the first black candidate. Oscar Stanton DePriest was elected the first black alderman in the city on a campaign platform that appealed to women's concerns and included ending discrimination in schools.

Perhaps one of her most important legacies was her intellectual insight about the intersectionality of labor, race, and gender. She presented papers at scholarly conferences about the status of black club women, the myriad social and economic problems blacks and women faced, and the importance of educational opportunity. She became a member of and a regular presenter at the conferences of the Afro-American Council and the National Negro Business League. She also flourished as a writer, providing commentary for several newspapers and journals. She was recognized for her intellectual insight and joined an illustrious female and male group of some of the "great thinkers" and "leading writers" of the race.[7] Booker T. Washington depended on her to highlight the work of black club women and provide an intellectual counternarrative to the caustic criticism of W. E. B. Du Bois, Ida B. Wells-Barnett, and other prominent blacks of his advocacy of industrial education. She appeared with him in numerous publications, including one of the most comprehensive discussions on club women in *The Colored American from Slavery to Honorable Citizenship*, which was edited by J. W. Gibson and W. H. Crogman in 1903. She also promoted the industrial model as a national educational paradigm in speeches and written commentary.[8]

She paid a price for her association with Washington. North of Jim Crow, many black Chicagoans were less enamored than their southern counterparts with the Tuskegee principal and his accommodation to white interests. They rendered scathing public criticism of him, blocked his nominees to federal political appointments, and attacked his supporters, including Barrier Williams. They vilified her in the press and branded her a race traitor. But long before Washington died in 1915, many Chicagoans had softened their opinion of her and of Washington and had turned to the more pressing problems of escalating racial discrimination, the rise of the ghetto, and how to handle the migration of the thousands of southern blacks who had already begun to descend on the city.

*   *   *

Barrier Williams's tenure as an activist spanned more than three decades. She earned her professional credentials between the rise of industrialization in the late nineteenth century and the advent of the worst race riots in the country at the end of the second decade of the twentieth century. She spent nearly forty years in the second-largest city in the country defending women and African Americans and helping to shape the municipal policies that affected their lives. The geographical locale of the city certainly determined the outcomes of her efforts, providing unprecedented opportunity, intolerable constraints, or a combination of both. North of Jim Crow, she existed in the most integrated environment of the country. And even as race lines hardened in Chicago, limiting the mobility of blacks by confining them to segregated neighborhoods and restricting their access to employment by relegating them to the most menial jobs during the first two decades of the twentieth century, she continued to inhabit the intimate spaces of whites, visiting them in their homes, sharing meals with them, and holding membership in clubs. To be sure, she was not untouched by racism. The protracted and nasty battle for admission to the CWC took nearly two years, and some white members threatened to leave the organization in protest when she was admitted. Discrimination in the suffrage movement forced her to challenge the racially exclusive policy of one of the largest female political organizations in the city.[9]

Fannie Barrier Williams was an aristocrat with classed-based ideals, and her class analysis and promotion of industrial education did not always endear her to black leaders. A philosophy rooted in her early life in Brockport and her linkages to the national community of elites often appeared to be much more aligned with the views of whites than they were with the black masses she professed to assist. She sometimes blamed the poor for their own plight, chastised black mothers for their ineptness, and championed the creation of protective associations to prevent the encroachment of poor blacks in elite black neighborhoods. In addition, she argued that the industrial education model was the most effective means of educating illiterate and unskilled blacks throughout the country at a time when "philanthropic and southern white crusaders for universal public education wished to substitute education for older and cruder methods of socialization and control," as historian James Anderson points out.[10]

But race, gender, and class do not provide an adequate framework for an examination of Barrier Williams's life and views. In that version, she becomes a marginalized figure who united with white women and men simply because she had never endured the horrors of slavery and the continuous assaults of racism and discrimination. She also becomes a prisoner of geography because she was a northern-born aristocrat who shared few things with the black masses. The facts of her life disprove such a limited analysis. Despite her small-town, privileged upbringing in the North, she taught in southern schools for more than a decade, she was a labor activist and broker in the industrialized city of Chicago, and she experienced the race and gender bigotry that universally haunted black women.

This biography argues that Barrier Williams was a transformative agent of change. Her story is a multifaceted and untold account that complicates our understanding of the gendered intersectionality of race, class, and region during one of the most progressive but volatile periods in American history. She was an undisputed leader, a savvy negotiator, and an effective liaison between blacks and whites who in many ways was the most significant female architect in the Progressive Era to shape the direction of the discourse about the progress of the black community and the reform activism of club women.

1. North of Slavery

Brockport

After a white mob lynched Richard Dixon and destroyed much of a black district in Springfield, Ohio, in March 1904, the editors of New York–based weekly *The Independent* decided to examine "the negro problem" through a series of three articles.[1] All of the writers were anonymous because of "concern [for] their social if not personal safety," and all were women, highlighting the significant impact of women's voices in shaping racial discourse at the dawn of the twentieth century. The narrators viewed race and gender in unique and vastly different ways, illuminating how deep the racial fissure had become nearly four decades after the end of slavery. They included a southern "colored" woman's autobiographical sketch of "The Race Problem—An Autobiography," a southern white woman's "Experiences of the Race Problem," and the "Observations of the Southern Race Feeling" by a northern-born white woman who had relocated to the South.[2]

The series also revealed a glaring omission. The sole black voice originated from the South, and the only northern voice was that of a white woman. Because there was no northern black woman's voice in the series, the editors, whether by design or not, had created a racial geography that gave whites privilege, allowing them regional mobility, while containing, constraining, and limiting the spatial place of blacks to the South. Nearly four months after the three articles appeared, the editors acknowledged their failure to recognize the significant regional differences among blacks, and they printed the one response to the magazine that "discusses a phase of the negro problem not touched upon by the three anonymous women, and often generally overlooked by the American people."[3] The author of the only essay they were not "obliged to reject" was Fannie Barrier Williams. She had captured their attention because there was no other public black female figure whose life had been so thoroughly shaped by geographical mobility and the fluidity of race relations in the nineteenth and early twentieth centuries.

With the publication of "A Northern Negro's Autobiography," Barrier Williams became the only one of the four women who was publicly identified as an author. She was also the only one who was born in the North, had lived in the South, and called the Midwest home. Her background illuminated the centrality of place, race, gender, and class in defining identity. Introducing herself to readers, she declared: "I am a Northern colored woman, a mulatto in complexion, and was born since the war in a village town of Western New York. My parents and grandparents were free people."[4] The autobiography added a unique dimension to the discussion by contextualizing and nationalizing race and gender, highlighting the gradations of skin color and class in the black community, contesting the national homogenized perception of African American women, and recasting the narrative about black life before and after the Civil War.

Fannie Barrier was born on February 12, 1855, in Brockport, New York, to mixed-race parents in an overwhelmingly white community. Although she came of age at a time when the vast majority of blacks were enslaved, the Supreme Court had declared that blacks were not citizens, and few blacks had access to the ballot, her birthplace offered a respite from the ideological turmoil that gripped the nation and would eventually led to civil war. Brockport was north of slavery, and according to census records, no resident of the town had ever owned enslaved people. More important, the village was a secure and supportive place for Barrier. Although white citizens overwhelmingly outnumbered blacks, she never felt out of place, threatened, or intimidated. Unlike many northern and southern communities Brockport designated no racially divided public spaces. As a result, Barrier enjoyed an unsegregated childhood and early adulthood that was free of residential, educational, religious, and social separation along race lines. She recalled in the *Independent* article that there was such an interracial intimacy that the "associates, schoolmates and companions" with whom she and her two siblings Ella and George engaged "were all white boys and girls." The interactive "relationships," she insisted, "were natural, spontaneous and free from all restraint. We went freely to each other's houses, to parties, socials, and joined on equal terms in all school entertainments with perfect comradeship. We suffered from no discriminations on account of color or 'previous condition' and lived in blissful ignorance of the fact that we were practicing the unpardonable sin of 'social equality.'"[5] The northern location of Barrier's hometown of Brockport and the convergence of several social, political, and economic factors sheltered her and greatly restricted the negative impact of racism and discrimination on her life.

*   *   *

In 1822, the northwestern upstate New York village of Brockport became one of eighteen towns that made up Monroe County.[6] When Brockport incorporated in 1829, it was still sparsely populated; only 791 people lived there in 1830.[7] The village was bordered by Rochester to the east, Lake Ontario to the north, and Buffalo to the west and was located in close proximity to the seat of an abolitionist movement that drew liberal-minded whites to the area. Many like Hiel Brockway and James Seymour, two of the village's founders, migrated from New England towns in Connecticut, Massachusetts, and Vermont.[8] Slavery never manifested in Brockport because by the time the village was established, legislation had already been enacted to gradually emancipate all those held in bondage. In 1827, the state permanently ended slavery altogether. According to local historian William Andrews, the white residents who settled there had little appetite for the practice. They were more liberal in their perceptions about race, and mixed-raced blacks and even members of racially mixed households were among the first inhabitants.[9]

From the time of its establishment, the village was swept up in the economic evolution generated by the rapid growth of commerce and industry, the revivalism of the Second Great Awakening, and the expansion of democratic ideals in politics and education. The rise of industrialism fueled economic engines and offered new areas of opportunities, particularly after the state legislature authorized the building of a canal in 1818 to link the eastern and western parts of upstate New York. In addition, western New York was the site of one of the most intense evangelical revivals in the country. The sheer force and concentration of the movement transformed perceptions about human freedom and the advancement of the abolitionist platform. It also reshaped the institutional landscape of the area by leaving in its wake a number of strong and active churches, and it influenced the religious associations of generations of western New York residents by spawning and legitimizing new denominations. Other movements changed the social landscape in upstate New York. The movement for universal male suffrage provided broader access to the political world for white men, and the push to democratize education expanded the public sphere for females. In Brockport, several primary and common schools and a private institute that both females and males attended had been established by the 1840s.[10]

Barrier proudly boasted in the *Independent* article that her father, Anthony J. Barrier, was intimately tied to the development of the village and its people. Born to a Frenchman and a free black woman on November 29, 1824, in Philadelphia, Anthony Barrier came of age in the community at a time when villagers were recovering from the depression of 1837 and the population more than doubled when Brockport merged with the nearby town of Sweden in 1850.[11] His mixed European and American or mulatto heritage proved less of a distinguishing marker to insulated villagers than it did for the census takers. He was, as Barrier contended, racially amorphous, living in an unsegregated environment and centered in the social and economic fabric of the village.

Several factors contributed to his privileged place. His presence presented few challenges to the overall social order. There was no perceived usurpation of white power like that feared in more urbanized areas such as nearby Rochester, where the "free colored" population was segregated in the Third Ward from the white majority. There were no distinct wards or districts for blacks in rural Brockport, where 99 percent of the population was white in 1830. Even a decade later, when the white population dipped slightly to 98 percent, the twenty-six black residents posed no real threat.[12]

In addition, as the economic prosperity of the 1820s gave way to the depression at the end of the 1830s, most residents devoted their energies to economic recovery rather than to devising ways to separate themselves from their few black neighbors. The creation of the Erie Canal catalyzed the spread of industrialization throughout the region, and until the canal was completed in 1925, Brockport was the western terminus. That commercial enterprise ensured that the village and its inhabitants benefited in several ways: the cost of production was decreased and economic development in the town increased. Even when the canal was completed and the final terminus shifted to Buffalo, the enterprise of more than 360 miles continued to expose the village to new commercial business, making it one of the major stations on the only east-west transportation route until railroads developed in the early 1850s. The canal brought continuous traffic. Passengers disembarked and marketable goods were loaded and unloaded at the village dock. Businesses near the canal serviced both local residents and business and tourist customers from canal traffic.[13]

Villagers enthusiastically promoted literacy and education, and as a result, the population was one of the most literate in the area. By 1840, only five whites over the age of twenty could not read or write, making the illiteracy rate in the village the smallest of the twenty communities in Monroe County.[14] The high literacy rate generated interest in local, state, and national news and fueled the development of educational institutions. The first newspaper was published in 1827. The *Brockport Free Press* became the main vehicle through which villagers were socially and politically connected to state and national issues. Although it had a short run, other newspapers soon filled the void. The *Brockport Recorder*, the *Monroe Republican*, the *Brockport Watchman*, the *Brockport Weekly Journal*, and the *Brockport Gazette* all began publishing before 1858.[15] The village also joined the surging interest in schooling that manifested in the early decades of the nineteenth century. The most prominent educational facility was established in 1835. Brockport Collegiate Institute combined the religious vision of the Baptist Missionary Convention and the business acumen of Hiel Brockway.[16]

But the economic boom that lured many to settle and seek prosperity in the area ended two years after the Brockport Collegiate Institute opened. As the nation descended into a depression, businesses closed and commerce and transportation declined. One of the major casualties was the institute. The school encountered financial obstacles as contributions decreased. Finally it closed, and the bank foreclosed on the property.[17]

In the early 1840s, signs of recovery appeared. Stores, banks, and hotels began to thrive again and Brockport Collegiate Institute reopened in 1841 as an incorporated unit of the state system of New York.[18] Boat building flourished as the canal generated profitable business. Eighteen residents listed canal, lake, and river navigation as their job in 1840, and the number of people employed in manufacturing, trades, and agriculture grew rapidly.[19] Produce from local farms joined the output of the many foundries and manufacturing companies in shipments outside the region. The town became famous for the production of reapers. With the development of the McCormick Reaper in 1844, the village claimed fame as "the oldest manufactory of reapers and mowers in the world." By 1850, the most prosperous residents were farmers, some of whom were new arrivals.[20]

Anthony Barrier staked out a claim in the economic recovery. He established a career in a profession that proved to be quite profitable. His barbershop was located in the lucrative village core on the corner of Main Street. His choice of career reflected his entrepreneurial acumen and his awareness of the developing beauty culture.[21] His newspaper advertisements in the 1850s emphasized the specialized services of "Hair Dressing, Shaving, Champooing [*sic*]" as well as the more luxurious and refined "Oils and Perfumery." The reference to oils and perfumery suggest that he engaged in retail as well, expanding his business and providing a shop where men could purchase items that made them feel (and smell) better.[22] It was, as Barrier noted, "a good business" that served him well for nearly fifty years.[23]

He was successful in part because of his skill at maintaining cordial and trusting relationships with his clients. He built a solid customer base that included local consumers and canal traffic, and his business benefited from the merger of the village with the neighboring community of Sweden in 1850, making Brockport part of one of the largest towns in Monroe County. The town had a population of more than 3,600 in 1850, the year of the merger. Seventeen black men and an equal number of black women lived in Sweden with 1,785 white men and 1,804 white women.[24]

Christian piety fueled the soul of the people. Residents embraced the Second Great Awakening that swept through the country in the early part of the nineteenth century. Led by charismatic evangelists, the religious revival that encompassed a large swath of upstate New York challenged and changed the cultural core of the area and influenced it for the remainder of the century. "Aflame with the fires of revivalism and reform, upstate New York before the Civil War (along with parts of New England and the Western Reserve) earned itself a reputation as a 'burned-over district,'" historian Judith Wellman wrote. She notes that the spiritual flame and success of the movement was so intense that "it also spawned Mormonism, Millerism, and the organized women's rights movement."[25] The broad reach of the religious movement ensnared the illiterate and the literate alike. Long before her engagement in the women's movement, well-known former Ulster County slave Sojourner Truth, for example, was so engulfed by the awakening that it influenced her life for decades. Shortly after her freedom from bondage, she aligned herself with the Methodist Church. Historian Nell Painter argues that when she moved to New York City, "she and her associates bore the hallmarks of the perfectionism she had accepted in the late 1820s: dressing and living plainly, and listening to 'the Spirit'—a voice representing communication and power."[26]

Lawyer-turned-evangelist Charles Finney was perhaps one of the most well-known and successful of the evangelists of the Second Great Awakening. His brand of fiery religious instruction found fertile ground in places such as Rochester. Finney arrived in the city in the fall of 1830 and spent half a year preaching primarily in Presbyterian churches and in public and private prayer gatherings that reached a broad range of people. Interest reached such a fevered pitch that the intense church services quickly spread to the secular areas of the home. Women thrived in that secular arena, a gendered space that provided the base for their assumption of a public role that eventually led to the women's rights movement.[27]

Finney was so successful because he spoke to the "common folk" whose lives were in the midst of major economic and social transformation. His disciples sought to find meaning and control in their everyday lives by flocking to hear his sermons. Most found enlightenment in the break with pessimistic Calvinist doctrine of original sin. The new emphasis on perfectionism and free will encouraged followers to delve deeply into questions about personal salvation, faith, and the ways that individuals could influence their own fate and to some degree the lives of others.[28]

Brockport was greatly influenced by the religious movement. In the wake of Finney's departure, it too became part of "the prevailing western analogy" that viewed the village as lodged "between the fires of the forest and those of the spirit."[29] Multiple denominations spawned the establishment of a number of churches. By 1830 the Methodists, Baptists, Presbyterians, and Episcopalians had all organized in the village. So enduring and significant was the awakening in the village that a number of denominations continued to emerge between 1840 and 1850. The Free Will Baptists organized in 1844, and the Catholics held their first mass by 1848. Congregants attended Sabbath worship services and Sunday school. In addition, mission schools, revivals, and lectures provided weekly immersion in religious study and activity.[30]

Anthony participated in the heightened interest in religion. He joined the First Baptist Church, one of the oldest institutions in the village. Originally established in 1828, it was located in the village core. It thrived for nearly a decade with a congregation of 169 members, but it was decimated by the economic depression of 1837. Congregants struggled for nearly two years, but so overwhelmed by financial problems, the group dissolved in 1839. A strong desire to resurrect the church, however, encouraged several members to dedicate themselves to creating the Second Baptist Church in 1841. Fifty-four people joined. Within a year, the congregation had grown to ninety members, of which Anthony was one. He was baptized on March 26, 1842. He continued as a member of the Second Baptist Church for almost fifty years.[31]

Although at the local level of Brockport, the rhetoric of free will that permeated the religious awakening promoted spiritual equality and embraced without limitation a mixed-raced man like Anthony, it did little to alter the intolerant racial dynamics of state and national politics. National laws did not recognize an intermediary racial category between white and black. Propertyless nonwhite males could not vote in New York. The explicit racial terms of political engagement that the state legislated in 1821 specified that "universal" male participation in politics was limited to white men, revealing how the interrelation of the hierarchies of race, class, and gender played a significant part in defining citizenship and the status of blacks and women in the state. The growing national conflict over the increasing power of the proslavery South and fear of the prospect of a mass migration of southern blacks in the 1840s certainly contributed to the heightened distress in the North. Historian Leslie Harris notes that the rhetoric of the delegates to the 1846 state constitutional convention demonstrated "that little had changed in conceptions of black political equality in the twenty-five years since the previous convention restricted black suffrage."[32] Many of the discussions focused on topics such as divine right, inalienable rights, the privileges of citizenship, and the inherent inferiority of blacks. The delegates who wanted to retain the property limitations on black men were in the majority. Fear of a substantial increase in the black population led one delegate to insist,

> If we invite all the blacks, who are to come from the south, by giving them this political power, which they cannot have till they reach this state, the next ten years will bring thousands of them among us, if they have in fact the ambition of ruling with our race, which has been ascribed to them by their special friends on this floor.
>
> Is such an accession to our population desirable? In the name of the people of St. Lawrence county, I answer no! . . .
>
> Suppose the thousands of emancipated blacks of the south, are, by an offer of all the privileges of citizenship, invited to settle in this state, must they not labor for their support? Will not their labor be brought in direct competition with that of our white laboring classes? It must of necessity and one of two things must result.—Either, this competition must reduce the price of labor, or our white laborers must make room for our new black citizens, by emigrating to other states.[33]

Another delegate argued that the franchise was not an inalienable or natural right but a privilege that blacks had not earned. "To permit the Ethiopian race to become an important portion of the governing power of the state! To allow that race, the farthest removed from us in sympathy and relationship of all into which the human family was divided, to become a participant in governing, not themselves, but us!" could not be tolerated, he declared.[34]

The views of delegates from New York City and St. Lawrence County perhaps summed up the most pervasive reason for the subjugation of blacks. The New York City delegate told his colleagues that "negroes were aliens—aliens, not by mere accident of foreign birth—not because they spoke a different language— not from any petty distinction that a few years association might obliterate, but by the broad distinction of race—a distinction that neither education, nor inter- course, nor time could remove—a distinction that must separate our children from their children for ever."[35] The St. Lawrence County delegate noted that "it was the destiny of the black race ever to occupy an inferior social position to the white. It was the latent decree of the Almighty, and nothing could change it." To "admit the blacks to a participation in the government of the country," he continued, meant that they were "on terms of social equality with us—and that could only be done, by degrading our own race to a level with them."[36]

This was not new rhetoric, nor was it unique among northern "free" states like New York. Racist ideas based in both religion and science had manifested to such a degree by the 1840s that racial ethnology took center stage in the national discourse about black inferiority and human bondage. The majority of northerners and southerners embraced the idea that blacks were inherently inferior.[37] The unification of these ideas demonstrated in many ways that even with an escalation in intersectional strife, white northerners and white south- erners were unified in racial ideology.

White solidarity marginalized the few white supporters of black political equality so much that the verbal linkages of the latter of democratic principles and the ideals of the American Revolution did little to sway their colleagues. Even a Madison County delegate's insistence that the discrimination ran counter to the Declaration of Independence's proclamation "that all men are created equal, and endowed by their Creator with certain inalienable rights, among which is life liberty, and the pursuit of happiness" and that the "distinction in the exercise of the elective franchise, on account of color or complexion, is invidious and anti-republican" could not triumph over the prejudice of most of the convention members.[38] Ultimately the 1821 state law that limited suffrage for black men to those who possessed at least $250 worth of property remained in place.[39]

This usurpation of rights did not go unchallenged by blacks. Frederick Doug- lass, the runaway slave who had settled in neighboring Rochester, and his colleagues Martin R. Delany and William Nell, who co-edited *The North Star* with him, used the pages of the newspaper to bitterly complain about the impediments to black equality.[40] For example, coverage of the sixty-six delegates who attended the National Colored Convention in Troy, New York, in 1847 highlighted mounting organized protest among blacks. Attendees represented the seven northern states of New York, Massachusetts, Connecticut, Pennsylvania, New Jersey, New Hampshire, Vermont, the Midwestern state of Michigan, and the upper South state of Kentucky. The overall theme was "eradicating the foul spirit of caste."[41] Of particular concern was the increase in racialized rhetoric at state convention meetings and the implementation of state policies that encouraged social, political, educational, and economic divisions along race lines.

These grievances certainly resonated with Anthony as he carved out a place in Brockport that was impinged upon by the convictions of state legislators and by state laws and national politics. Despite the fact that he could obtain social privilege in Brockport as a mixed-race man, state law now grouped him with other blacks and prevented him from legally participating in the "universal" political rights his local white male friends enjoyed. What he thought about the racially charged convention debate or the state voting law remains unclear, but he was surely keenly aware of how intimately linked electoral politics was to citizenship rights. Male villagers elected several local citizens to state government posts and sent one to Congress. Levi Pond and H. P. Norton served in the state legislature in the 1830s, and Jerome Fuller was elected to the position in 1842. Five years later, his constituents sent Fuller to the New York State Senate. Perhaps the most successful politician in the area during this time was Elias B. Holmes, who was elected to the U.S. House of Representatives in 1844 and 1846.[42]

Still, Brockport's insulation engendered privilege and afforded Anthony the ability to lead a relatively unencumbered life. So when he met and married a young mixed-raced woman named Harriet Prince, he had few fears about their future. Harriet, who had been born on March 12, 1835, in Sherburne, a small community in southeastern Chenango County, New York, was eleven years Anthony's junior. Her father, Noah Prince, seems to have been a white man who originated from Sherburne. Her mother, Philantha Macy Prince, who was listed as a mulatto in the 1850 census, was originally from Connecticut and moved to Sherburne. In addition to their shared racial ancestry and regional background, Harriet and Anthony had both attended school and were literate.[43]

Harriet and Anthony married in 1849. The announcement of their nuptials appeared in the April 20th edition of *The North Star* that year. This listing in a national antislavery newspaper reflected their stature as a couple and in many ways captured the essence of the privileged and intimate relationship that the two had developed within the black and white communities.[44] The ceremony was held at the predominantly white First Baptist Church and was officiated over by a white minister, Rev. C. N. Chandler. The announcement did not mention the race of the couple.[45]

The couple settled into married life. During the first year, they listed no real estate property. In this they were not unlike a number of their neighbors. And like the wives of many of their white contemporaries, Harriet followed the traditionally defined path for women; she did not work outside the home. As a result, her worldview, like that of her white female neighbors, was narrowly defined to the private and often invisible feminized space of domesticity and child rearing. Over the next six years she gave birth to three children and devoted her life to their welfare. George was born in 1850. Ella arrived in 1852. Fannie, the last child and second daughter, was born in the winter of 1855.[46]

The economic status of the family changed with the birth of the children. Shortly after George was born, Barrier's father began the process of increasing the family's wealth and affirming his political citizenship through the creation of a real estate portfolio. By the end of 1850, he had purchased a 20-acre tract for $450 from fellow church members Abram and Catherine Peck.[47] Two years later, he purchased a parcel of land on Erie Street for $650 from Francis Haight, who would become a member of the Board of Trustees at Brockport Collegiate Institute, and his wife.[48] Five years after the birth of Fannie, the declared value of the family's real estate and personal property was $1,500, situating them squarely among the affluent of the community.[49] Anthony's success in business and his successful property accumulation ensured the family's security and encouraged his youngest daughter's confidence in his ability "to take good care of his family."[50]

Anthony's assets provided the family with the accoutrements of wealth and softened the blows of financial misfortune when they occurred. Harriet and Anthony developed "a taste for good books and the refinements of life" and sent their children to Brockport Collegiate Institute.[51] Even when a fire swept through the financial district in the town center in February 1853 it posed few problems. Although Anthony's barbershop, which was valued at $50, was destroyed and he carried no insurance, he was able to recover fairly quickly and rebuild the business.[52]

Affluence also enabled the family to offer assistance to friends and relatives. By 1860, three young adults had joined the family at the home on Erie Street. They appear to have been relatives or acquaintances of Harriet. They listed no real estate or any other type of capital. Two were a couple that was classified as mulatto and, like many in Harriet's extended family, had been born in New York and Connecticut. Their gender roles resembled those of their hosts: the wife listed housekeeper as her occupation and the husband identified as a barber, suggesting that he might have been working for or apprenticing with Anthony. The other tenant was a female whose last name was Prince and was listed as the household servant. The move for her was probably motivated by the search for an improvement in economic status. The young woman appears to have been the same one who a decade earlier had lived with Harriet's mother Philantha Prince in Sherburne. In 1850, the 55-year-old Prince was listed as the sole head of a family that included two males aged seventeen and twenty-one, a fourteen-year-old female, and a two-year-old child. Ten years later, Philantha Prince was living alone and was struggling to maintain a modest lifestyle. Fending for herself with only $350 worth of real estate and personal property, Philantha became a washerwoman. Eventually the burden proved too difficult and by 1870 she had left Sherburne and relocated to Brockport to be near her children and grandchildren.[53]

Life for Fannie's parents was certainly busy as they juggled tending to small children, managing a household, running a business, and assisting relatives. Still, she noted, they were both publicly active. By the time she was five years old, her mother had begun moving out of the private feminized space of her home and claiming a public place in the religious community. She joined First Baptist in 1860.[54] Eventually, she would begin teaching "a large Bible class of women in the same Sunday school" as her husband.[55] Her activities certainly contributed to the immersion of her children in church culture. All three joined First Baptist. The two youngest, Ella and Fannie, became members in 1866. The oldest, George, joined the congregation in 1867.[56] Their distinction as "the only colored family in the church" solidified their religious commitment and served to further illuminate their social standing in the community.[57]

Harriet's emergence into public life continued over the next decade and extended beyond the confines of the church. As her children reached adulthood, she increasingly delved into the masculine world of the marketplace by assuming a larger role in the economic life of the family. Her husband made his last land purchase, a piece of property on the corner of Monroe and Utica Streets, from Sanford Goff, a longtime fellow member of First Baptist, in 1869.[58] By 1876, it was Harriet who was solely responsible for the buying and selling of property for the family.[59]

Over that same time period, Barrier's father also increased his public visibility. Like his wife, he first began in the church, making a bid for the office of collector and treasurer at First Baptist in 1864. This paid position was one of the most important administrative posts in the church. Recognizing his adeptness in financial matters and his prominent and respectable place among congregants, the majority white membership easily elected him. He was so successful in the position that he became the most consistently elected treasurer and one of the longest-serving ones in the church's history before 1890.[60] During his decade-long tenure, the fortunes of First Baptist steadily grew. Fifteen new members joined the year he took office, for a total of 575. Worship services moved from a leased property to a permanent structure that was purchased with $10,000 of church funds.[61] By 1870, he was collecting tithes from a membership list of more than 600 and managing a budget of over $2,000. When he left office in 1874, the church had over 700 members. In recognition of his industriousness, competence, and dedication the church frequently increased his salary. He was paid $23 during his first year; three years later, his stipend had increased to $35.[62] When his yearly term expired in 1872, members "unanimously elected" him to the position again and increased his stipend to $50.[63]

Because of unfolding national events, Anthony also broadened his geographical advocacy of black equality. During the 1840s and 1850s, rhetoric about the increasing number of slaves who ran away and sought refuge in the North grew louder, and a power struggle between slave owners and non-slave owners led to the passage of the federal Fugitive Slave Law in 1850. Anthony's life and those of his family became intimately intertwined with blacks on the national scene. The new law strengthened the rights of slave catchers and slave owners and threatened the lives of free blacks in the North and the South. It also provided new ammunition for abolitionists and galvanized the movement against slavery. Anthony joined the efforts of Douglass to assist black fugitives and, like his white neighbors, welcomed Douglass's appearance in Brockport in December 1856. According to the village newspaper, *The Brockport Republic*, Douglass addressed a supportive "large and highly intelligent audience" at Concert Hall.[64] All who attended agreed that "slavery is a moral and social evil—unrighteous in principle and practice."[65] But few had as much at stake as Barrier's family did. In 1857, shortly after Douglass's visit, the legal status of blacks became clear. Dred Scott, a slave who was sold to an army surgeon and taken to the free territories of Illinois and Wisconsin, filed suit in Missouri claiming that his residency in both geographical regions had made him free. The state denied his claim. Eventually the suit made its way to the Supreme Court. The justices sided with the state and argued that Scott had no legal rights. Moreover, the justices argued that he, like all other blacks, was not a citizen. In spite of the Court's denial of citizenship status for blacks, Barrier's parents "were public spirited and regarded as good citizens" in Brockport.[66] But they could not escape the geographical and political realities of state and national politics. In spite of their privileged position of prominence in Brockport, neither they nor their children were citizens of the country where they were born.

The assault on their security escalated as the sectional conflict over slavery reached an impasse. When the southern states seceded from the Union, adopted a constitution, and elected a president to preside over the Confederate States of America, Barrier's parents must have envisioned a less stable future for their family. Their concern grew as the Civil War that began in 1861 immersed their white neighbors in the conflict. From the beginning, Brockport residents rallied and demonstrated their patriotism by supporting the Union. At an early meeting at Concert Hall, more than 100 volunteers from Brockport and surrounding areas joined Lincoln's call to create a coalition of strong Union forces.[67] Many of those volunteers joined several regiments that were organized or located in the vicinity of the village, including the 13th Regiment, New York Infantry and the 8th New York Cavalry.[68]

Anthony engaged in the battle in another way. Led by his own race consciousness, he traveled 100 miles to Syracuse, New York, in 1864 to attend the National Convention of Colored Men at Wesleyan Methodist Church. There, along with other delegates, Anthony endorsed abolitionism, universal suffrage, and black equality.[69]

When the war finally ended, the fate of Anthony, Harriet, George, Ella, and Fannie became much more clearly tied to the nearly 4 million former slaves who gained their freedom in 1865. All blacks, regardless of geographical location, became citizens under the Fourteenth Amendment.[70]

*   *   *

Even during the most tumultuous years of the war and its aftermath, Barrier and her siblings were sheltered from the racial turmoil that surrounded the community. Unfettered access to Brockport Collegiate Institute made them as racially amorphous as their parents and afforded them continued social interaction with white peers. The race of the children who attended the school was never listed, so it is unclear whether they had other black or mixed-raced classmates. Class, gender, religious affiliation, and residential location trumped race in defining the identity of students.

Familiar faces greeted the Barrier children as they arrived at school each day because most of their classmates, teachers, and administrators lived in the village and shared similar class traits and ideals.[71] Most of their parents owned property or had accumulated enough financial resources to be able to pay the fee for their children to attend the school. The cost for day school students like the Barrier children was $6.00 in tuition and 35 cents for incidentals per term. Parents of students who boarded at the school paid $200 for a full year, or three terms.[72] The parents of the school's students had primarily professional jobs or specialized in a craft. For example, both children of the principal, Malcolm McVicar, attended and so did the daughter and son of carpenters.[73] Many of the students attended First Baptist Church, as did some teachers and administrators, and at least one member of the Board of Trustees was a member there. Two of the administrators also taught Sunday school and one of the nine faculty members attended the church.[74]

Religion was such a strong influence in the school that all students attended scripture reading and prayer service each day. Bible classes were held weekly that explored "the views of different religious sects" but adhered to "the fundamental truths of Christianity."[75] A Sunday church service was mandatory for students on the campus.[76]

Social familiarity and residency in Brockport allowed the Barrier children to escape the restrictions many black children faced. Few states had a viable public school system during the first half of the nineteenth century, and of those that did, most preferred to organize segregated black institutions rather than permit blacks and whites to attend the same school.[77] As a result, many black parents supported segregated schools because they believed that the amount of racism and discrimination their children faced put them at greater risk of marginalization and labels of inferiority.[78] That happened in the neighboring city of Rochester, where black activists campaigned for an all-black school specifically to counter the effects of institutionalized racism.[79]

Even more important was the fact that the prevailing racist and sexist ideology that governed most black women's lives had little effect on Fannie and Ella. To be sure, they benefited from residing north of slavery and attending a more liberally defined educational system than their southern counterparts could, but many of their northern black female peers had difficulties gaining full admittance and acceptance in public and private educational institutions. A few did find access to private institutions, but those were often fraught with racial problems. For example, in 1833, many white parents reacted with anger when Prudence Crandall, a white Quaker teacher in Canterbury, Connecticut, admitted a black female student into her all-white female academy. They withdrew their children in protest. When Crandall reopened the academy as an all-black female institution, she was harassed, arrested, and convicted of providing instruction to nonresident blacks. Eventually local residents vandalized the school, forcing her to close the doors to an important vehicle for the education of black females.[80]

Fannie and Ella escaped those kinds of assaults because of the insularity of the community and the villagers' high regard for their family and aversion to racial segregation. Former principal Malcolm McVicar, speaking as a representative of the American Baptist Home Mission Society, recalled in 1897 during a presentation to the Virginia Baptist State Convention in Salem, Virginia, that he had been "working for the colored people" for decades. "I have stuck to them and will stick to them until I die," he told the audience. One example that he highlighted to demonstrate his long-term commitment to black equality was a recollection of an event that occurred at the school during his tenure as principal. "During her early life in New York state, Fanny [sic] Barrier Williams was seated in the school with a white patron of the school. He wished her to have a seat in another place," presumably because the patron did not want to sit near a black student. School officials were so offended at this demand for segregation that "we told him that she could have another place by going to another place."[81] In other words, there was no separation of the races at the institute, and only if she left to go somewhere else that practiced segregation would she be separated from the others.

That kind of environment provided many opportunities. Although girls in Brockport were limited by gender norms, they had almost as much access to education as their male peers. When Fannie and Ella enrolled in the 1863–1864 academic year, six of the eleven teachers were female. At nearly every level, from Collegiate Department, which provided advanced preparation for college, to the Primary Department, the number of female students either surpassed or was almost equal to the number of males. The aggregate number of females enrolled for each of the terms in that school year exceeded the number of males: there were 205 females in the student body of 353. Even though the Collegiate Department was one of the few venues where men were prepared differently than women, there was a combined total of eleven females to the twelve males in both the junior and senior programs over the three terms of that school year. Males who were enrolled in the "Gentlemen's Classical" tract were destined for college, while the "Ladies Classical" courses were "designed for such as wish, in addition to the ordinary English course, to pursue the study of Latin." The largest number of women was concentrated in the Academic Department, where women outnumbered men by a margin of seventy-nine to thirty.[82] Many students who attended the school (eighty females and seventy-one males) were not enrolled in any of the categorizations; they were listed as unclassified.[83] The high number of females who attended the institute was certainly due in part to the increase in young northern men delaying entry or dropping out of school because they were enlisting in the military during the waning years of the war. But it was also because parents who could afford it were interested in expanding opportunities for their daughters. More educational facilities in the Northeast, like the institute, had begun to respond to the insistence of parents that education for their daughters combine professional training with an emphasis on household management and motherhood. And young women seemed eager to explore the new opportunity. Even by December 1865, eight months after the end of the war, the number of young women outnumbered the number of males in Barrier's class of 173.[84]

Just as gender had a limited impact on the status of Fannie and Ella at the school, age differences played a limited role in the school's programs. Although three years separated Fannie and Ella, they remained in the same classes throughout their course work, and George, who was five years Fannie's senior, matriculated with boys in the same department as his sisters. Records for the three terms of the 1863–1864 school year suggest that they had all completed the requirements of the Primary Department and moved to the Preparatory

Department in a class of twenty-six girls and twenty-four boys. By the winter term of 1864–1865, the class had grown to include thirty-four girls and thirty-one boys. In the fall of 1865 they advanced to the Academic Department.[85] In the first year of that program, they enrolled in courses that included math, grammar, history, government, and philosophy. The second year was more rigorous. They completed the math and philosophy courses that they had begun in the first year and advanced into courses that included geography, Latin, botany, and literature.[86]

The end of the Civil War and the reunification of the nation had a profound impact on enrollment at the institute and exposed the Barrier children to a much broader regional range of students. The number of students more than doubled in the Academic Department. Ninety-eight ladies and seventy-five gentlemen were taking courses in the fall of 1865. Some students came from communities as far south as Richmond, Virginia, and from as far west as East Troy, Wisconsin.[87]

Fannie and her siblings were exposed to a broad array of opportunities to develop skills in writing, oratory, and the arts and an appreciation of the importance of physical fitness. Students who prepared compositions engaged in weekly "rhetorical exercises."[88] Payment of extra fees that varied from $1.50 to $15.00 offered access to lessons in piano, organ, bass, and guitar. The school argued that music was an important part of the educational experience "not only as an art and an accomplishment, but as a means of promoting health and happiness." Creative courses such as a class in oil painting enhanced artistic proficiency.[89] And young women were encouraged to engage in "various athletic games" for "healthful exercise."[90]

There was a literary culture at the school as well that most likely played a significant role in Barrier's subsequent engagement in literary clubs, her voracious appetite for reading, and her pursuit of a professional career as a journalist and writer. Students had access to a library and reading room that contained "a good variety of miscellaneous books for general reading" and "a fine collection of standard works for reference." For more advanced Collegiate and Academic students there was also a reading room that included daily newspapers like the *New York Times*, *The Rochester Democrat*, and *The Brockport Advertiser*; nearly twenty weekly and monthly magazines such as *Harper's New Monthly Magazine* and *Godey's Lady's Book and Magazine*; and quarterlies such as *The Christian Review* and *The North British Review*. The Gnothesophia Literary Society held weekly meetings "for improvement in extemporaneous debate and criticism and such other exercises as tend to fit its members for real life, and accustom them to parliamentary usages."[91]

The access of girls and women to the resources of the institute played a significant role in the development and implementation of a formalized teacher curriculum that catered to their pursuit of professional careers. The regents of New York State recognized that the institute's teacher training program serviced the educational needs of the state's children and provided a subsidy that assisted twenty students at the institute with their professional development. Instruction was free for students who contracted "to engage in teaching [in] district schools a reasonable length of time," maintain student status at the institute for a full term, and adhere to the rules and regulations of the institute. The course of study the regents approved reflected the trend toward the professionalization of teaching. The institute's board promoted a series of lectures that emphasized the "Science of Common School Teaching" and formalized the school's coursework. The training women received at Brockport Collegiate Institute accorded the profession of teaching the prestige and legitimacy that had not been available to the previous generation of women.[92]

The professionalization of teaching gained momentum at the same time that the educational system underwent a significant shift in postwar New York State. Educators and legislators in the state began to place greater emphasis on school consolidation, consistency in curricula, and credentialing of schools. With the passage of the Normal School Act of 1866, the state began to move away from simply subsidizing teacher training programs and toward establishing a uniform system of normal schools with a curriculum designed to substantially increase the pool of teachers for common schools. The mandate proved beneficial to Brockport Collegiate Institute. The strong belief that the school would become an important regional facility emboldened supporters; buildings were already in place at a prime location in northwestern New York. The school's boosters approached the state legislature with a plan to enter the new standardized teacher training system, and in 1866 the institute reopened as the State Normal and Training School at Brockport.[93]

The new Normal and Training School married state and local educational interests, standardized the curriculum, and made Brockport an important regional center for instruction. It also gave Barrier unprecedented access to a professional career. An early brochure to market the new school sold it as a collaborative partnership between an expanding state educational system and the local community. The town's location, surroundings, and amenities were important in promotional materials for the facility. The brochure painted Brockport in the same way that the Collegiate Institute had in 1863. It was a genteel place "noted for its quiet beauty" that was "situated in the midst of an extensive and delightful agricultural district." The visual design of the school highlighted the physicality of the space. The buildings were "upon a slight elevation," offering "a fine view of the village." Secluded but not isolated, the facility offered both the amenities of the city and the tranquility of a village. There was ample transportation in and out of the region via railroad routes to nearby cities. In addition, "the depot, the post office, and several churches" offered necessary services, all within walking distance. But, even with its considerable offerings, the village was unlike commercialized industrial centers such as Rochester because it was "entirely removed from the dust of travel and the noise of business."[94]

The school offered programs that focused on the pedagogy and the practice of teaching. The Normal School began instruction with "a thorough drill in the primary and academic studies conducted in accordance with the most approved methods of teaching." The goal of the Training School components were "to test the ability of pupil-teachers, to reproduce the drill they have received in the Normal School, and to give them an opportunity of practicing in their profession, both as to methods of teaching and governing, under the supervision of skilled teachers, whose duty it is to criticize their work, commend their excellencies, point out and correct their errors, and suggest to them the sources and means of improvement."[95]

The school was so successful that it attracted a wide variety of female students. A large percentage came from outside Brockport. In addition to surrounding communities such as Spencerport and Clarkson, they came from places such as Niagara Falls to the west, Kendall to the north, Attica in the southwest, and Penfield, located on the eastern side of Rochester. Their denominational affiliations were also diverse: they were Catholics, Presbyterians, Episcopalians, Methodists, Congregationalists and Baptists. And the age range was broad: the youngest students were fourteen and the oldest were twenty-three.[96]

After participating in the "middle class" graduation exercises in June 1868, Barrier officially entered the Normal School in the fall. And for the first time, she was the only Barrier child enrolled in the school: Ella and George do not appear on the roster of students that year.[97] The distinction set Fannie, the youngest of the three, on a course that made her the first member of her family to matriculate from a state-funded and -accredited institution of higher learning.

Several factors contributed to her entry into the normal school. Class records for 1865 listed her as age eleven, but census records suggest that she may have been only ten that year. Thus, in 1868, she became eligible for admission to a program that required students to be fourteen years old. In addition, she demonstrated a keen intellect; she had the proficiency needed to successfully complete the "examination in spelling, reading, writing, geography, and arithmetic (as far as roots), and to analyze and parse any ordinary English sentence" that was required of all students. Finally, she benefited from state subsidies for the education of teachers. She attended free of charge and had unlimited use of textbooks; in exchange, she agreed to dedicate herself "to the business of teaching in the schools of this State."[98]

Those who entered the Academic Classical Course along with Barrier took an array of classes over a four-year period. They included grammar (in which

Barrier excelled, earning a score of 91 in one term); literature; history; ancient geography; penmanship and composition; various math and sciences courses that included geometry, algebra, trigonometry and astronomy; modern languages and rhetoric; logic and philosophy; and drawing.[99] In addition to the rigors of the academic curriculum she also could express artistic talent in drawing, painting, and music classes.[100]

By the spring 1870 term, it was clear that Barrier had been a good student, met all of the requirements of the program, and enjoyed the intellectual stimulation and camaraderie that the educational institution offered. That June, at just sixteen years old, she joined more than twenty students who presented orations, essays, and music at the graduation exercises. The topics of most speeches ranged from the esoteric ("Night Brings Out the Stars," "Society," "Pandora's Box," and "Mirrors") to the practical ("Book Making") to the reflective ("Monuments of the Past"). Barrier, in contrast, presented an essay that pointed to the future: "All the World's a Stage." *The Brockport Republic*, which deemed the speech "very fine," highlighted her curiosity about the expansive nature of the world and pointed to her desire to explore borders beyond the quaint little town that had nurtured, sustained, and shielded her since birth.[101]

In the end, the school had provided her with the necessary skills to pursue the personal, public, and professional life that was not available to her mother's generation. Harriet had married at fourteen, after which she supported her husband as a homemaker. By the age of twenty-five, she had produced three children. This would not be the fate of her daughter. Education provided a ticket to a world beyond domesticity. "After I was graduated from school," Barrier wrote, "my first ambition was to teach."[102] Through teaching she would find not only economic opportunity and intellectual stimulation but also geographical mobility.

Like a number of her classmates who eventually settled in places such as Illinois and Michigan, Fannie eschewed the security of remaining in Brockport and the promise of employment. She decided instead to strike out on her own. "I could easily have obtained a position there at my own home," she recalled, but full of ambition and high hopes for the future she decided instead "to go out into the world and do something large or out of the ordinary."[103] The establishment of segregated black schools in southern states provided the incentive, beckoning her and drawing on her professional teaching skills, her intellect, and her race consciousness. She would fill a critical need for a black population that was struggling during and after Reconstruction to reduce illiteracy rates. At the same time, she would enlarge the geographic scope of her network among the black educated elite.

2. "Completely Surrounded by Screens"

A Raced Identity

A young and determined Barrier left the insulation and security of Brockport in 1875 to teach in the black school system in a South confronted with Reconstruction and marked by stark contrasts with other regions of the country. She first went to Hannibal, Missouri, a small town on the Mississippi River in Marion County on the northeastern edge of the state, and then to Washington, D.C., where the largest and most cohesive group of black elites resided. These moves proved to be some of the most disconcerting, confounding, and valuable times in her life.

Considered a border state during the Civil War, Missouri had a conflicted racial and ideological history. It claimed neutrality and remained in the Union, but a large percentage of the population included southerners from both lower and upper South states who supported the Confederate cause. Nearly 10 percent of the state's population had been black slaves prior to the war, and one of the highest prewar concentrations of slaves in the state was in Marion County. By the end of Reconstruction, there was vehement opposition to the assertion of black rights in Missouri. The assault began as white Democrats began to regain control of politics shortly after the end of the war.[1] Embracing the southern redemption movement, Missouri, like many lower South states, had effectively removed Republicans from office by 1876. During this period, the legalization of segregation intensified as racial oppression became more entrenched. For example, in 1874, white Missourians defeated a Civil Rights Bill that would have enabled black students to attend predominantly white schools.[2]

Undeterred by the political turmoil and increased racial animosity, black Missourians were determined and ultimately successful in their quest for educational opportunity. The all-black Lincoln Institute was established in Jefferson City in 1866, and an institutionalized black public school system soon followed.

Hannibal became the site of one of the earliest public educational facilities built for blacks when the state mandated racially segregated schools in 1868. The Douglasville School in that city opened in the fall of 1870. But with few blacks trained as teachers, the school staff consisted of a white administrator and white instructors. Student attendance was erratic as more parents felt uneasy with the all-white personnel and about the inadequate curriculum. One group of parents was so concerned that they petitioned the school board to hire black teachers. Their efforts were successful, and in 1874, the board hired Joseph Pelham as the first black principal and two black female teachers.[3]

Barrier arrived in the town one year later. Probably lured to the area by her familial relationship with Pelham (he was her brother-in-law), she was one of a second group of black teachers that he recruited. Pelham had been born in Virginia to a large family that migrated to Detroit, Michigan, and carved out a prominent and successful niche in the city in the newspaper industry and in politics. After attending school in Detroit, he migrated to Missouri. He began his career in Independence, Missouri, and later moved to Boonville and married a teacher there. By the time he took the job as principal of Douglassville School, Barrier's brother George had united the Barrier and the Pelham families by marrying Delia Pelham, Joseph's sister. George moved to Detroit a year before Barrier became a resident of Hannibal in 1875.[4]

Hannibal was vastly different from Brockport in many ways and proved to be an inhospitable place for a northern-born elite mixed-raced woman who had lived in a prosperous and unsegregated egalitarian environment. Although there were far more blacks living in the town of over 10,000 inhabitants, prejudice and the entrenchment of injustice had created deep racial fissures and intolerance. The town's more than 1,600 blacks endured institutionalized segregation in the school system and in everyday life. Barrier settled in the town shortly after the economic depression of 1873 dealt a devastating five-year blow to the economic engines that drove the nation. In response, the Hannibal School Board cut teachers' salaries and shortened the school term. Barrier earned a meager $25 a month, $15 less than white teachers who were employed in 1870, and taught less than eight months, a reduction of nearly two months from the 1870 requirement.[5] In Hannibal, she became raced for the first time. She was denied the privileges of her class and was forced to acknowledge the gendered and raced constraints upon black woman-hood. Reflecting on her anguish and torment, she wrote in 1904 that "until I became a young woman and went South to teach I had never been reminded that I belonged to an 'inferior race.'"[6] That label of inferiority had a profound impact on her. It challenged the principle of equal access that she had come to understand and highlighted a clear disparity between her and her white friends in the North. She confessed that she had primarily pursued employment in the region because "I had known of quite a number of fine young white women who had gone South to teach the freedmen, and following my race instinct, I resolved to do the same."[7] But her optimism dissipated because the South she inhabited was much more narrow and confining for her than it was for her white colleagues. "It was here," she wrote, "for the first time that I began life as a colored person, in all that term implies."[8] Bemoaning the loss and security of her northern unfettered world and lamenting the dehumanizing effects of racism, she asserted that

> no one but a colored woman, reared and educated as I was can ever know what it means to be brought face to face with conditions that fairly overwhelm you with the ugly reminder that a certain penalty must be suffered by those who, not being able to select their own parentage, must be born of a dark complexion. What a shattering of cherished ideals! Everything that I learned and experienced in my innocent social relationship in New York State had to be unlearned and read-justed to these lowered standards and changed conditions. The Bible that I had been taught, the preaching I had heard, the philosophy and ethics and the rules of conduct that I had been so sure of, were all to be discounted. All truth seemed here only half truths. I found that instead of there being a unity of life common to all intelligent, respectable and ambitious people, down South life was divided into white and black lines, and that in every direction my ambitions and aspirations were to have no beginnings and no chance of development.[9]

So intolerable was her stay in Hannibal that by the time she wrote to family friend Frederick Douglass to congratulate him on his new appointment as U.S. marshal in the District of Columbia in March 1877, she had already mapped out a plan for fleeing the town.[10] By the fall of 1877, she had relocated and joined Douglass in the nation's capital. With this move, Barrier began to recognize the distinctive differences between the geographical regions. Nearly twenty years later she opined that "there is something in the land of the south and in its civilization that make it the most interesting portion of our country." Plagued with "so many social contrasts, so many contradictions, so much good cheer and so much sadness, so much hope and so much despair, and above all such warmth of welcome on the one hand and so many repelling prejudices on the other, that you are scarcely sure of your beliefs."[11] That analysis only emerged after she had enjoyed the fruits of a sophisticated and cosmopolitan southern mecca of black aristocracy.

*   *   *

The migration to Washington reunited Fannie with her sister Ella, intimately connected her to the largest contingent of blacks that she had ever known, and helped her understand how a raced person could exist within the confines of the privileged world of southern black culture. Ella, who graduated in 1871 from the Elementary English program at Brockport Normal and Training School, had been hired in the "Colored Schools of Washington" in September 1875, where

Figure 1. This photograph is believed to be of Fannie Barrier as a young woman and may have been made when she lived in Washington, D.C., from 1877 to 1887. Courtesy of Moorland-Spingarn Research Center, Howard University.

she developed a long and productive professional career.[12] As the older sister, Ella's presence two years before Fannie arrived minimized the burden of Barrier's relocation and proved to be an important resource for the younger sister's application to the public school system and her entrée into the very tight-knit circle of black elites.

More urban and populated than either Brockport or Hannibal, Washington offered multiple social, cultural, and employment opportunities.[13] For the first time Barrier was immersed in a racially separate and cohesive community. The solidity created a race and class consciousness unlike anything that she had ever encountered in her overwhelmingly white northern home town. The well-defined black aristocracy of prominent and powerful women and men shared many characteristics. They were primarily mixed race, educated, and refined. Although many were southerners, a number of them hailed from the North or had spent considerable time there. Some of the most distinguished included the Cook family, Mary Ann Shadd Cary, Richard Greener, Charlotte Forten Grimké and her husband Francis J. Grimké, and Frederick Douglass, who had relocated to the area.

The Cooks had a long history of leadership. John Francis Cook had helped establish one of the oldest black churches in the city, Fifteenth Street Presbyterian Church, in 1841 and led what became known as the "black 400" aristocratic society in Washington. His three sons, who all graduated from college, played a central role in education, business, and medicine in the city for decades: George F. T. Cook served as superintendent of the black public schools; John Cook was a trustee of Howard University and was employed as a tax collector; and Samuel LeCount Cook became one of the most successful physicians in the area.[14]

Mary Ann Shadd Cary, a native of Delaware, had lived in Canada for more than a decade before the Civil War and had co-founded the *Provincial Freeman* there, a newspaper that was committed to assisting the black refugees who fled the Fugitive Slave Law of 1850. Hers was a caustic voice against discrimination, and she was a staunch civil rights activist. She moved back to the United States after the death of her husband and subsequently migrated to Washington. She found employment in the city's public school system, first as a teacher then as a principal. She also earned a law degree at the Howard University Law School and became active in the budding women's reform movement.[15]

Richard Greener was born in Philadelphia and earned a degree at Harvard in 1870. Shortly after he graduated, he moved south. He first became principal of the black high school in Washington, D.C., then relocated to Columbia, South Carolina, to accept a post as the first black faculty member at the University of South Carolina in 1873. When the university closed in 1877 he returned to Washington, where he began working for the federal government in the Treasury Department and became a professor at Howard Law School. He was dean of the law school from 1878 to 1880.[16]

Charlotte Grimké was also a native of Philadelphia. Her family included some of the most influential abolitionists and women's rights advocates in the country. Like them she became an activist, making speeches, writing, and engaging in civil rights issues. She moved to the sea islands of South Carolina to teach blacks during and after the Civil War. After the war she worked for the Treasury Department. In 1878, she married Francis J. Grimké, the nephew of abolitionists Sarah and Angelina Grimké.[17]

Francis Grimké was one of three sons born to a white slaveholder and an enslaved mixed-race woman in Charleston, South Carolina. He attended public schools in the city and eventually moved north to further his studies at Lincoln University. After graduating in 1870, he entered Princeton Theological Seminary and became an ordained Presbyterian minister. He and his wife became two of the most prominent members of the Washington elite when he accepted the position of minister of the Fifteenth Street Presbyterian Church in 1878.[18]

The black elite found camaraderie and solace among themselves, creating a separate world from the masses that included a number of educational, social, and civic pursuits.[19] Literary societies dominated their intellectual interests, while musical concerts and parties provided social stimulation and reinforced class consciousness and boundaries. When *The People's Advocate* noted that "Washington has nothing to boast of in the way of literary organizations," several blacks answered the call to change that perception.[20] They created a number of literary groups, including the Monday Night Literary Society and the Bethel Literary Association. Organized sometime in the early 1880s, the Monday Night Literary society catered to its educated, affluent, and business-minded membership, which included public school teachers such as Barrier, administrators and faculty at Howard, and other professionals. Longtime family friend Frederick Douglass, who had moved to Washington in 1878 after his appointment as U.S. marshal in the District of Columbia by President Rutherford Hayes, was one of the most famous members. Francis J. Grimké, Charlotte Forten Grimké, and Richard Greener were also members. The society studied the works of Ralph Waldo Emerson, Charles Dickens, and Shakespeare.[21] In addition to its mission as an educational circle, the society also seemed to act as a respectable meeting place for singles. For example, when Douglass hosted a lavish end-of-the-year celebration that highlighted the social importance of the society at his home in June 1883, many single men and women attended. Several unescorted female guests, including Barrier, her sister Ella, and fellow teacher Marion P. Shadd, joined in the festivities with unattached young men such as Samuel Laing Williams, a native of Michigan who was a pension office employee. That evening, they spent time on the "croquet lawn" before gathering in the parlor for a program that included music, recitation, speeches, and dinner.[22]

The much more egalitarian Bethel Literary and Historical Association was perhaps the most well known of the black societies in Washington. Unlike the Monday Night Society, Bethel embraced the literate populace, regardless of class, and operated less like an elite social club. While the membership in the two organizations may have overlapped, Bethel's mission was broader.

Organized in 1881 by Bishop Daniel Payne of the African Methodist Episcopal Church, the association's primary purpose was to serve as "a forum in which maturity of thought, breadth of comprehension, sound scholarship, lofty patriotism and exalted philanthropy could find a cordial welcome."[23] The size and outreach of the association and its open forum format attracted a considerable following and contributed to the association's longevity; it lasted for more than three decades. Meetings were initially held twice a month but quickly grew to once a week on Tuesday evenings.[24] In the early years, presentations by men and women demonstrated their commitment to race and gender issues and to nationalism and history. The first presentation, "Who Were the Ancient Egyptians and What Did They Accomplish?," spoke to the attempt to highlight the diasporic heritage of black Americans and to illustrate the accomplishments of early Africans.[25] Some of the most distinguished intellectuals in the nation sought an opportunity to present to the association, attracted by Bethel's critical analysis and debating style. Contributors from Ohio and South Carolina and newspaper editors vied for space. In addition to Frederick Douglass, Henry McNeal Turner was a frequent guest. Over the years literary topics broadened to reflect Victorian ideals of "True Womanhood" and "True Manhood" as well as the social, political, and economic issues the black community faced in the latter half of the nineteenth century.[26]

Bethel's more egalitarian forum encouraged women to participate. Although the group did not elect its first female president until 1892, women did hold administrative posts and made presentations. For example, a woman was elected second vice-president and treasurer in 1887.[27] Emma Merritt, demonstrating an early interest in women's reform, discussed temperance at the February 1884 meeting. In her well-prepared speech, she used statistical evidence to illuminate the debilitating effects "of drunkenness on the individual and society."[28] Other women found a space as well. Mary Ann Shadd Cary joined a panel of six men to discuss the merits of a presentation on persecution in the South and advocacy of westward migration.[29] While it is unclear whether Barrier was a member of Bethel in its infancy or attended any of the meetings, she certainly was influenced by it. Newspapers reported on each event and many of her aristocratic cohorts attended and participated in the meetings. In later years she demonstrated her high regard for the organization by returning as a presenter.[30]

The elites who participated in the various clubs, societies, and organizations of the city usually worshiped together as well. These religious institutions not only met the spiritual needs of their members but also acted as social centers of coordinated activity. Union Bethel AME (later Metropolitan AME), Fifteenth Street Presbyterian, Nineteenth Street Baptist, and St. Luke's Protestant Episcopal, for example, were some of the most noted and exclusive institutions in the city to highlight the association between social class and religious affiliation. The churches served as both a barrier between their members and the black lower class and a bulwark against white discrimination. Since the elite were highly critical of the emotionalism displayed in the majority of black churches, their churches adopted a sophisticated and intellectual liturgical style that confirmed their class status and educational attainment and ensured that the illiterate would not attend.[31] Barrier's connection to the elite black culture in the city led her to insist in later years that black aristocrats worshipped differently from the masses because their style of worship symbolized enlightenment's triumph over the demonstrative displays of emotion that were so prevalent among the uneducated.[32]

The stark class differences in the city's black community also meant that the religious institutions in Washington were bound to the black elite in terms of geography. The churches of the elite physically segregated them from the black masses because they were situated in the confines of the elite black sections of northwest Washington. And because prominent whites often befriended or at least demonstrated a "tolerant friendliness" toward elite blacks, they sometimes attended services.[33]

One of the most prominent churches was the Fifteenth Street Presbyterian, where Fannie and Ella attended and taught Sunday school. The church, which opened its doors in 1841, became a symbol of racial progress. Under the leadership of Grimké, one journalist described the church in 1881 as reflecting "our possibilities and excellences." This was primarily because, according to Willard Gatewood, the church "included a disproportionately large number of blacks who were highly educated, occupied the most lucrative posts open to their race in the federal and District governments, and held membership in Washington's most exclusive social organizations."[34]

The city's black elite actively engaged in a number of cultural activities as well. One favorite seemed to be hosting receptions and participating in home visits. When Pinckney B. S. Pinchback, who had served as Louisiana's lieutenant governor in 1871–72 and acting governor of Louisiana during a short period in the winter of 1872–73, held a reception at the home of Robert Harlan, a member of one of Washington's premier black families, in honor of leap year, it was an elaborate affair that welcomed prominent black elites.[35] They also held parties and opened their homes for New Year's Day celebrations. Guests often enjoyed feasts and joined in lively conversation. Meetings in private homes were of particular importance for welcoming young single women into the aristocratic community. Often the small gatherings in homes were as much about maintaining certain rituals of formal introduction to elite black society as they were about fostering an environment for and assembling an aristocratic cohort of women. Barrier attended one such event at the home of Mrs. Smallwood in 1880.[36] Adhering to elite etiquette, Smallwood also included two other sisters who more than likely were single and had recently arrived in the city.[37] Even the annual summer vacation was celebrated just before aristocrats fled the heat of the city in favor of places like Sandy Spring on the eastern shore of Maryland and Cape May in northern New Jersey. Many northerners returned home each summer to visit family and friends, as did Fannie and Ella. Although these festivities were sometimes hosted in private homes, many were held in churches. For example, the Fifteenth Street Presbyterian Church threw a gala "in honor of those of their number, teachers and others who are about to leave for their homes on their annual vacation." Coordinated by a committee of women that included Fannie's sister Ella and the minister's wife, Charlotte Forten Grimké, the celebration included music, food, flowers, and various performances. The minister served as master of ceremonies, and several prominent members of the church gave speeches.[38]

Although the black aristocratic culture in Washington connected Barrier to both the southern and national black elite communities and provided her with a socially derived class network from geographical areas that spanned the nation, that connection could not limit the association that she had with less affluent blacks or with the racism they faced in their daily lives. While black aristocrats certainly could minimize the impact of discrimination on their own lives and voluntarily segregate themselves from the black masses, the fullest illumination of their racial imprisonment and powerlessness was visible when they faced the entrenched segregated environment of the city. Unlike Brockport, with its low black population and residential egalitarianism, Washington's neighborhoods contained and limited black interaction with whites, forcing Barrier into a racialized cultural experience. Employment and business opportunities were more often than not determined and segregated by race. Even blacks who held lucrative positions in the federal government found that those jobs had limits. Although as scholar Jacqueline M. Moore points out, "the civil service gave two things to a black employee: economic security and the prestige of white-collar employment" and elevated his or her status in the black community, they were still constrained by race.[39] The editor of *The Washington Bee*, W. Calvin Chase, noted the problems many black government employees faced. Forced to perform menial labor and domestic chores rather than the skills for which they were hired, many black government workers felt trapped by the discriminatory actions of their employers. Fear of losing their jobs kept them in what Chase argued was "a new kind of slavery."[40] Like Barrier's father, some blacks found entrepreneurship the best means of economic success. One of the most successful routes to economic stability for blacks was in the hotel industry. Few white hotels opened their doors to blacks, and those that did were unappealing to aristocratic guests. In response, James A. Wormley, one of the most prominent blacks in the city, established the Wormley Hotel in 1871.[41]

If a raced class identity forced Barrier to face a collective racial experience, then economic imperatives compelled her to acknowledge the limitations of a raced gender identity. When she entered Washington's education system, the vast majority of the teachers were female and segregation in education was entrenched. Although calls to integrate the schools had always been part of public discourse in the city, its parallel and separate educational systems continued to expand. Even blacks who were unwilling to send their children to ill-equipped schools shortly after the Civil War and who had argued that an integrated system offered black children the best opportunity began to advocate for a separate system in the post-Reconstruction years.[42]

The very nature of segregated schools highlighted two primary issues that illustrated the complexity of southern segregation. First, black teachers found themselves constrained by race. When Barrier applied for a teaching position in Washington she became raced, since her skin color determined that she was only eligible to teach in black schools. Second, in spite of the racialized implications of a dual educational structure, she and other black teachers gained cultural capital by engaging in a respected field of employment for single black and elite women in the late nineteenth century.[43] As a teacher she maintained her social class standing, and her normal school training and skills were valuable and much-needed commodities. Because teaching provided respectable employment and paid for expertise, it proved to be one of the most lucrative occupations for black women. And the school system of the nation's capital was highly regarded and provided African Americans with one of the best educations in the country. The salaries of black teachers in the city were comparable to those of their white counterparts, unlike in other southern cities. Blacks also held positions on the school board along with whites.[44]

In addition, because few southern institutions were devoted to the training of black teachers, job opportunities abounded for northerners like Barrier for the critical period during Reconstruction. School systems in cities such as Washington welcomed northern female graduates of normal schools and academies. For example, Louise Smith, who was trained in Norwich, Connecticut, began her teaching career in Washington in 1869. Mattie Hoy was educated in New York and found employment in the school system in the fall of 1873. Even those from across the northern border found opportunity. Marion P. Shadd, a native of Chatham, Ontario, Canada, was the cousin of Mary Ann Shadd Cary. When her father died in 1866, the family relocated to Washington, where her parents had lived before migrating to Canada in the 1850s. While Shadd's brother attended Howard, eventually earning degrees in 1878 and 1881, she was enrolled in a high school for black children. Initially held in the Fifteenth Street Presbyterian Church, the school later moved to the Sumner Building. By the time that she was sixteen, she had been sent north to attend the Framingham Normal School in Massachusetts. In the fall of 1877 she returned to Washington and found employment in the city's public schools.[45] Barrier, Shadd, nine other black teachers, and three sub-assistants were confirmed by the Board of Trustees for positions in the Seventh Division in that year. More teachers were hired in that division in 1877 than in any other division in the system.[46]

All of the northern-trained women had arrived at an opportune time, just before a local push to turn inward to find a way to decrease dependence on northern schools for teachers for the primary grades. The Washington school system became one of the first in the South to successfully do so. In the November 11, 1879, minutes, the Board of Trustees of Public Schools of the District of Columbia officially recognized its ongoing and lucrative relationship with the Myrtilla Miner School for black children. Established by abolitionist Myrtilla Miner in 1851, the school had played an important and necessary role in serving the educational needs of black children since before the Civil War. Although it closed briefly during the war, it reopened and became part of the Washington school system for black children. Because of the "important and intimate relations of this institution and the Board" the school eventually became a teaching institution that supplied large numbers of black female teachers throughout the 1880s.[47]

In August 1877, two months before Barrier was hired, the Seventh Division Sub-Board contracted with the Institution for the Education of Colored Youths to erect a ten-room building on 17th Street Northwest at P and Q streets. The school housed the Public High School for Colored Children and the Miner Normal School. The construction of the building ensured that "the female graduates of the Public High School for Colored Children shall, upon recommendation of the Principal of said High School and the Superintendent of Colored Schools, and the approval of the Trustees of the Miner Normal School, be entitled to admission to said Normal School, and upon the successful completion of the usual course, and passing the required examination for teachership in the Public Schools, shall be given the preference over all other candidates for positions of teachers in the primary grades of the Public Schools for Colored Children of Washington, Georgetown, and the District of Columbia."[48] The partnership effectively limited outside competition with local teachers and essentially locked many northern black female professionals out of the city's school system.

Teaching offered single women like Barrier some real financial returns. The average salary in 1877 was $64.44 per month. By 1883, Barrier's annual salary of $700 amply supported her elite lifestyle. Her housing costs were minimal because she and her sister boarded in the home of a respected and prominent black family, as most young single elite black women did.[49] As a result, she and

Ella were able to live the sophisticated and aristocratic life to which they had become accustomed without depending on family assistance.

Teaching was also hard work. The work day was intensive and the schools were overcrowded. Classes began at 9 A.M. and ended for most at 3 P.M. A fifteen-minute recess did not give teachers respite, for they were charged with watching their students. Most students were poorly prepared, and the curriculum the administration dictated encouraged specific methods of teaching reading, spelling, math, geography, and history. Most black parents were eager to educate their children and insisted that they attend school. As a result, the schools were filled beyond capacity and the student-teacher ratio was high. In 1877, the year Barrier was hired, more than 17,000 black and white students attended public schools. Nearly 6,000 were black. The Seventh Division had the highest number of regular teachers: ninety teachers taught 5,500 students in that division. Each teacher had an average of sixty-one students in his or her classroom.[50]

Barrier remained in the system for nearly ten years.[51] Because of a dramatic increase in the number of students, an Eighth Division was created, and she moved into it in 1882. She and fourteen other women taught in the Randall Building that year.[52] In 1884, Barrier had sixty students in her fourth grade class.[53]

The Washington Bee recognized the grueling conditions under which black teachers operated, reporting that Barrier's sister Ella had such a "weak constitution" that she couldn't possibly survive in her position. "The position of teacher is [such] a constant drain upon the system," the paper opined, that "few ladies can stand it." So it was recommended that she and others like her "assume the responsibility of governing the home of some good man" to "escape the bondage of the school room."[54]

The *Bee*'s scathing assessment and gendered attack on Ella was not unusual. Because black parents and the local community had a deep interest in the success of black public schools and entrusted their children to teachers for much of the day, black newspapers such as the *Bee* scrutinized and provided their own personal assessments of individual professionals. Sometimes biased and often critical, the biographies praised those perceived as good teachers and lambasted those deemed incompetent. Although there were no clearly defined criteria, the reports assessed the personal traits of teachers as well as their methodology and pedagogy. For example, one teacher was noted as being "a painstaking teacher, but is devoted entirely too much to the book." Another was said to be conscientious and hardworking, "at times a little prudish, but generally solid and earnest . . . is a good grammarian and mathematician, and in teaching draws in both studies largely upon the natural ability of their pupils in preference to the routine and parrot-like book method." Still another was commended for being "an honest hard working teacher" but then derided because she did not have "the qualities of making her mark as a teacher much beyond the grade now taught by her—first."[55]

Perhaps it was grueling nature of the work or because, as the *Bee* noted, "her heart is not in the work" that Barrier sought an alternative to her career as an educator. The same year the newspaper reported on the state of teaching for black women, Barrier showed signs of making a gradual departure from the teaching profession. A long-term interest in art, particularly painting, that perhaps had its genesis at Brockport Collegiate Institute or at the normal school encouraged her to seek ways to further develop her skill. To the chagrin of the editor of the *Bee*, Barrier had found a way to combine her career with a personal pursuit while still employed with the school system; she used its leave policy as an opportunity to enhance her artistic talent. Clearly disturbed by the practice, the paper opined that "she has some artistic talents and aspirations, and uses to a certain extent the public school in furtherance of that end."[56] And indeed she did, in part because it seems she had burned out on the profession, she was single and mobile, and the country was experiencing an artistic rebirth.

Washington joined the culturally enlightening movement. Members of the art community in the city had long pushed for an art school and a museum to showcase America's cultural interests. But little had occurred until the five-story building that housed the Corcoran Gallery and studio space opened in 1874. Built by white businessman William Corcoran, the gallery showcased European art and the eclectic talent of local artists, essentially solidifying the city's place in the art world. The building also included space for art classes.[57] But many blacks found the environment uninviting. To avoid discrimination, some engaged in a cultural circuit of their own making, depending on sporadic courses offered by itinerant artists or participating in private home tutoring to indulge in their interest. They even found ways to display their myriad talents through fair exhibitions such as one held at Bethel Hall in 1886.[58]

Barrier's interest in the creative arts was more than an indulgence. She wanted to become an artist. It was so important to her that she probably began searching for a skilled art teacher soon after she arrived in the South. Initially she found it impossible to locate one. But her persistence paid off when she eventually convinced a "white art teacher to admit me into one of her classes."[59] Her joy at finding a progressive-minded teacher quickly gave way to the reality of living in the segregated South. By "the second day of my appearance in the class I chanced to look up suddenly and was amazed to find that I was completely surrounded by screens," Barrier remembered. Irritated and resentful over the partition that separated her from the white students in the class, she demanded that the screen be removed. Her demand fell on deaf ears, and the instructor told her that the segregation "was made the condition of my remaining in the class."[60] While Barrier had lived in the South amid the inequities of racial segregation for some time, she was terrified of simply accepting the inevitability of racial inequality. So she refused to negotiate with those who sought to enforce the parameters of racial inequity or acquiesce to notions of white supremacy, stubbornly clinging to the social justice ideal that racial caste should not determine how and where she was taught. In the end, though, she found that the persistence of racism and discrimination was so pervasive and entrenched there was little that she could do to combat it. Ultimately she concluded that since "I had missed the training that would have made this continued humiliation possible," the only viable option for her was to leave the class.[61]

However, Barrier refused to abandon her dream of classroom art training, so she looked to the North. When she was granted a short-term leave from her teaching duties in 1884, she moved to Boston and enrolled in the New England Conservatory of Music.[62] The nearly 20-year-old institution beckoned women from all over the North and the South. Founded by Eben Tourjee in February 1867, the New England Conservatory joined several schools that opened in the post–Civil War period, including Oberlin Conservatory and Peabody Institute in Baltimore.[63] All benefited from the heightened interest of the arts, the demand for women's education, and the push to include aesthetic education in the curriculum of public schools.

The New England Conservatory also reflected a shift in the business of advertising, promoting, and implementing aesthetic programs. At the conservatory, the individual model of tutoring, which limited enrollment, gave way to a prototype that catered to a class model of instruction. The strategy proved successful and introduced hundreds to music and the arts. The school boasted that it was the largest music school in the country, and it attracted enough students to build a dorm that housed some female students on campus rather than in scattered boarding facilities throughout the city. The facilities also offered students practice rooms, parlors, and a library. By the time that Barrier arrived in 1884, nearly 2,000 students had been enrolled in or attended the conservatory. Although graduation rates remained low, many young women seeking careers in teaching and an enhancement of their cultural awareness flocked to the school.[64]

Barrier attended the conservatory for two terms, enrolling in the School of Fine Arts. The goal of the program was "to enable those wishing to make a special study of art, independently, or in connection with other studies, to secure the best facilities under competent teachers." The diverse program included elementary and advanced courses in drawing, painting, wood carving, and art embroidery. Students could also enroll in the College of Music and the School of

Elocution and Dramatic Art.[65] Barrier feasted on this large and varied number of courses. During her first term she enrolled in the Drawing Department, the Painting Department, and the Music Department, taking piano with John D. Buckingham, drawing with William Briggs, and painting with Mary E. Carter. In the second term she advanced her interest in music by continuing the piano studies with Buckingham.[66] Barrier was so proud of her achievement at the conservatory that she produced a crayon sketch of her parents and sent it to them as a gift. One store in Brockport displayed one of her pieces to showcase her talent and celebrate her success.[67]

The openness and egalitarianism that Barrier found so enlightening in the North and provided her with the opportunity to pursue her dream proved to be a double-edged sword. Founder Eben Tourjee, who had been an antislavery supporter and had come of age during the height of the abolitionist movement, ensured that black students could enroll at the conservatory. And, participating in the growth of economic enterprises in both the North and the South, he marketed the school nationally, encouraging a multi-regional growth in student population and an enlarged customer base. This coalescence of economic interest across the regions in the post-Reconstruction period was not limited to the northern institutions such as the conservatory. Southern businessmen who had formulated a plan to emerge from the aftermath of the Civil War as a New South looked to join with the industrial might of northern businesses.[68] While this dual process provided significant benefits for southern businessmen, the conservatory's push to embrace southerners and boost profits in education had detrimental consequences for Barrier. Students and their parents publicly criticized and objected to integrated classrooms and any notion of social equality. Caught between his commitment to the business of education and his personal liberal views, Tourjee adapted, accommodated such criticism, and ultimately sacrificed the egalitarian nature of the school. Pragmatic economics triumphed over idealism, and Barrier's educational aspirations were cut short. She was asked to leave the conservatory because she was black. However, she did not direct her anger toward Tourjee or hold him responsible. Instead, she attributed her dismissal to regional influence, insisting that it was the entrenchment of white supremacy that had penetrated northern reasoning and affected the northern educational and economic systems. "Even here, in the very cradle of liberty," she complained, "white Southerners were there before me, and to save their feelings I was told by the principal of the school, a man who was descended from a long line of abolition ancestors, that it would imperil the interests of the school if I remained as all of his Southern pupils would leave, and again I had to submit to the tyranny of a dark complexion."[69] In other words, she had come to experience the tension between her perceptions of the North based on her experiences while

growing up in Brockport before the Civil War and the economic realities of a
North that had reconciled with the South in the post-Reconstruction period. The
dismissal was a cruel blow and was terribly disconcerting to a woman who had
idealized her northern upbringing, often highlighting the distinct geographical
characteristics as a means of differentiating it from the racist South. With little
recourse, she returned to Washington to resume her teaching career.

* * *

Barrier returned to a city that was still reeling from the maelstrom concerning
the marriage of her dear family friend Frederick Douglass in January 1884 to
Helen Pitts, a white woman. The union and the local and national media furor
that it generated illustrated Barrier's inability to escape the entrenched schism
of the racial divide in either the North or the South. It also illuminated the
contentious debate among blacks about interracial marriage and highlighted
the ambiguous place mulattos occupied among blacks and whites. While their
backgrounds were very different, Barrier and Douglass both were able to trace
their ancestry to white lineage. Barrier's paternal grandfather was a Frenchman who married a black woman; her maternal grandfather was a white man
who married a mixed-race women. Douglass, a former slave, was the child of
his master and a slave woman. While their mixed heritage moved them into
a different caste from the darker-complexioned black masses and exposed the
fallacy of the ideology of racial purity, it did not provide unrestricted privilege.
Unlike the community of Brockport, the South and many areas in the North
were much less tolerant of marriages between blacks and whites.[70] Even Pitts's
father, an abolitionist, refused to recognize the marriage and rejected Douglass
as his son-in-law. Moreover, Douglass's own children felt betrayed. Scholar
William McFeely suggests that for them the marriage "seemed formally to have
repudiated his family—his children, their mother, and their mother's people—all
black people."[71]

His children were not alone in their views. Shortly after the ceremony was
conducted by Francis Grimké in the parsonage of the Fifteenth Street Presbyterian Church, *The People's Advocate* printed a column entitled "Must We
Intermarry?"[72] Angry over the suggestion that intermarriage was the only means
of acceptance for blacks and that black men should follow Douglass's example,
the paper editorialized that

> Much of the prejudice from which the Negro and his descendents [sic] suffer is
> the result of a belief that the Negro is absolutely an inferior being, and possible
> only of a very limited degree of culture; that the progress he has shown has been
> entirely superficial. . . . This belief, which is the foundation of all our trouble about
> equality of recognition, must be controverted. The issue cannot be shirked or

dodged. It must be squarely met. Obliterating the color line by absorption does not meet it; it simply rids the country of the Negro—that's all; the prejudice against the Negro remains.[73]

As for the status of black women, the editorial noted:

> Now that our sisters and daughters are growing to greater loveliness and comeliness than ever; now that all the womanly graces are theirs, with the added lustre of culture, let us treat as idle words the advice of the *Independent* to prefer white ladies, even though it be thought following the example of so eminent, so worthy so able an American as Frederick Douglass.[74]

In a survey of opinions in newspapers throughout the country, the *Advocate* found some support for Douglass's marriage, but the vast majority fell into two unsympathetic camps. The first highlighted black notions of leadership and the role of a race man. Douglass was accused of abandoning the race. For example, one weekly noted that "Fred Douglass, the great leader and champion of the colored race, has made the fatal error of his life. He has forfeited his claim to the leadership of his race by a foolish and unwise step. . . . This step has impaired, if not totally destroyed, Mr. Douglass' usefulness as a race leader." Another paper went further and accused Douglass of rejecting the race by not wanting "to be identified with the dear people."[75] The second camp illuminated the race and gendered dynamics that shaped black lives and perceptions. In their minds, Douglass had simply rejected black women. One noted that "among all the women of his race he finds none fit to be Mrs. Fred Douglass." Another reported that "while we believe it to be the privilege of every man and every woman to choose whom they please for a life companion, we at the same time consider the step taken by Mr. Douglass, occupying the position which he does, as a reflection upon the colored ladies of the country."[76]

Interest in the Douglass marriage remained a topic for more than year. The June 13, 1885, issue of *The Washington Bee* carried a story from the *Saturday Union* in Massachusetts that revealed that even the most enlightened religious circles bowed under the weight of southern social custom. When the couple attempted to attend one prominent Presbyterian church, they were refused acceptance for fellowship. "There has been a general stampede from the church," the paper reported, adding that "if Douglass persists in sharing his religious devotions in company with his own wife, there will soon not be a single fashionable worshipper in the church."[77]

Barrier's personal views about interracial marriage suggest that because of her own background, she both accepted Pitts and championed interracial marriage in general.[78] Her correspondence with Douglass in later years and her essays in newspapers and journals about race support this analysis. So the assault on

Douglass must have weighed heavily on her mind and made her appreciative of the fact that her own courtship and subsequent marriage drew less public scrutiny. Her future husband was also a mulatto, and the wedding was performed in Brockport, where social etiquette allowed her to combine her black and white heritage without fear of reprisal.

Barrier met Samuel Laing Williams in Washington through the aristocratic black social circle they both inhabited. They certainly attended the Monday Night Literary Society at the same time and more than likely socialized on numerous other occasions as well. They had much in common. The child of a black woman named Nancy and a white Englishman, Samuel was born in Savannah, Georgia, sometime between 1854 and 1859. While his early life is difficult to trace, it seems that he left the South as a young child and moved to Chicago with the Laing family. According to the 1870 census, the family's residence in the Fifth Ward included 62-year-old David and 60-year-old Ann Laing; three adults, Ann Richard, David Laing, and Henry Richard, all of whom were between the ages of twenty-four and thirty-one; a nine-month-old boy and sixteen-year-old Samuel Williams, who was listed as a domestic servant. All of the family had been born in England except for Henry, who was from Massachusetts; the child, who was born in Illinois; and Samuel, who was born in Georgia.[79] The family eventually moved to Columbiaville, Michigan, a small lumber and farming village located northeast of Flint in Lapeer County. Like Brockport, its population was overwhelmingly white.[80] And like Brockport, its economy was linked to the development of the transportation industry. With the arrival of the railroad in the early 1870s, the business center grew to include general stores, hotels, a harness shop, a wagon shop, and a foundry. The foundry, which opened in 1874, was owned and operated by David Laing. He had at least four years' experience in the business; he listed iron founder as his occupation while living in Chicago. That experience contributed to his economic success and made him a prominent citizen in the community. He and his wife Ann had all the trappings of an upper-class lifestyle. Ann did not work outside the home, and they employed a 20-year-old servant named Nancy Johnson to assist with household chores. They also served as guardians to a four-year-old granddaughter named Clara and Samuel, who in 1870 was a 25-year-old college student who was known as Samuel Williams. Williams later adopted the name S. Laing Williams.[81]

S. Laing Williams's connection to the Laings and his own determination to succeed meant that he fared well in Columbiaville. The studious young man received a good education at the local preparatory school, then entered the bachelor of arts program at the University of Michigan in Ann Arbor in 1877. By all accounts, the years he spent in Ann Arbor were good ones and influenced him personally and professionally. Although he was reportedly the only black male in his class, he excelled at the university. He was hard working and serious, and he enjoyed literature. He was described as "genial" and as having a "dignified personality," and he was well liked by his classmates.[82] He found employment in the summer to earn income to support his studies. One of those positions was as the enumerator for the Columbiaville census in June 1880. After earning his AB degree in 1881, he moved to Greensboro, Alabama, to become the principal of Tullibody Academy, a private school for blacks that had been established in 1873.[83] The following year, he acquired a position as an adjudicator with federal Pension Claims Bureau in Washington, where he earned an annual salary of $1,200. The position provided a steady income, exposed him to an aristocratic black southern community, and offered him the opportunity to pursue his interest in law. Shortly after arriving in the city, he enrolled in law school at Columbian University (now George Washington University). Although he was admitted, he encountered racial challenges from his classmates. He faced the anger of many whites at the Law School because he was, one source claimed, "the first colored man that ever gained admission to that University." But the adversity did not deter him. He performed well and was awarded "one of the College prizes for the best legal thesis." S. Laing received the bachelor of law degree in 1884 and graduated with the master of law in 1885.[84]

An ambitious and shrewd man, S. Laing moved quickly to enhance his economic prospects and distinguish himself in his chosen field. He enrolled in postgraduate courses at Columbian soon after he graduated. He also passed the bar and was officially admitted to the practice of law in Washington, D.C., during the summer of 1885. He then focused his attention on returning to his midwestern roots and searching for more rewarding opportunities. He resigned from his position at the Pension Office and moved back to Chicago in the fall of 1885. The city was now a bustling industrial corridor. In January 1886, he passed his examination and was admitted to the Illinois bar.[85] In the summer he formed a lucrative partnership with Ferdinand Barnett, a well-established and highly regarded attorney who had founded and edited *The Chicago Conservator*, a black weekly. Together they opened what one newspaper referred to as "a new and elegant office" that was, according to many, "the finest law office in the city."[86] Still, S. Laing had an affinity for Washington. His engagement to Barrier encouraged him to visit often.

Fannie Barrier formally resigned from her teaching position in the Eighth Division of the Washington public schools on April 12, 1887. Although her resignation was not effective until the end of the school year in May, her teaching responsibilities took a back seat to the more pressing personal matter of preparing for her upcoming nuptials.[87] Eight days after she tendered her resignation, she married S. Laing. The Williams-Barrier wedding took place at the home of

Figure 2. Samuel Laing Williams and Fannie Barrier married in 1887 in Brockport,
New York. He was a graduate of the University of Michigan in Ann Arbor and
Columbian Law School (now George Washington University) in Washington, DC,
a lawyer and a leading social and political activist in Chicago. Source: Booker T.
Washington, ed., *A New Negro for a New Century: An Accurate and Up-to-Date
Record of the Upward Struggles of The Negro Race* (Chicago: American Publishing
House, 1900), 69.

the bride's parents in Brockport on April 20, 1887, at 1 P.M. It was a grand affair that reflected the class status of the bride's family and of the couple. Nearly thirty family and friends attended the exclusive, intimate, and "very pleasant event." Flowers and plants adorned several rooms of the home where guests gathered. The bride wore a white satin dress that was highlighted by lace trimming. Barrier's sister Ella was the bridesmaid. The minister of First Baptist, J. H. Mason, presided over the ceremony as the couple took their vows in the parlor beneath a floral arch.[88] After the nuptials, the bride and groom opened gifts "that lacked nothing in beauty or value" and dined on an "an ample wedding feast."[89]

The wedding generated considerable attention in the press, which presented the event using language that was congruent with the racial utopia Barrier had longed for ever since leaving her home town more than a decade earlier. Her father's prominence and strong connection to the community invited the extensive coverage. Describing the bride as the "youngest daughter" of "our well known citizen Mr. Anthony Barrier," *The Brockport Republic* highlighted the social status of the Barrier family and made no mention of the race of the couple or the family.[90] Reflecting back on the event in 1904, Barrier Williams boasted that "my own family and my husband were the only persons to lend color to the occasion. Minister, attendants, friends, flowers and hearts were of purest white."[91] Holding the wedding in the one place that reminded her of the potential for racial harmony restored her confidence in her ability to connect and interact with whites on equal terms. The relationships with her white cohorts for the short time she was home reaffirmed the memories she had of the strong white support network she had left behind during her sojourn in the South. She fondly recalled that it was the bonds of friendship developed with former white classmates that sustained her in the bleakest moments and provided the support and assistance she needed in preparation for and during her wedding. Angered by the racism that had plagued her as an adult, she turned to those childhood memories and friends to assuage the bitterness. "After the buffetings, discouragements and discourtesies that I had been compelled to endure," she lamented, "it was almost as in a dream that I saw again my schoolmates gather around me." They welcomed her home and "manage[ed] every detail of preparation for my wedding." They decorated the home with flowers and demonstrated their affection and fondness by "showering me with gifts, and joining in the ceremony with tears and blessings."[92]

Barrier Williams wasn't the only one caught up in the vision of a racial utopia. *The Cleveland Gazette*, a black weekly, viewed the marriage as a potent indication of the future of race relations. The paper focused its attention on S. Laing rather than on his new bride, highlighting his stature and regional residency. Whereas Barrier Williams's father's prominence in predominantly white Brockport ensured coverage by the white newspaper without any mention of race, the

Gazette, a black paper, promoted S. Laing as a symbol of the success that elite blacks believed was vitally important for alleviating racism. He was recognized as "the distinguished attorney of Chicago, who was married to Miss Frances Barrier last week, in Brockport" and noted as "the student whose entrance into Columbia [*sic*] college some years ago caused the white students to threaten to leave. But some of the same students were his best friends when he was married."[93] Ultimately, the ceremony that joined the southern-born attorney and his northern bride signified the merger of race, region, and class and became a metaphor for the triumph of black aristocratic aspirations over white animosity and antagonism.

But first the couple had to relinquish the serenity of their utopian dream by traveling back into the racially bifurcated world of the South. Less than six hours after the ceremony, Fannie and S. Laing left Brockport and boarded a train bound for the South. Embarking on a "wedding tour," they headed back to Washington to be properly presented as a couple to the black aristocratic society that had welcomed and embraced them for more than a decade. There they would enjoy "several receptions" hosted by "intimate and influential friends."[94] After the festivities, the couple shifted their sights to one of the fastest-growing regions in the country and their new home of Chicago.

3. Creating Community in the Midwest

Chicago

Even before Fannie and S. Laing Williams completed their wedding tour in Washington and settled into their home on Calumet Avenue in Chicago, they had been introduced to the city's black community. The *Western Appeal*, one of the leading black newspapers in the Midwest, announced the nuptials. Listed on the front page under "Knots & Tours: Matrimonial Linkings and Spring Migration of Prominent People," the notice highlighted S. Laing's prominence in the community and solidified the couple's place among the city's elite.[1] More important, the announcement was a first step in the public ritual of introducing the two as a unit to the local and regional community and served as the first significant vehicle for securing Barrier Williams's place in the privileged and cultured circle of black midwestern aristocracy.

The aristocracy that would ultimately determine Barrier Williams's stature centered on two distinct and overlapping groups. The first was the small socially conscious group of black families who had arrived in Chicago before the Great Fire that destroyed much of the city in 1871.[2] Often referred to as the "old guard," many had escaped from the oppressive racial politics of the South. They were only a small part of the 6,480 blacks who made up a little over 1 percent of city's ethnically diverse population in 1880.[3] The most prominent of those was Mary Jones, the widow of John Jones, who had been the most successful black man in post–Civil War Chicago. Born Mary Richardson, the mixed-race daughter of a blacksmith, she was from Memphis, Tennessee. Her husband John was also a southerner and of mixed-race lineage. He had been born on a plantation in North Carolina to a German father and a mixed-race mother. He was sent to Memphis to fulfill an indenture to a tailor, but he eventually migrated to Alton, Illinois, where he married Mary in 1841. The couple moved to Chicago sometime in 1845 or 1846. Life in pre–Civil War Illinois was not easy. The black population hovered around 300 in 1850. But even with so few black residents, restrictive codes limited their rights. Blacks could not vote, serve on juries, or testify against whites. They also could not serve in the militia. The Fugitive Slave Law of 1850 that mandated that northerners return escaped slaves to their owners added to the inhospitable environment. The Joneses valiantly fought against these injustices. John publicly spoke out against the Black Laws that severely restricted black social, economic, and political opportunity and participated in several conventions that petitioned for black rights. He attended a national convention of freemen in Cleveland in 1848 and was elected vice-president of the convention. In 1853 he traveled to Rochester, New York, to attend a meeting where representatives from eight states discussed ways to promote black self-sufficiency. The couple also became staunch abolitionists and helped hundreds of runaway slaves reach Canada. They hosted Frederick Douglass when he traveled through the area, and John wrote several letters to Douglass, one in 1847 decrying the flogging of a black man accused of being a spy and another in 1853 about the flourishing Underground Railroad in the state. Mary played an equally active role. The couples' granddaughter recalled that her grandmother "harbored and fed the fugitive slaves that these men bought to her door as a refuge until they could be transported to Canada. In fact she stood at my Grand-father's side—her husband John Jones—until their early Chicago home became one of the Underground Railway Stations. It was she who stood guard at the door when these pioneer abolitionists were in conference—with the slaves huddled below in the basement."[4]

Advocating for black rights and engaging in the abolitionist movement certainly contributed to the couple's financial hardships during those early years in the city, but they managed to prosper anyway. With the assistance of sympathetic whites John learned to read and find adequate employment. He saved his money and subsequently opened his own tailoring shop, catering primarily to wealthy whites. He accumulated enormous wealth and influence and parlayed his success into the realm of politics.[5] In 1871, when he was elected to the Cook County Board of Commissioners, he became the first black man to hold an elected position in the county. After his death in 1879, Mary, who had considerable financial resources and connections among the city's prominent residents, assumed her husband's position in society and became the aristocratic matriarch, presiding over the black elite for nearly two decades.[6]

The Joneses' gallant and successful battle for black rights benefited late-nineteenth-century migrants like Barrier Williams. They enjoyed the fruits of an early struggle that culminated in collegial interactions between the races and social, political, and economic opportunities for black residents. By the

1880s, overt segregation had decreased for the most part, and laws had become much more consistent about protecting black rights. Black men continued to vote and participate in politics long after the Fifteenth Amendment was passed and Reconstruction ended. Three black men served in the Illinois House of Representatives in the period 1876 to 1890. In 1885, the city of Chicago passed a civil rights law that demonstrated a move toward racial democratization.[7] As a result, optimism remained high. For example, Ferdinand Barnett's weekly, *The Chicago Conservator*, proudly noted that "Chicago was a pretty fair place for Negroes to live and that there was little friction between the races."[8]

Another reason for confidence was the fact that by 1890 Chicago had become the second-largest city in the country and a center of industry.[9] In the aftermath of the Great Fire, the economic engines that drove the city attracted both big business and a multiethnic workforce. Fueled by the growth of the grain and meatpacking industries and the increased production in manufacturing, merchandising, and publishing, the city became a lucrative and efficient financial powerhouse.[10] As a result, the city's population soared. From 1880 to 1890, the black population alone more than doubled, from 6,480 to 14,271.[11] Even with this increase, the proportion of blacks in the city remained the same as it had for a decade, near 1 percent of the total, because so many whites and immigrants moved to the city. In 1880, nearly half a million whites lived in the Chicago. But more than 200,000 of those were foreign born. Ten years later both figures had doubled: the city had 1,084,998 white residents, of which 450,666 were foreign born.[12]

The new generation of elite blacks had much in common with the old guard, but they advocated a clear shift in strategy and pushed for programs designed to assist them and the rest of the black community. Collectively they faced far less racism than the old guard had. Nearly all had been born free; for them, the memory of slavery was less poignant. Almost all of the men of the new generation had come of age at a time when voting rights were assured. Most arrived with college degrees and had the skills they needed to develop prosperous businesses. The women were as well educated as the men and were much more visible in public life than the women of any previous generation. Many, like Barrier Williams, had graduated from normal schools or attended other academic institutions. For this group, interracial cooperation was integral to their mission of dismantling any vestiges of segregation. Because a number of them had lived in predominantly white communities and earned degrees in schools that were predominantly white, they were more integrated with the white community than any generation of blacks in history. They were opposed to racial separation of any kind and strenuously and successfully objected to a proposal to build a black YMCA in 1889. The defeat came at the hands of the new generation of aristocrats because they believed that race-specific designations invited submission to segregation, and in this case the old guard supported them.[13] *The Chicago Conservator* perhaps best captured the group's sentiment: "As a race let us forget the past so far as we can, and unite with other men upon issues liberal, essential, and not dependent upon color of skin or texture of hair for its gravamen."[14]

The members of the new generation distinguished themselves from the black masses by highlighting their differences from the poor who were unemployed and members of the working class who held jobs as servants in white homes or hotels. When physician Daniel Hale Williams told a group that "the great mistake which white people make is to judge the whole Colored race by the sleeping car porter (who is not half so black as he has been painted)," he expressed a characteristic sentiment of the black elite, who took pride in their mixed-race lineage, their light skin, and their professional occupations.[15] The union of the old guard and the new generation in Chicago created an aristocratic clique that was known as the "black 400," like the Washington black elite. This group influenced the direction of black social and political reform in Chicago until the turn of the century.[16]

Barrier Williams easily transitioned into this culture. Her credentials as a northern aristocrat who had been embraced by Washington elites certainly added to her profile in the Chicago group. S. Laing's residency in the city in the early 1870s and his law partnership with Ferdinand Barnett also eased the couple's transition. Fannie and S. Laing quickly built a coalition of like-minded friends and gained the favor of Mary Jones. Barnett and his wife Mary, Lloyd Garrison Wheeler and his wife Sarah, Charles Bentley and his wife Traviata, and Daniel Hale Williams were perhaps some of the most important members of the couple's inner circle.

Ferdinand Barnett and Lloyd Garrison Wheeler had lived, for the most part, in Chicago for at least a decade before Barrier Williams arrived and provided a bridge between the old guard and the new generation. Born in Nashville, Tennessee, in 1855, Barnett had lived for a short time in Canada. Several years later, the family migrated to Chicago, where he attended high school. After receiving his diploma, he went south to teach for two years. Upon returning to the city, Barnett entered the Union College of Law, earning his degree in 1878. That same year he began publishing *The Chicago Conservator* with James E. Henderson and Abram T. Hall.[17]

His wife, Mary Graham Barnett, was one of Barrier Williams's most important contacts because of the law partnership their husbands shared. Mary may have been a long-term acquaintance of S. Laing; they had attended the University of Michigan during overlapping years. She graduated in 1880, a year before he did, becoming the first black female to earn a degree at the university. After her marriage to Ferdinand in 1882, she assisted him with *The Chicago Conservator*. In addition to her professional activities, she was a musician and raised the couple's two sons. Unfortunately, illness plagued her, and in 1888 she died of heart disease.[18]

Lloyd Garrison Wheeler, the first African American admitted to the Illinois bar, was originally from Ohio but spent his formative years in Canada. In 1870, he moved to Arkansas, where he filled several Reconstruction-era political appointments; he became the attorney for and served as a member of the Board of Commissioners of Pulaski County. His marriage to Sarah Raynie Petit, a niece of Mary and John Jones, gave him entrée to the most powerfully connected family in the city. After Jones's death, Wheeler managed the tailoring business and assumed a leading role in civic and political activities.[19]

Charles Bentley and Daniel Hale Williams were both medical professionals who found success and prosperity in the city. Bentley was born in Cincinnati, Ohio, in 1859. As a young man he reportedly played in the band of Janesville, Wisconsin, resident Charles Henry Anderson. He settled in Chicago sometime in the 1880s. By 1887 he had earned a degree in dentistry at the Chicago College of Dental Surgery.[20] When Charles Anderson's wife died, he relocated his family to Chicago, where his daughter Traviata married Bentley. Like her father, Traviata had a keen interest in the arts. She studied with a renowned organist and became an accomplished musician. However, the duration of her friendship with Fannie Barrier Williams was nearly as short as that of Mary Barnett; Traviata died in the early 1890s.[21]

Daniel Williams was the most nationally successful of the Chicago group. Born in 1856, he was a native of Hollidaysburg, Pennsylvania. He migrated to Chicago in 1880 after attending school at the Classical Academy of Janesville, Wisconsin, where he worked as a barber and boarded with the Anderson family. The smart and driven young man came to Chicago to enroll in Chicago Medical College, a predominantly white institution. He lodged in the home of Mary Jones while pursuing his degree and became intimately tied to the matriarch of the elite community. When he graduated in 1882, she provided assistance that enabled him to start his medical practice. By the last decade of the nineteenth century, he was recognized as one of the most renowned physicians in the country.[22]

Barrier Williams spent much of her initial years in Chicago engaging in activities with this community of women and men. They attended numerous parties, receptions, musicals, and lectures together. Their parties and receptions were as elaborate, sophisticated, and high fashioned as those in Washington. Detailed descriptions of fine food and of the hair styles, clothes, and jewelry of the women and men appeared in the newspaper. Dress suits and pompadour coifs for the men and silk and diamonds for the women were common. Aristocrats from as far away as Nashville and New Orleans attended. One soirée featured one of the most recognized men in the country, Pinckney B. S. Pinchback, the first black man to serve as governor of Louisiana.[23]

The socialite identity certainly suited Barrier Williams and offered numerous benefits. But she was an energetic and professionally trained teacher who had worked and been self-sufficient much of her adult life. Marriage to S. Laing had enabled her to leave behind the arduous work of teaching but it did not take away her passion for art. The artistic training that she gained in the South and the North and her ambition and skill proved to be quite advantageous to her personally and professionally. She was already known for her oil paintings in Washington, and she quickly became one of the best-known black female artists in Chicago. Capitalizing on a network of social connections, she marketed her talent as a portrait artist. Her skill with crayon, oil, and watercolor drew so much praise and so many clients that she told a reporter from her studio on Calumet Avenue that she was "over-crowded with orders" and gleefully reported that "I have no time for rest."[24] At the time of the interview, the subject of her crayon portrait was white Unitarian minister James Villa Blake. Also on display was a completed portrait of Lloyd Wheeler's wife Sarah.[25]

Barrier Williams also had a thirst for intellectual stimulation that manifested in two ways. The first was her interest in learning a language. When Cyrus F. Adams, an itinerant lecturer and teacher whom Barrier Williams had met in Washington, offered a six-week course in the reading, writing, and speaking of German, she enrolled. She excelled in the rigorous course, which met four hours a day five days a week. One reporter noted that "no English is permitted in the class room . . . all explanations of words or grammatical combinations being given in German." And while "Professor Adams does not claim that one can master the German language in six weeks . . . any person of average ability after a six weeks' course, can converse in German on almost any everyday topic." Barrier Williams had developed enough proficiency by the time the class ended to "read a selection" at a concert that Adams hosted at Lincoln Hall on a Monday evening in March 1888.[26]

The second and perhaps most significant manifestation of her intellectual interests originated in literature. Her parents' love of books ensured that she was exposed to literature at a young age, and this certainly played a role in her interest in reading. Her education at the Collegiate Institute and the Normal School provided a strong foundation as well. S. Laing was also noted for his "literary tastes" as a student at the University of Michigan. That common interest had drawn the couple together at the Monday Night Literary Society in

Washington, played an important role in their courtship and marriage, and led them to replicate their southern experience in the Prudence Crandall Literary Club in Chicago.[27]

In many ways the Prudence Crandall Literary Club, which S. Laing and his friend Lloyd Wheeler established sometime in 1887, was modeled after the Monday Night Literary Society: its members were a tight-knit well-educated group, and the club format included posh social gatherings and classical readings.[28] But the very name of the club signaled a raced, gendered, and regional perspective that the Monday Night Literary Society lacked: it was a tribute to Prudence Crandall's stand against racism and sexism in the North in the first half of the nineteenth century. When she was harassed for admitting a black female student to the Connecticut school that she headed and was forced to close the school, she reopened it as an all-black female academy. For this courageous act, she had become an iconic figure among the black northern educated elite. Crandall welcomed the honor. Barrier Williams proudly told a reporter that she had "written us a kind letter" acknowledging the club's existence.[29]

Following a long tradition that scholar Elizabeth McHenry suggests "constituted an attempt to complicate and reformulate both individual and group identity," the club added to the intellectual climate of the city and joined a growing number of organized lyceums.[30] Church groups and secular organizations met often to develop "mutual improvement" and "mental culture." For example, in the summer of 1889, the Garden City Lyceum began holding Monday evening sessions, apparently after disbanding at an earlier time. It welcomed women and men and solicited anyone who was interested in the lyceum's broad objectives for membership. Those included "a thorough diffusion of knowledge amongst its members in art, natural science, history agriculture and horticulture, music and literature, mental and moral philosophy."[31]

But the Prudence Crandall Club was by design distinctly different from any other literary club in the city. It was the most exclusive and by January 1888 had become "the leading social society." Membership, which was by invitation only, catered to the elite, although according to Barrier Williams, "any friends" could "attend the meeting who [were] interested in the work." The twenty-five "working members" determined the structure, readings, and programs. They included Mary Jones, Daniel Hale Williams, couples such as the Wheelers, the Barnetts and the Bentleys, and other prominent members of the community. One of those was George F. Ecton, who was elected to the Illinois House Representatives in 1886 and served two terms.[32]

The club's practices of elocution, public readings, recitation, and performance excluded the unschooled, the illiterate, and the timid from its ranks, creating an invisible barrier. Most of the assigned readings and lectures highlighted European works, although some American literary works were selected as well. While the larger group met weekly, five smaller sections met monthly in the privacy of homes. The smaller groups were organized around a number of broad topics. S. Laing, who was something of a literary scholar, as evidenced during his years at the University of Michigan and the library he and Barrier Williams had in their home, led the literary section. His responsibilities included selecting the readings, presenting papers on readings, and guiding discussions. During the first year he adopted the textbook *History of English Literature*, which included various types of literature. In preparation for his duties he often provided "a connecting link between the meetings, including a resume of the last lesson, with a study of the new subject matter."[33] The philosophy section was led by Lloyd Wheeler. He used John Fiske's *Destiny of Man* as the text and led discussions of evolution. Charles Bentley led the science section. As a practicing physician, he was well versed in chemistry and included experiments as an integral part of his instruction. The music and art section was led by Ferdinand Barnett. Members read biographies and studied the history of art, paying particular attention to early Egyptian art. Architecture, particularly in Greece, was also a popular topic. During the 1888 session, members also examined various schools of music.[34]

The influence of Barrier Williams and Mary Jones on the development of the club was clearly visible from the outset. One of the most important sections of the club was the women's group. Led by Jones, it was a conscious-raising association that united the core group of black women for the purposes of self-improvement and the protection of women and children.[35] Lectures, readings, and presentations from nationally and locally prominent black women informed them and shaped their agenda. Black medical personnel spoke to them about health and hygiene. Several of the women in the section, including Mary Jones, hosted meetings and receptions for women members of the club.[36]

The women's section of the Prudence Crandall Literary Club gave women a space for intellectual stimulation and the development of a collective female political voice. From this base, women began to cultivate and share ideas about participating in and shaping civic reform in the city. Public relations and advertising became critically important to their success. They worked closely with the black weeklies that had regularly chronicled the activities of aristocrats, but they also sought to move beyond the small racialized audience of the weeklies. They engaged in a campaign to do something that no other generation of black women had accomplished: they created a strategy for defining and representing themselves in the mainstream white press. One of the first opportunities came when the *Chicago Tribune* developed an interest in "Cultured Negro Ladies."[37] In an attempt to educate white readers about the distinct social gradations among blacks and call attention to the activities and perceptions of the black

aristocracy in Chicago, a reporter interviewed two members of the club, Mary
Jones and Fannie Barrier Williams. By way of introduction, the reporter wrote:

> Although some interest is occasionally shown in the progress of negroes in the
> South, the condition of those members of the race who live among us excites
> little if any attention. We have given them freedom, the franchise, and oppor-
> tunities for education but we are not curious in regard to the use they make of
> these gifts. We forget rather than ignore them. To the mass of whites they are
> waiters, barbers, merry clowns, and—nothing more. All the rest—their hopes,
> their ambitions, and their disappointments, their homes, their struggles, and
> their personal advancement—are buried in the oblivion that shrouds a race apart.
>   With a desire to learn something more of these people the writer called upon
> a few of them, saw their homes, talked with them of their interests and plans for
> improvement, and sought to learn their views concerning their relations with the
> world. As the race still lingers under the misfortune of being generally represented
> by its lower elements care was taken to secure a just picture of the brighter side."[38]

The piece was an orchestrated public relations experiment that Barrier Williams and Jones carefully crafted with the assistance of the *Tribune* reporter, who
visited them in their homes. When the reporter visited Barrier Williams, he was
quite impressed by her demeanor and her surroundings. "She is a young woman
with soft voice and well-bred manner," he wrote, adding that her "broad brow
and kindly eyes bespoke intelligence." Her home contained a "cozy parlor that
was spotlessly neat and tastefully furnished," "a library [with] a well filled book
case," and a "sitting-room, with its tasteful adornments and simple comforts."
She was "a cultured colored lady" whose appearance and residence demonstrated
an "unaffected refinement." That was precisely the image that Barrier Williams
wanted to project. The importance to her of self-representation and recognition
of her elite status were evident in Barrier Williams's statement to the reporter that
"my acquaintance here belongs to the better class and are usually educated."[39]

Like several black elites in Chicago, Fannie Barrier Williams eschewed traditional black religions. Most members of this group concentrated on dispassion-
ate philosophical and scientific study rather than participating in the emotional
religiosity that working-class blacks viewed as integral to their lives. When asked
by the *Tribune* reporter whether the club "was an outgrowth of any church,"
Barrier Williams smiled and replied, "We are freethinkers, and don't belong to
the church usually." This revelation startled the reporter, who responded, "You
surprise me. I supposed that all the people of your race were religious." To the
chagrin of the black intelligentsia, the question illustrated the reporter's failure
(and the failure of most whites) to recognize the distinct class stratifications in
the black community and the cultural superiority of the black elite. Barrier Williams quickly rejected the implication: "Most of them are . . . but not all. Some

of us are interested in science and we no longer accept all the old ideas."[40] By making religion a determining factor in the social hierarchy, Barrier Williams equated the vast majority of blacks with traditional religious institutions, "old ideas," and irrational and illogical thought. In contrast, the black aristocracy, according to her analysis, represented enlightenment, rational thought, and new ideas.

Although not all black elites abandoned mainstream religious institutions, those who did were attracted to more nontraditional denominations such as the Unitarians, primarily because of that denomination's rejection of a doctrinal system and its emphasis on education, free will, and the goodness of humankind. The Unitarians also welcomed mixed-race congregations in the Midwest, at least in theory although not always in practice. The Unitarians, whose denomination was still relatively new in the region in the 1880s, espoused racial equality and championed the rights of women. The Bentleys and the Wheelers were members.[41] So strong was the connection between the Prudence Crandall Club and the Unitarians that the speaker for the final meeting of the 1888 season was Jenkin Lloyd Jones, the founder of and minister at All Souls Unitarian Church in Chicago. His presentation was "The Great Paintings of The World."[42]

The interview with the *Tribune* reporter also highlighted the clear awareness of Barrier Williams and Jones of the problems the unfettered and rapid growth of industrialization had created for women and children and their interest in seeking the reform measures to ameliorate these conditions. Longer work hours limited family time, and the kinds of labor-intensive jobs that were available to black women and men paid very little, trapping them and their children in a life of poverty. Barrier Williams insisted that "moral education" was the key to a better home life.[43] Jones agreed. She argued that because mothers were so central to the cohesiveness of the family, the lessons needed to begin them. "Women need to understand the laws of motherhood," declared Jones. Jones viewed the coalescence of knowledge about science, the environment, health, and pregnancy as "a means to the cultivation of a better race." She and the other members of the women's section studied "pre-natal influences" and the ways that educational guidance could assist them with their "crusade against evil."[44] They adopted the model of the Moral Educational Society of Chicago, an influential organization made up mostly of women that was created in 1882 and dispensed "information on marriage and parenthood, the abolition of vice, and the moral training of youth."[45]

Jones's statement about creating a "better race" reflected the conflicting and contradictory ideals of aristocratic black women. In formulating a homogenized standard of womanhood they sought to promote the notion of black female

respectability. At the same time they adopted a supremacist ideology that de-
monized and stigmatized the poor black women. Ultimately, their prejudice led
them to embrace a normative gendered construct that rejected a working-class
ideal of womanhood. The elite black women of Chicago were more than willing to lay claim to moral authority and saw themselves as the main source of
progress for their race.

While Jones insisted that the status of women determined the character and
disposition of a race, she also argued that black men shared responsibility for
the problems that plagued the black family. "We want more justice to women
. . . and more virtue among men," she told the reporter. Stressing the distinct
but complementary gender roles of black women, Jones highlighted sexual
differences and argued that virtuous men protected their women and helped
create and shape a positive environment for their wives and children. Protected
women were morally astute and produced healthy productive children. Defense-
less and unprotected women were vulnerable and could descend into vice and
other evils. It was of this group that Jones spoke when she noted that "too many
children are born vicious."[46]

Jones also emphasized that alcohol consumption was detrimental to the black
community. Not surprisingly, she was a strong advocate of prohibition. Believing "that drink is responsible for most of the evil in society," she, like women in
the Women's Christian Temperance Union (WCTU), argued that alcohol was a
powerful enemy of women.[47] It invaded the sanctity of the home and shattered
the cohesion and structure of families. Men who drank abused their wives
and victimized their children. Women who drank destroyed their respectable
womanhood, their home, and their children. More important, their actions
reflected poorly on the black community as a whole.

While women in the Prudence Crandall Club linked themselves to the national movement against alcohol consumption, the successful and powerful
Women's Christian Temperance Union did not embrace them. When asked "Do
any of your women belong to the W. C. T. U.?" by the reporter, Jones replied "I
do not know of any."[48] The WCTU had been established in 1874, and although
the organization often encouraged interracial cooperation, Jones implied that
it rarely occurred among black and white women in Chicago.[49] "Can it be that
these ready allies are forgotten by the women who in nearly every town in the
county have united their sisters in a common cause?" the reporter asked.[50] Like
a number of predominately white women's organizations in the last decades of
the nineteenth century, the W. C. T. U did not embrace black women as equals.
When there was a branch of the organization it was usually segregated, afford-
ing white women the opportunity to associate in the company of their peers
without crossing racial boundaries. However, there was one notable exception
in the city.

The newly formed Illinois Woman's Alliance (IWA) created the first in a series of significant opportunities for Barrier Williams to publicly engage with white women since leaving Brockport. The IWA, which was organized in 1888, played a major role in the labor movement and women's municipal activities in Chicago until 1894. The organization significantly altered how women interacted with corporations and city government. Historian Mari Jo Buhle argues that "during its brief life the IWA stood as a model institution of cooperation between the local woman's movement and the Socialist-influenced Trades and Labor Assembly."[51] Even more important was the fact that the IWA crossed racial boundaries and embraced black women's concerns at a time when few labor organizations or white female reform associations did. It provided a bridge between Barrier Williams, the women's section of the Prudence Crandall Club, and the world of public reform activism.

The IWA was the product of the vision of Elizabeth Morgan and Corinne Stubbs Brown. Morgan and her husband had immigrated to the United States from England in 1869. After they arrived in Chicago, she quickly became active in the labor movement, where she found her footing in the Chicago Knights of Labor. Brown, a native of Chicago, was employed in the public school system as a teacher and principal. Even after her marriage to a prominent banker she remained committed to labor issues. Both women had helped build and shape the local Ladies' Federal Labor Union No. 2703 (LFLU) an affiliate of the American Federation of Labor. The initial impetus for the organization was concern about the negative impact of the working conditions of women and children in many of the factories of the city. While labor issues were their primary concern, Morgan and Brown also wanted to improve the overall lives of working women and children and broaden their focus to include the social, economic, and political issues that related to the circumstances of women's lives. Toward that end, they called seventy women from various clubs to a meeting at Palmer House and created the IWA in November 1888. The LFLU and twenty-five other organizations comprised the IWA, including a reading club, a flower club, a press association, an Ethical Ladies' Union, a temperance association, several church groups, a Single Tax Club, and the Prudence Crandall Literary Club. The organization adopted "Justice to Children, Loyalty to Women" as its motto.[52]

The organization cited an ambitious five-pronged agenda that was spelled out in Article II of its constitution and by-laws.

> SECTION 1. The objects of the Alliance are to agitate for the enforcement of all existing laws and ordinances that have been enacted for the protection of women and children, as the factory ordinances and the compulsory education law.

SEC. 2. To secure the enactment of such laws as shall be found necessary.

SEC. 3. To investigate all business establishments and factories where women and children are employed, and public institutions where women and children are maintained.

SEC. 4. To procure the appointment of women as inspectors and as members of boards of education, and to serve on boards of management of public institutions.

SEC. 5. The work of the Alliance shall also include correspondence with the authorities of other localities where factory and educational legislation has been obtained.[53]

The IWA was the first group to unite the agendas of a labor group and reform-minded club women. The coalescence created one of the most powerful lobbying machines in the city. "It is hard to say," Brown noted at an annual meeting, "just how much influence we have, but I believe we ought to let the public know the women are ready to protect women and defend themselves."[54] The alliance made women's concerns public issues and reformulated the expectations of municipal government. Public welfare shifted from something that had relied on private charity to a civic-minded challenge to everyone that demanded an actively engaged government. In July 1889, the organization initiated a publicity campaign to convey their agenda. They wanted to improve sanitation by pushing for free bathing facilities in city parks. They focused on safety and the sanctity of Victorian womanhood by demanding that the city place a matron in every police station. They highlighted the unique needs of women workers by supporting factory inspection. They demonstrated the importance of the education, supervision, and welfare of children when they lobbied the state to build a school for dependent children.[55]

Three representatives of the women's section of the Prudence Crandall Literary Club attended the founding meeting of the IWA: Lottie McCary, Viola Bentley, and Fannie Barrier Williams.[56] Their involvement highlighted common concerns among black and white women. The members of the Prudence Crandall Literary Club were just as committed to education, health and hygiene, and labor issues as white women were. Enforcing labor laws and compulsory education laws would ensure that black parents had access to safe jobs and black children had the opportunity to attend adequate schools.

Barrier Williams quickly became immersed in the IWA. She was elected vice-president in November 1889 and served on a committee that focused on the health and hygiene of the poor. She also was a member of the Free Bath Committee, which launched an organized campaign for city-funded public baths.[57] The long and arduous campaign fostered camaraderie between women of different racial and economic backgrounds and established the IWA as a formidable politicized force. Involvement in this public civic project enabled

Barrier Williams to develop new skills, such as petitioning and negotiating with male city officials. The committee corresponded with mayors in major eastern cities that already had public baths, such as Boston and New York. They also met with city commissioners in locations that seemed to be the most feasible sites for the baths. Often the women encountered resistance from male administrators such as those in West Park, who were "adverse to the petition on the ground that it would cost too much and there were not funds available." Others delayed open discussion of the issue or offered only "useless sympathy for the movement."[58] The committee sustained its campaign for nearly five years and was finally rewarded with success in 1894, when the first public municipal bath opened in Chicago.[59]

The alliance between the Prudence Crandall Literary Club and the IWA proved to be a defining moment in Barrier Williams's public and political activism. Her affiliation with both organizations helped her build ties to the constituency that would ultimately play a major role in her career as a clubwoman and lecturer and engendered a politicization that shaped her civic involvement for the next three decades. Her membership in the IWA provided a vehicle for navigating the political arena among white women. Ambitious and savvy, she cultivated relationships with some of the most prominent middle- and upper-class white women in the city through club work. In addition to her associations with Morgan and Brown, she became acquainted with Caroline Huling, who had established the Cook County Suffrage Association and was elected president of the IWA in 1889. She also interacted on occasion with members of the exclusive Chicago Woman's Club such as Celia Parker Woolley and Ellen Henrotin as they joined forces with the IWA to lobby the judicial system on behalf of women.[60] Fannie Barrier Williams's relationships with black and white women and the skills she honed in the Prudence Crandall Literary Club and the IWA solidified her place as one of the most influential black women in the city.

* * *

While Barrier Williams's stature in Chicago grew, she still remained deeply rooted in Brockport. In the late 1880s, the time she spent in the village became more important because of the declining health of her father. When she and S. Laing visited in late August 1890, Anthony Barrier fell and his physical condition quickly deteriorated. He was diagnosed with paralysis, and he never recovered. He died on August 27, 1890, at the age of sixty-five. Remembered as "an honest, conscientious and straightforward man, well meriting the widespread respect which he commanded," Barrier was eulogized at First Baptist, the church where the family had found fellowship, friendship, and solace for nearly half a century. He was the first member of the family to be buried in the village cemetery.[61]

Six months after the death of her husband, Barrier Williams's mother Harriet traveled to Chicago to visit her daughter.[62] It was an exciting time. The city had been named the site of the World's Fair and preparations were already under way. In addition, her daughter had begun work on a project that changed the delivery of health care services for blacks and whites in the city, illuminated her skills as a savvy negotiator, and advanced her career as a labor activist.

Barrier Williams and S. Laing began assisting their friend Daniel Hale Williams achieve his dream of establishing a hospital and a nursing program long before Harriet arrived in Chicago. The availability of health care had become a critical concern for blacks during the last decades of the nineteenth century. Racism and discrimination contributed to inadequate health care, high morbidity and mortality rates, and unsanitary living conditions. Concerns about the spread of disease and the impact of disease on the black community, particularly women and children, pushed the community to look for ways to solve the problems it faced. One of the key issues was the fact that there were too few hospitals in the city, particularly those that accepted black patients. There was also a citywide shortage of black nurses. The number of black nurses was so minuscule that most black women never even considered careers in nursing.[63]

In 1887, Daniel Hale Williams was appointed to the Illinois State Board of Health, where he closely monitored the problems the lack of access to medical care and the shortage of black doctors and nurses created for blacks. Although he had attended integrated schools and had opened an integrated practice, he was well aware that few black doctors had the same opportunities. Williams proposed that an interracial hospital be established in Chicago that catered to blacks and whites but remained controlled by African Americans.[64] Many in the black community, including S. Laing and Fannie Barrier Williams, supported the idea, but others vehemently opposed it. The opposition was led by John G. Jones. Born in Ithaca, New York, in 1854 Jones became a practicing attorney in Illinois in 1884, devoting most of his time to criminal law. He quickly rose to prominence. He was a friend and colleague of Edward Wright, a powerful black politician in the Republican Party. On several occasions, Jones clashed with Daniel Hale Williams and his ideas about the hospital.[65] He remained one of their most vocal critics for more than a decade.

This was not the first time controversy had erupted among the elites. While the group may have shared a collective class orientation about racial equality, they differed about how best to protect black interests and help the black community. The views of integrationists like Jones were steeped in a traditional late-nineteenth-century black ideology that viewed any attempt to erect separate institutions for blacks as a rejection of equal rights and as submission to segregation. Others, like Williams, argued for compromise, seeing validity in joining forces with whites as a means of building institutions that served black interests and promoted self-help. The conflict between supporters and opponents of the proposed new hospital often led to bitter public exchanges. Contentious meetings inflamed the rhetoric and polarized the community. Jones had been the leading opponent of the proposal for a black YMCA in 1889 because he argued it segregated blacks and infringed on their equal rights.[66] But in the two years since the successful derailing of the YMCA, the landscape had changed. Supporters of broad-based racial coalitions who now found merit in institutions developed and operated by blacks had skillfully crafted arguments about the necessity of building facilities in black neighborhoods. The Prudence Crandall Literary Club was one of those groups that provided a cohesive base of supporters backed by a powerful organization to combat Jones and his opposition forces. While the club did not officially enter the fray, the proposal had originated from member Daniel Hale Williams. The co-creators of the club, S. Laing Williams and Lloyd Garrison Wheeler, became vocal advocates and defenders of the proposed hospital, and several members of the women's section looked favorably on the proposal because it fit their commitment to protecting the health of women and children.

Jones faced this well-organized and politically savvy group as he attempted to derail the proposed hospital. In April 1891, when he, Bishop Cornelius Lennox, Sam Thompson, and several other prominent black men held an "indignation meeting" with the primary "purpose of condemning the establishment of a Colored hospital," Jones found himself embroiled in a debate about his own governance and authority. The *Western Appeal* reported that "the door was guarded and very few except those who were friendly to the cause were admitted."[67] But a few supporters of the hospital did manage to enter. The meeting was so contentious that Jones verbally abused S. Laing and forced him out of the meeting when he questioned the legitimacy and secretive nature of the proceeding. Williams's supporters protested and left the meeting. Angered and frustrated, Jones and his associates passed a resolution suggesting that most blacks in the city condemned the planned hospital.[68] But the resolution blatantly misrepresented the wishes of the black majority, the *Western Appeal* claimed, since "there were [only] twenty people left in the 'mass meeting.'"[69] Jones's conduct at the meeting astonished many of the elite and reinforced their sense that he was out of step with their push toward self-help. They derided him for his outburst and fervent opposition by mimicking those who had nicknamed him "indignation Jones."[70] Eventually Jones's conduct alienated him. His argument that the creation of racially separate institutions would stymie black progress provided an opportunity for supporters to marshal their forces, refine their argument, and neutralize him.

When Jones attended a large public meeting about the proposed hospital that included Fannie Barrier Williams, S. Laing Williams, Daniel Hale Williams, Lloyd Garrison Wheeler, and Charles Bentley, he was clearly in the minority. Nevertheless, he raised numerous objections and questioned the principle and practical aspects of operating a hospital conceived of and administered by blacks. His attempt to persuade the crowd revealed his fury and illuminated how deeply entrenched the rhetoric and actions of each side had become. Jones's first tactic was to stir up controversy by reminding blacks of their own identity and the long struggle for inclusion. He angrily asked "Are we self-respecting people, or aren't we?" When that drew little response he stepped up his negative campaign, revealing his pessimism about the future of the black community if they approved the creation of the hospital. "I'd let colored people die in the streets," he declared, "and be eaten up by flies before I'd put them in a separate hospital!"[71] The remarks roused some support from audience members, but the committee quickly responded that anyone who required medical attention, regardless of race, ethnicity, or religious affiliation, would be admitted to the hospital. Emphasizing racial and ethnic equality, they projected a forward-looking enterprise that would not exclude whites and people of other races.[72]

But Jones refused to back down. He redirected his attack by focusing on the employees of the proposed facility. "What about the nurses?" he asked.[73] The question was not simply rhetorical. It illuminated the gendered nature of black women's work and raised an important staffing issue. While the decision had already been made to staff the hospital with black and white doctors, there had been little discussion about the nursing staff. At the time, there was a great shortage of black nurses because too few schools would accept them and even fewer hospitals offered training to black students. Thus, the majority of the nurses at the hospital would be white. Would white nurses work with black nurses on a daily basis? Would they receive equal salaries? Would white nurses only tend to white patients and work with white doctors? Would black nurses only tend to black patients and work with black doctors? One of the most important reasons that Daniel Williams wanted to create the hospital was his knowledge of the case of a black woman, the sister of a Methodist minister, who had been refused admittance to training schools because of her race. Williams believed that the hospital would legitimize the profession for black women and provide new economic opportunities for them.[74]

Williams received overwhelming support from black women for an all-black staff of nurses. Women members of the Prudence Crandall Literary Club championed the idea, as did many black women throughout the city. Barrier Williams was one of the strongest and most vocal advocates. The two organizations to which she had the closest ties, the women's section of the Prudence Crandall

Literary Club and the IWA, were interested in the health and hygiene of mothers and their children. More important, Barrier Williams's involvement in the IWA had dramatically increased her interest in the labor movement. Because of that perspective, she saw the proposed hospital as an employment opportunity for black women. After a heated debate about the status of nurses Barrier Williams argued that the hospital would certainly help with the shortage and enable black women to practice in the profession. She saw racism as the heart of the problem. "There are other training schools for white women, but none at all for colored women. Why let white women take any of the few places we'll have open, at least at the start?"[75] She pointed out that "Dr. Bentley has to have teeth to work on or he can't be a dentist . . . and our nurses will have to have patients to train on or they can't become nurses."[76] In the end, supporters of the hospital project won the day.

Financing such a venture necessitated cooperation across class, gender, and race lines. Daniel Williams's professional work as a physician enabled him to enlist the aid of the working class. But for monetary support he looked to elite black women and men with whom he had business and social connections. He knew that he could depend on members of the Prudence Crandall Literary Club. Barrier Williams became intimately involved in the project. She operated as a liaison fund-raiser among black and white groups, raising more than $2,000. Lloyd Wheeler held rallies to alert black people in the West and South sides of the undertaking, and James Madden, a black bookkeeper, became the auditor. Mollie Green of the West Side and Connie Curl of the South Side headed auxiliaries that raised funds for the hospital. They hosted events such as ice cream socials to educate the community and generate contributions.[77]

Daniel Williams, Barrier Williams, and others procured aid from a number of prominent whites as well. Businessman Philip D. Armour, the meatpacking mogul, contributed a generous donation and influenced his friends to donate as well. Florence Pullman (the daughter of the inventor of the Pullman sleeping car) contributed too. Some white ministers also viewed the project favorably, including the powerful and influential Jenkin Lloyd Jones.[78]

In May 1891, Provident Hospital opened in a three-story brick structure on the corner of Dearborn and Twenty-Ninth streets. A crowd of supporters attended the opening of the first and only interracial medical facility in the city. The gala event included speeches that reflected the successful conclusion to a yearlong struggle to deliver better health care to African Americans, create employment opportunities for black women, and forge alliances across race and class lines. Rev. J. T. Jenifer of Quinn Chapel highlighted the fact "that the color line had been disregarded in the plans of the hospital," while Jenkin Lloyd Jones "congratulated the colored people" and praised them for taking "a step toward the goal of the highest good will toward their follow-men."[79]

The Chicago Tribune also celebrated the success. The paper scolded the white community for inept policies that inhibited racial progress. "White people," the paper opined, "have been trying to wipe out the color line for years, but it has come to be the privilege of the colored folks of Chicago to make the opening attack on race discrimination. The first patient of the new Provident Hospital will be an Irishman."[80] More important, "Before last night the colored people had no place here where they could send their sick ones to be built up by doctors of their own race and where young colored women could be trained for nurses. The other hospitals may pretend to receive all the sick and the maimed that come to them, but dark patients and white nurses have never been found who will establish themselves on terms of mutual good-will."[81]

The interracial cooperation that was so clearly displayed with the creation of the Provident Hospital signaled the progressive nature of the Midwest. Although Chicago was still considered to be an outpost of the West, Barrier Williams had found there the promise of advancement that she was denied during the years she spent in the South. Over the next decade she built a formidable network of white colleagues in which she could develop her skills as a writer, a lecturer, and a reformer. The alliance with the IWA proved to be only the first in a series of calculated steps Barrier Williams took to build a strong local coalition that eased her entry into the segregated world of the white female club movement. Before the end of the century she would be one of only a few black women to speak before an international and predominantly white audience as the nation celebrated the 400th anniversary of the discovery of its continent, and she was the only black woman to gain membership in one of the most prestigious and powerful white women's clubs in the country.

The second step was rooted in her religious ideology. Although she had been raised a Baptist in a predominantly white church, she refused to be limited by denominational or racial strictures. She had attended a segregated black Presbyterian church in Washington. In Chicago, she found a unique combination that demonstrated a coalescence of race, class, and religion and provided the same kind of camaraderie and support that her family had enjoyed in Brockport. For her, the congregation of All Souls Unitarian Church fulfilled her progressive vision of an intellectually stimulating, racially broad-minded, and integrated community.

4. Crossing the Border of Race

The Unitarians, the World's Fair,
and the Chicago Woman's Club

On the fourth Sunday in July of 1890, Barrier Williams was the guest speaker at All Souls Unitarian Church. It would not be the last time that she would appear in the pulpit, but this presentation topic, "Prudence Crandall Philleo," had a particular meaning.[1] It honored the memory of Crandall, who had died the previous January. Crandall married Baptist minister Calvin Philleo shortly after she was forced to close her school for black girls in 1834. When the couple left Connecticut, they eventually migrated west and lived for a time in Illinois. Crandall's life story was a strong illustration of a principle that Barrier Williams held dear: a dedication to promoting education. The admiration for Prudence Crandall's accomplishments was clear in the name that her husband and Lloyd Wheeler gave the club they had co-founded three years earlier. And because Crandall's Quaker background was at the heart of her antislavery activism and commitment to black rights, Barrier Williams saw a clear link between Crandall's social justice ideals and the religious ideology she embraced.[2] All Souls presented Barrier Williams with an institutional venue for advancing black progress in the same way that Crandall's educational institution had done so for young black girls in the early nineteenth century.

All Souls was part of the Unitarian movement that began in the Northeast and found its footing in the Midwest in 1849 when the few Unitarian ministers located in the region held their first conference in Chicago. Rapid growth encouraged a second meeting seven years later.[3] By the time Fannie and S. Laing Williams arrived more than thirty years later the denomination had become firmly entrenched. In Chicago, Jenkin Lloyd Jones had built one of the most successful religious institutions in the city.

Jones, who was born in 1843, acquired his deeply religious and freethinking ideas from his Welsh parents, who were liberal Christians. They immigrated to the United States when he was one year old and settled on a farm in Wisconsin. Though his formal education was limited, he was exposed early to religious study. Several of his uncles had been Unitarian ministers, and his father had led church services. During the Civil War, Jones enlisted in the Union army. After the war, in 1866, he entered the Preparatory Department at Meadville Theological School in Pennsylvania. After graduating in 1870, he married Susan C. Barber, a secretary at Meadville. The two formed a formidable team that lasted until Susan's death in 1911.[4]

The first professional years for the couple were nomadic and sometimes difficult. Initially Jones found a position as a minister in Winnetka, Illinois, where he preached at Liberal Christian Church. But that appointment proved incompatible with his style of leadership. The couple moved to First Independent Society of Liberal Christians in Janesville, Wisconsin, where they flourished. With Susan's assistance, Jones published *The Sunday School*, a monthly devoted to religious education and creative methods of teaching theology to children. He also established the Mutual Improvement Club. The club pulled women into the public life of church work, social service, and reform. Similar to a lyceum, it offered readings, discussions, and lectures in topics such as classical literature, art, and poetry. There were also lectures and sections on current events. As regional and national interest in women's issues increased, suffrage, temperance, and civil service reform discussions were held often.[5]

The couple also participated in the Western Unitarian Conference. Established in 1852, the conference covered a large territory that encompassed the old Northwest and parts of western New York State. As a result of the expansive geographical territory, regional as well as ideological differences threatened the cohesiveness of the group. Debates over oversight grew as Midwestern members, motivated by their own unique regional circumstances, questioned church authority, teachings, and doctrine. Debates over slavery and the role of blacks in society also caused much concern, pitting individuals, local communities, and the national organization against each other.[6] By the end of Reconstruction, however, many of the differences had been resolved. To be sure, regional distinctions remained: Midwestern Unitarians were in a constant struggle for power and control with their northeastern colleagues, the seat of Unitarian dominance. The impact of the dissension, however, was minimized primarily because of Jones's enthusiasm for increasing the membership of midwestern Unitarians. Serving as missionary secretary to the Western Conference from 1875 to 1884, he advanced the conference and the relevance of Unitarians in the Midwest. Jones was so successful in those nine years that the financial situation and strength of nearly every entity in the conference improved. The number of "active societies" more than doubled and the number of ministers in the conference increased. In addition, under his tenure the debt of associated churches was significantly reduced. He also edited the Unitarian magazine *Unity* for six years.[7]

While Jones was an exceptionally effective administrator, his travel throughout the conference was what gave him the insight he needed to develop his own idea of what would make the "ideal church."[8] During his tenure, he traveled more than 120,000 miles, met with countless parishioners, and preached hundreds of sermons. On November 1, 1882, he presented the sermon "The Ideal Church" to a small group of congregants who were the remnants of the Fourth Unitarian Church in Chicago, which had dissolved after the Great Fire of 1871. In the aftermath, many residents had been displaced and the minister had left. By the end of the decade, the church building had been sold. Jones told the small audience of about twenty-five that he envisioned

> a free congress of independent souls. It is to lead in the campaign for more truth rather than to indolently stand guard over some petty fragment of acquired truth . . . it will be the thinker's home. The student of science will handle no discoveries that it will not prize and indulge in no guesses that it will not respect. Oldest India and newest America will hold no gem of thought that will not be welcomed into its sacred Scriptures. The skeptics will be the cowards who dare not exercise the reason God has given them. Over its portals no dogmatic test is to be written to ward off an honest thinker or an earnest seeker.
>
> This church must emphasize the Universal Brotherhood; it will stand upon a grand emphasis of the great word of the century, Unity. It will seek to welcome low and high, poor and rich, unbeliever and believer.[9]

A little over a month later, on December 8, 1882, the Church of All Souls, Unitarian was born with Jones as the minister.[10]

Many in Chicago shared Jones's vision of a multiracial Christian institution that eschewed rituals and dogmas. The membership and the use of the facilities increased so substantially by 1886 that a new structure was built. Resembling a home more than an institution, the chapel that was built on the southeast corner of Oakwood Boulevard and Langley Avenue did not look like the traditional church building that was used only on Sunday. Jones argued that those structures lacked the warmth, friendliness, and accessibility needed to combat the cold corporate industrial culture of the city and the workplace. These churches, he argued, were impersonal, uninviting, and intimidating. So he and his congregation built a homelike structure that linked the church to the community in both design and theology. Jones argued that if the community "is the larger family," then the church "must be made the larger home."[11] When the church opened, Frank Lloyd Wright, the famed architect who was the nephew of Jones, suggested that his uncle had indeed succeeded in his quest to create a nonsectarian unit. The design, he noted, looked "in no way like a church, more like a 'Queene Anne' dwelling."[12]

All Souls didn't operate like a church. The facilities were open seven days a week and were designed to serve the community. All Souls hosted a reading, lecture, and discussion group known as the Unity Club that met several times a week. In keeping with its intellectual mission, the church offered a reading room and a library. The reading room was open every day and the library was open four days a week. The library had extensive holdings, including noncirculating reference works and a circulating list that included fiction, poetry, biographies, and books about travel, history, religion, and the arts and sciences. It also offered a number of periodicals.[13] By the 1890s, the church was functioning as a combination settlement house, educational facility, and religious institution. It provided classrooms, a gymnasium, a kindergarten, study clubs, and a manual training school.[14]

The church's design and programs in many ways combined Jones's personal, religious, and political beliefs with his professional mission. Ignoring the segregation that was so prevalent during the period, he argued that in his "ideal church" blacks were equals. From the beginning blacks found a place in the church. Although they did not always experience the ideal situation that Jones imagined, they were actively engaged in the church.[15] As the church grew, so did the interest of the new generation of aristocratic blacks. In 1888, prominent blacks such as Lloyd Wheeler and his family were among the church's 116 members. By the early 1890s, the membership had more than doubled to 250 families, and S. Laing and Fannie Barrier Williams were among them.[16]

Counting black members among his congregants was only a small part of his mission. Jones defied the conventional practices of the midwestern metropolis by socializing with blacks on a daily basis, visiting them in their homes and participating in their clubs. He encouraged his congregation to do the same. His ease with blacks both professionally and socially was probably why he received an invitation to speak to the Prudence Crandall Literary Club at a meeting held in the home of Mary Jones in the spring of 1888.[17]

In Jones and the Unitarians, Barrier Williams found a spiritual paradise. The religion catered to the educated elite, appealing to her aristocratic sensibilities. Unitarians rejected the Trinity and the notion of inherent evil, offering salvation through good deeds instead, which was quite different from the Bible-based approach and the emotionalism that characterized many mainstream black religions. Congregants embraced reform, promoted solidarity across race lines, and supported a range of black issues.

Perhaps no Unitarian endeavor was more significant for Barrier Williams than the commitment to the education of southern blacks. Tuskegee Institute became one of the most promising projects of Unitarians.[18] By 1890, pleas for monetary assistance from Booker T. Washington, the institute's principal, had begun to appear in a broad range of Unitarian publications. In November of that year, a letter from Washington designed to familiarize the community with the school and to elicit support was published in *The Unitarian: A Magazine of Liberal Christianity*. He wrote, "Everyone who cares for the progress of the colored people of the South should know of the work that is being done by the Normal and Industrial Institute for the Training of Colored Teachers, located in Tuskegee, Alabama." Appealing to the reform sensibilities of Unitarians, he pointed out that "as a result of the training received here," students had "in a word reformed whole communities."[19] Washington's persuasiveness was evident a year later. An article entitled "How to Help the South" appeared in the November 1891 edition of *The Unitarian* that listed ways to provide financial assistance to southern groups in Florida, Texas, North Carolina, Tennessee, and Alabama. Tuskegee was the only one of the five that was secular and specifically addressed the educational needs of black children. The author commented that "if the education and elevation of the colored youth of the South seem most important to any, I can cordially recommend the work of the Tuskegee Normal School, under the charge of Mr. Booker Washington, Tuskegee, Ala."[20]

Within two months the magazine began a promotional campaign for the school, devoting a page to "A School for Industrial Education in the South" and making a plea for more assistance. After providing a history of the school and its mission the article discussed the financial hardships the school's students faced. "The students are wholly unable to pay anything for *tuition*," the article declared, urging "the friends of negro education" to provide scholarships for 355 students who had no financial resources. "Without these scholarships, the institution will be forced to turn away a number of worthy young persons who are too poor to pay for an education." To demonstrate the Unitarian community's commitment to the school, the National Unitarian Conference at Saratoga, New York, passed a supportive resolution: "*Resolved*, That the National Conference recognize the broad, unsectarian, educational work of the Tuskegee Normal and Industrial School, under the presidency of Booker T. Washington, and cordially commend it to the support and confidence of our churches."[21]

Unitarians in Chicago embraced the cause. Jones published a letter from Washington in the November 1889 issue of *Unity* requesting "the payment of $50 a year for the education of some worthy young man or woman at the Tuskegee Normal and Industrial Institute." The article highlighted the success of a former graduate in his efforts to help a community ravished by poverty. Jones introduced the letter by noting that "Prof. Washington is well known to the

Unitarian workers of the country, and enjoys their confidence. We hope his appeal will not fall on deaf ears."[22]

S. Laing Williams answered one of those calls for assistance. In March 1892, he responded to a request from Washington for books for the school library. "I noticed your call for certain books needed in the library of your splendid school. I at once interested my self in trying to supply the needs as best I could. The enclosed catalogue of books is the result of my efforts. The books have this day been expressed to you."[23] Williams's relationship with Washington, which developed at first through charitable assistance to Tuskegee, evolved very quickly into a lifelong personal friendship.

Barrier Williams was also attracted to the Unitarians because of the group's inclusion of women. That provided the context for the development of a lifelong friendship and partnership in Barrier Williams's life. While she was living and teaching in Washington in the late 1870s and early 1880s, Celia Parker Woolley was fast becoming a seasoned club woman who actively engaged in social activism and reform. Woolley's membership in the Chicago Woman's Club (CWC), one of the oldest, most exclusive, and most elite women's clubs in the city, solidified her place among white aristocratic women and in the burgeoning women's reform movement. By the time that she met Barrier Williams, she was intimately tied to the Unitarians and was a member of organizations such as the CWC that collaborated with the IWA. More than anyone else, Woolley introduced Barrier Williams to a circle of prominent white women and to a professional career as a lecturer.[24]

The two women had much in common. Like Barrier Williams, Woolley had come of age in the mid-nineteenth century, when educational opportunities for women were expanding, providing the basis for professional careers. Each spent their youth north of slavery, Woolley in the Midwest and Barrier Williams in the Northeast. Both were greatly influenced by liberal religious teachings that originated out of the Second Great Awakening. And they both married men who supported their goals and their professional careers.

Woolley was born in 1848 in Toledo, Ohio. Shortly after her birth, her family moved to Michigan, eventually settling in Coldwater. Her parents were educated, prosperous, and liberal minded. Her father, Marcellus Harris Parker, was a professional architect, and her mother, Harriet Maria Sage Parker, was a homemaker. Woolley attended Lake Erie Seminary in Painesville, Ohio. She graduated from Coldwater Female Seminary in 1866 or 1867 as one of the first four young women from the collegiate department.[25] By the age of twenty she had married J. H. Woolley, a Coldwater dentist ten years her senior. Seeking intellectual stimulation, she devoted time to the Ladies' Library Association. In that organization, she strategized and campaigned for a public library. In 1870

Figure 3. Celia Parker Woolley was one of Fannie Barrier Williams's closest and dearest friends. A Unitarian minister, reformer, and activist in Chicago, she opened the Frederick Douglass Center to assist the black community. Courtesy of Andover-Harvard Theological Library, Harvard Divinity School, Cambridge, Massachusetts.

she became involved in the movement to enfranchise women by joining and serving as secretary of the Branch County Suffrage Association.[26]

In 1876, the Woolleys left Coldwater and moved to Chicago. While her husband built his dental practice and engaged in numerous professional activities, she pursued an interest in literature and writing and plunged into club work. Finding a home on the Reform Committee of the CWC, Woolley presented papers and participated in discussions about the role of women. From 1888 to 1890, she served as president of the CWC. She also joined the Woman's Social Science Association of Illinois.[27] In the late 1880s, she gained membership in another exclusive club, The Fortnightly, where she cultivated relationships with some of the most prominent women in Chicago, including Bertha Honoré Palmer, wife of business magnate Potter Palmer; Ellen Henrotin, wife of banker and broker Charles Henrotin; and Catharine Waugh McCulloch, a graduate of Northwestern University Law School and a practicing attorney.[28]

She also established an enduring religious affiliation. Long immersed in liberal religious ideals, she and her husband sought an enlightened and progressive church. They joined Third Unitarian Church shortly after their arrival. She and Susan Barber Jones assisted with the creation of the Women's Western Unitarian Conference. When Jenkin Lloyd Jones solicited support for his goal of establishing an institutional church that provided a unique blend of religion, education, social reform, and interracial cooperation, she and her husband became members of All Souls.[29] Woolley was highly regarded for her writing skills, and she became the assistant editor of *Unity* in 1890. In 1892, Woolley was appointed as pastor of a church in Geneva, Illinois.[30] At the same time, Chicago was preparing for the thousands of U.S. and foreign visitors who would descend on the city to see the World's Columbian Exposition.[31]

*   *   *

When Congress officially voted to endorse Chicago as the site of the World's Columbian Exposition on February 24, 1890, the city became "the most representative of modern urban places" and part of the larger vision of "a perfect city."[32] As a commemoration of the discovery of America 400 years earlier by Christopher Columbus, the World's Fair as it came to be known, also made Chicago one of the most visible cities in the world. The fair took place in two stages, first with a dedication ceremony in October 1892 and then with a variety of festivities, conferences, and entertainments that began on May 1, 1893, and continued for six months.[33]

Black Chicagoans were excited by the fair and the possibility of heightening their own status. Local newspapers began publishing articles highlighting black success shortly after the announcement. For example, in May 1890, the *Chicago Tribune* devoted three columns to "Chicago Colored People," specifically focusing on regional differences between the midwestern city and the South. Providing detailed biographies of prominent men such as Lloyd Wheeler and Daniel Hale Williams, the paper opined that their success proved that "the rapid progress he [the black man] has made in the North is due beyond doubt to the free air that laps him." Concluding that "Chicago, [which] pushes ahead of the band in every procession, naturally leads in this instance," the article geographically set the city apart from racist southern states like Mississippi where "the negro influence is kukluxed out of existence."[34]

But the article failed to address the racism that seemed to plague the fair from the beginning. There was no clearer evidence of this than in the announcement of the selection of national committees and boards for the fair. With only a few exceptions, the commissioners from each state and territory were white and the members of the Board of Lady Managers, which was led by Bertha Palmer and was created by Congress in April 1890, were all white as well. In addition, most of the local committees in cities and states were overwhelmingly white. Black Americans felt slighted because they were not adequately represented and because there appeared to be little or only token discussion about ensuring black representation.[35] Attacks from the black media began immediately after President William Harrison sanctioned the event and Congress appropriated the funds. The *Indianapolis Freeman*, for example, noted that the fact that "no Negro is on the commission implies that no one Negro in any state of the Union had the required qualities to represent one-fourth of his state or one-eighth of the nation."[36]

Black women expressed particular outrage about the racial makeup of the Board of Lady Managers. This was due in part to the historic nature of women's participation in the event.[37] The omission of black women meant a devaluation of their progress, their accomplishments, and their intellect.

The first complaint originated from a local black women's organization, the Woman's Columbian Association (WCA). At the first meeting of the Board of Lady Managers in November 1890, Lettie Trent, head of the WCA, questioned the legitimacy of white female hegemony.[38] The WCA issued the following resolution on behalf of black women:

> Whereas no provisions have, as yet, been made by the World's Columbian Exposition Commission for securing exhibits from the colored women of this country, or the giving of representation to them in such Fair, and WHEREAS under the present arrangement and classification of exhibits, it would be impossible for visitors to the Exposition to know and distinguish the exhibits and handwork of the colored women from those of Anglo-Saxons, and because of this the honor, fame and credit for all meritorious exhibits, though made by some of our race, would not be duly given us, therefore be it RESOLVED, that for the purpose of demonstrating the progress of the colored women since emancipation and of showing to those who are yet doubters, and there are many, that the colored women have and are making rapid strides in art, science, and manufacturing, and of furnishing to all information as to the education and industrial advancement made by the race, and what the race has done, is doing, and might do, in every department of life, that we, the colored women of Chicago request the World's Columbian Commission to establish an office for colored women whose duty it shall be to collect exhibits from the colored women of America.[39]

The resolution generated "considerable" discussion among the board members particularly when Mrs. John A. Logan, representing the District of Columbia, "requested that the board use its influence to have a colored woman appointed to collect and take charge of the exhibit of the colored people" and "moved to refer it to the Executive Committee of the National Commission."

Some members favored both the resolution and Logan's request. But, when it was recommended that a black woman be an alternate on the board, there was little support.[40]

Meanwhile, the Women's Columbian Auxiliary Association (WCAA), another local group of black women, had marshaled its forces. The president, Mrs. R. D. Boone, issued a letter to the Board of Lady Managers about the best way to include black women in the fair. "In the prosecution of our work," the letter stated, "we have consulted some of the best minds of our race. We do not in any way suggest a separate department in the coming exposition, for colored people, but we do believe there is a field of labor among the colored people, in which members of the race can serve with special effectiveness and success." To aid the committee in its efforts, the association enclosed a document that was "carefully outlined in a published prospectus for use of societies cooperating with us."[41]

The challenges from two black women's organizations in Chicago, the WCA and the WCAA, failed to bring the rapid change that black women in the city had hoped would come. The activities of these two groups highlighted how the absence of a citywide umbrella organization of black women's groups comparable to the CWC hindered black women's collective efforts to alter the situation. The CWC was so well organized and politically connected that its members dominated the Board of Lady Managers and much of the direction of the role of women at the fair.[42] Because black women did not have a comparable association, there was little that they could do except continue to appeal to the board and solicit assistance from CWC members.

The actions of the WCA and the WCAA also illuminated the ongoing divisions among Chicago blacks about how best to address their needs. The protracted fight over Provident Hospital and Barrier Williams's battle over the nursing program were just two examples of differences within the black community about how to challenge racism and discrimination. The two camps in those two battles were strikingly similar to the split between the WCA and the WCAA. The WCA insisted that a segregated unit for black women would be the best way to secure black female representation at the fair. The WCAA rejected any notion of segregation. Black women, the association argued, must be integrated into the main administration of the Board of Lady Managers.

By the time the board met again to seriously consider the issue of black female representation, other groups had jumped into the fray. In October 1891, the board's secretary, Susan G. Cooks, attempted to defend the board's actions and control the damage the absence of black women had created. The board drafted a letter entitled "To All Interested in the Colored People" and sent it to several newspapers, including *The State Capital*, which was published in

Springfield. In the letter, Cooks noted that when the board was first alerted to the issue, a committee of three consisting of Helen C. Brayton, Mrs. John A. Logan, and Mrs. Mary Cecil Cantrell was quickly assembled to discuss the matter.[43] The letter claimed that when the Executive Committee of the Board of Lady Managers met in April 1891, "in conformity with the wishes expressed by the colored women, in the report of the committee appointed to confer with them in November, Mrs. Mary Cecil Cantrill, of Kentucky, was appointed to represent the colored people on the committee."[44] But by the second meeting of the board, the once united coalition of black women had become two clearly divided camps. One argued that black women "should be treated separately and their exhibit placed by itself." The other called for "no unjust discrimination in color, but favored placing the colored women on the same footing with white women, giving them the same latitude and opportunity." To the dismay of the Board of Lady Managers, the "dissensions among the colored people" continued to grow. "Two factions had increased to four, and all were clamoring for a national representative. It was impossible to unite them, and but for this a national representative would already have been appointed," Cooks wrote.[45] Distressed, annoyed, and confused by the multiple voices from black female constituents, the all-white board ultimately decided to further victimize black women by accusing them of being unreasonable, irrational, and disorganized. Blaming them for their own failure to be represented, Cooks concluded with a request: "The Board of Lady Managers would most earnestly urge the leaders of the various factions to sacrifice all ambition for personal advancement and work together for the good of the whole thus seizing this great opportunity to show the world what marvelous growth and advancement have been made by the colored race and what a magnificent future is before them."[46]

While the rhetoric escalated, a small group of local white and black women had been strategizing about the best way to incorporate black women and minimize the negative publicity for the board. By the end of the year a plan was in place. At a meeting held in Chicago in December 1891 female state delegates engaged in a discussion with the National Board of Control of the World's Fair about the status of the plans for women's exhibits. Bertha Palmer detailed the specifics. Fannie Barrier Williams represented black women's interests at that meeting. A reporter for the *Woman's Journal* was particularly captivated by her presence. Highlighting her Victorian gentility and aristocratic background, she described Fannie as "a handsome and refined colored woman" who "is the wife of S. Laing Williams, the well-known lawyer." Referring to her as "a very intellectual woman" and "an artist," the article correlated her upper class status with her educational and creative achievements. The article acknowledged her "great work in connection with the new Providence [sic] Hospital and Training School for Nurses" and noted that she was a leader who was interested in interracial cooperation. Most interestingly, the article concluded that her request that "two of their race were appointed to some position where they could work in the interests of their people" was so persuasive that the National Board of Control instructed the director general, George R. Davis, to respond to her request by appointing two black women to the Bureau of Publicity and Promotions. Barrier Williams, of course, was recommended to fill one of the slots.[47] Although she did work in the administration of the exposition, it does not appear to have been in the bureau. Eventually she was tapped to evaluate paintings that were displayed in the Palace of Fine Arts.[48]

One of the slots in the bureau was filled by Mrs. A. M. Curtis, who had close ties to Provident Hospital. She was initially employed there as a nurse, and she eventually held the post of solicitor for the institution. Her husband, Austin M. Curtis, was the first intern at the hospital and later became the superintendent of the training school. She was appointed to a clerical position in the bureau, where she secured space for black exhibits and acted as the public relations liaison to the national black community. However, Curtis was set up for failure because the position was mostly ceremonial. She occupied a desk that sat in Bertha Palmer's office and seems to have had very little power to make decisions. She lacked adequate public relations skills so the few communications she had with the black public did little to assuage their anger about their underrepresentation in the administration of the exposition. She was heavily criticized and attacked in the press, and she eventually resigned.[49]

By then the battle over black female representatives had shifted from primarily a local issue in Chicago to a national issue. Hallie Q. Brown, who was scheduled to give a presentation at the Prudence Crandall Literary Club in April, was quite disturbed by the national discrimination against the black community and by the local Illinois board's dismissal of black women's concerns. When she sent inquiries to the Board of Lady Managers, she received few responses and those that did were opposed to appointing a black representative. In response, she penned an open letter to the black community that was reprinted in newspapers in other states, including *The Cleveland Gazette*. In the letter, she asked local communities to tell her "if the colored women or the colored people as a whole in your state and section have been called upon by your state lady managers to form auxiliaries and to organize for active work in the interest of the world's fair to be held in this city in 1893. If not, are they co-operating with any organized body sanctioned by the state lady managers? I share the common interest of the race in how far our women are expected to participate in the Columbian exposition. I adopt this plan to ascertain what influence has been brought to bear and what activity has been awakened throughout the country. An early reply will be appreciated by yours sincerely, Hallie Q. Brown."[50]

Barrier Williams had already taken a very public position on this issue and could do little more than she already had. One reason was that she was ill. In April 1892, four months after she appeared before the National Board of Control, she was suffering from an illness that lasted nearly a month.[51] Her growing involvement with All Souls and an extraordinarily busy volunteer and professional schedule probably contributed to the prolonged illness. She was still an active participant in the Prudence Crandall Literary Club, her labor activism in the IWA had escalated, and she had many responsibilities related to the administration of Provident Hospital, including soliciting funds, acting as a liaison between the hospital and the white community, and championing the nurses' training program.

The national battle to include blacks in the committees that governed the fair drew in Frederick Douglass and other black activists. In his official capacity as the commissioner of Haiti he arrived in the city in January 1893 to oversee the dedication of the Haitian Pavilion. While he was in Chicago, he also was one of the main speakers at a Prudence Crandall Literary Club commemoration held at Bethel A.M.E. Church to honor prominent men in the antislavery movement.[52] A secondary goal of this event was to provide a forum for discussion of black history and progress. Less than a month before the major festivities for the fair began Douglass returned to the city, staying, as he often did, in Barrier Williams's home.[53] Other black activists, including anti-lynching crusader Ida B. Wells, had come to Chicago as well. She, Douglass, Irvine Garland Penn, and Ferdinand Barnett each wrote short essays that were published together under the title *The Reason Why the Colored American Is Not in the World's Columbian Exposition.* The pamphlet generated considerable attention because it placed the omission of African Americans at the fair in national context by addressing the multiple ways in which African Americans were being oppressed throughout the country. It also offered a critique about the absence of black women on the board of lady managers, the resignation of A. M. Curtis, and the appointment of Barrier Williams in the Department of Publicity and Promotion.[54]

Less than a month before the exposition began in May 1893, Barrier Williams was appointed "clerk in charge of colored interests," becoming the primary black female liason between white female administrators and black women. Her salary was $50 a month.[55] The exact nature of the deliberations that led to Barrier Williams's acceptance of the position are not clear but the juxtaposition of her appearance at the Board of Control meeting, support from the white women with whom she had worked, and the divisions among local black women's groups certainly contributed to her appointment. For the white women who knew her, such as Ellen Henrotin, Elizabeth Morgan, and Corinne Brown, she represented a safe choice that would counteract the negative publicity that had hounded the Board of Lady Managers since it was created.[56]

The appointment increased Barrier Williams's public profile and solidified her place among white and black elite women. One of the important events for women at the exposition was the week-long World's Congress of Representative Women. The congress was a historic event for organized women and increased the profile of U.S. club women both nationally and internationally. It was planned and organized jointly by the World's Congress Auxiliary, the General Federation of Women's Clubs, and the National Council of Women of the United States. It attracted nationally and internationally known women leaders from around the world. When Fannie Barrier Williams was invited to speak at this event, she transitioned from a local figure to a national celebrity. White friends and colleagues who had positions of leadership on exposition committees ensured that she had a voice at the conference. Unitarian May Wright Sewall, who was president of the National Council of Women, was appointed chair of the Committee of Organization for the congress. Ellen Henrotin led the Woman's Branch of the World's Congress Auxiliary. Bertha Palmer, as mentioned, was president of the Board of Lady Managers. These three women were deeply involved in the planning and organization of the World's Congress of Representative Women.[57] Barrier Williams joined other black activist women speakers Anna Julia Cooper, Fannie [Fanny] Jackson Coppin, Sarah J. Early, Hallie Q. Brown, and Frances E. W. Harper.[58]

At 7:45 on Thursday evening, May 18, Barrier Williams presented "The Intellectual Progress of the Colored Women of the United States since the Emancipation Proclamation."[59] The title highlighted the significance advancement black women had made in the nearly thirty years since the end of slavery. This talk was one of the first times that Barrier Williams publicly presented the view that black women had a central place in the creation and shaping of the reform movement that sought to address the issues facing the black community. Keenly aware that her audience was both multiracial and international, she told her listeners that "less is known of our women than of any other class of Americans."

> No organization of far-reaching influence for their special advancement, no conventions of women to take note of their progress, and no special literature reciting the incidents, the events, and all things interesting and instructive concerning them are to be found among the agencies directing their career. There was been no special interest in their peculiar condition as native-born American women. Their power to affect the social life of America, either for good or for ill, has excited not even a speculative interest.[60]

Black women had made significant progress in many areas, she noted, including religion, education, and reform. And given "the same opportunity for the acquisition of all kinds of knowledge that may be accorded to other women . . . in the next generation these progressive women will be found successfully occupying every field where the highest intelligence alone is admissible."[61]

Demonstrating the influence of her work in the IWA and her commitment to activism on behalf of black women workers, she argued that the dearth of employment opportunities for black women was a serious impediment to their advancement. "Our exclusion from the benefits of the fair play sentiment of the country is little less than a crime against the ambitions and aspirations of a whole race of women," because "except for teaching in colored schools and menial work, colored women can find no employment in this free America."[62] She reiterated a theme that had its roots in her unsegregated childhood when she renounced categorization by race and highlighted the shared interests of black and white women. "We come before this assemblage of women," she remarked, "feeling confident that our progress has been along high levels and rooted deeply in the essential of intelligent humanity. We are so essentially American in speech, in instincts, in sentiments and destiny that the things that interest you equally interest us."[63]

Barrier Williams's presentation at the World's Congress of Representative Women and her relationships with Jenkin Lloyd Jones and Celia Parker Woolley provided her with another opportunity to speak at an exposition event, this time at the World's Parliament of Religions, a two-week conference that was held from September 10 to September 27, 1893. The parliament was conceived by Jones and other Unitarian ministers and was sanctioned by the General Committee on Religious Congresses of the World's Congress Auxiliary. The goal of the parliament was to move beyond "Christian denomination in this country" and embrace "an exposition of the world's material progress . . . elevated by a presentation of the spiritual beliefs of the world's religions." The primary mission was "to bring together in conference, for the first time in history, the leading representatives of the great Historic Religions of the world." The parliament attracted representatives of religious groups from around the world, including Catholics, Baptists, Congregationalists, Jews, Hindus, and Buddhists. An array of individual congresses was held under the umbrella of the World Parliament, including one that represented women and men in the African Methodist Episcopal Church. Several of the black women who had presented at the World's Congress of Representative Women spoke at the A.M.E. Congress, including Hallie Q. Brown, Anna Julia Cooper, Fanny J. Coppin, and Sara J. Early. Amanda Smith joined this group to speak on topics related to programs that would promote the success of girls and women. They joined male leaders such as Daniel Payne, Henry McNeal Turner, and Benjamin Tanner.[64]

Barrier Williams's presentation of the thirteenth day of the parliament transcended the boundaries of the individual congresses. Her speech, "What Can Religion Further Do to Advance the Condition of the American Negro?," revealed two ideological themes. The first highlighted her belief that there were distinctive and important differences between the concept of religion and the institutional structure of the church. The "power of religion pure and simple transcends all other forces that make for righteousness in human life," she argued. The church, on the other hand, was a vehicle through which religion could be institutionalized. But often the institution failed by sometimes providing opportunities for misguided people who "had no sort of preparation and fitness for the work assigned them" to become leaders. She especially pointed to the prominent role of black ministers in the South. "With a due regard for the highly capable colored ministers of the country, I feel no hesitancy in saying that the advancement of our condition is more hindered by a large part of the ministry entrusted with the leadership than by any other single cause. No class of American citizens has had so little religion and so much vitiating nonsense preached to them as the colored people of this country." Barrier Williams argued that those called to minister in the South should be "only men of moral and mental force, of a patriotic regard for the relationship of the two races." And they needed to embody three important characteristics: "the qualities of a teacher, the self-sacrificing spirit of a true missionary, and the enthusiasm of a reformer" if they were "to do much good as a preacher among the negroes."[65]

Her second theme was that religious leadership was central to minimizing the impact of racism and discrimination against blacks. Since the end of slavery, in spite of the best efforts of blacks to fully exercise their citizenship rights, they were denied at every turn when they "appealed to every source of power and authority for relief." She complained that "for the last twenty-five years we have gone to legislatures, to political parties, and even to church, for some cure for prejudice." She used the pulpit of the parliament to chastise leaders, noting that regional religious divisions played a crucial role in the social, political, and economic obstacles blacks faced. "It is a monstrous thing that nearly one-half of the so-called Evangelical churches of this country, those situated in the South, repudiate fellowship to every Christian man and woman who happens to be of African descent." For blacks, she continued, "the golden rule of fellowship taught in the Christian Bible becomes in practice the iron rule of race hatred." She asked, "Can religion help the American people to be consistent and to live up to all they profess and believe in their government and religion?" She believed that religion could because it was only through "the gentle power of religion that all souls of whatever color shall be included within the blessed circle of its influence." Believing that religion was one of the most powerful weapons against the racism that plagued blacks, she concluded that "it should be the province of religion to unite, and not to separate, men and women according to superficial difference of race lines."[66]

Both of her presentations at exposition events pleased her, as did the subsequent publication of her texts. "Please pardon also the expression of pride and satisfaction that in Dr. Barrow's book on the parliament of Religions I am given quite a large space together with my picture," she bragged to Douglass. Jenkin Lloyd Jones's book about the parliament, *A Chorus of Faiths*, reproduced excerpts from her text, and Barrier Williams wrote that "I can but feel gratified not so much that my words win with preserving as that the subject of them could have been deemed of so much importance."[67]

The publications certainly increased her national profile and generated numerous and profitable speaking opportunities. She employed an agent and the public relations machine of the Slayton Lyceum Bureau to promote her lectures.[68] And although she complained to Douglass about suffering from "'nerves' which sometimes are troublesome to the point of illness," her contract with the bureau commanded most of her attention and necessitated that she travel. Several months after she spoke at the World's Parliament of Religions, she had two invitations to speak in Wisconsin, where she would participate in a "Popular Lecture Course," and at least three lectures were being planned in Michigan. "I have accepted" the invitations, she told Douglass, "first because I shall be glad to have my words do missionary work if they can, second, because I think a change of scene may benefit me physically and third the possible remuneration promised me in excess of my necessary expenses."[69] These lectures increased her professional status, provided financial compensation, and gave her opportunities to speak to liberal whites and supportive blacks about the reform issues that were important to her.[70]

Her profile as a reformer-intellectual increased among women's groups and in religious circles, particularly among the Unitarians. For example, on February 18, 1894, she spoke to a Unitarian Church in Kalamazoo, Michigan, where the local press described her as "a colored woman of rare ability." She delivered the same speeches that she had presented at the World's Congress of Representative Women and the World's Parliament of Religions.[71] The large and "most appreciative" audience at the Unitarian Church in Ann Arbor, Michigan, where she spoke in April 1894, was "composed mostly of students and a number of the professors." Later she presented a "new and special lecture" for one of the few black audiences on her tour in Kalamazoo.[72] The following month, she spoke to "a large and deeply attentive audience" at Celia Parker Woolley's church in Geneva, Illinois, on "The Intellectual Progress of Colored Women since the Emancipation Proclamation." Woolley was an enthusiastic supporter of Barrier Williams's work. "Mrs. Williams is a thoughtful, cultured and impressive speaker, and her appearance upon the lecture platform presents the opportunity for the discussion of themes connected with one of the most important and interesting sociological problems of the day from the standpoint most needed. Our liberal societies, women's clubs and similar organizations should try to secure her services" she wrote.[73]

After an extensive season of lecturing and traveling, Barrier Williams was tired. She admitted to Douglass that she was "a little fatigue as a result of my unusual work this winter."[74] The work had also energized her and reignited her interest in crossing the entrenched racialized borders of women's clubs. Six months after she wrote to Douglass she and Woolley joined forces to implement a course of action that demonstrated their close bond and proved to be one of the most significant changes and challenges in both of their personal and professional lives.

* * *

Celia Parker Woolley, a longtime member of the Chicago Woman's Club, had stepped down as president of the club the year that Congress announced that the World's Fair would be held in Chicago. She continued to be an active member of the club, though. She served on the Art and Literature Committee from 1890 to 1893 and was one of eighteen directors from 1893 to 1894. In the fall of 1894 she was actively engaged in the work of a CWC committee that sought to create what would become the Chicago Political Equality League, an organization committed to pushing for equal suffrage for women.[75] However, Woolley wanted the CWC to move beyond reform activism and to begin shaping public discourse and policies about race. Thus, she began turning her attention to the goal of giving black women equal access with white women to membership in the CWC. Her friendship with Barrier Williams and their religious connection with All Souls played a key role in steering that interest.

The CWC, which was established in 1876, had nearly 700 members by 1895, making it one of the largest clubs in the country.[76] Like several other major white women's groups, the club had no formal statement or constitutional rule that limited its membership to white women. And although by the 1890s several members of the CWC had contributed to or been involved in work that benefited blacks, women often viewed the socially intimate spaces of the club as private, thereby cocooning themselves in a homogenized sanctuary free of racial tension and questions about social equality.

But that changed in November 1894 when Woolley, with the assistance of Ellen Henrotin, who had been elected president of the General Federation of Women's Club that year, and Grace Bagley, a member since 1889, introduced Barrier Williams's name for membership. They also introduced a resolution that would open the club to women of other races: "Resolved, that the Chicago Women's Club condition its membership on character and intelligence, without restriction of race or color." The resolution demonstrated that Woolley and her colleagues had carefully planned a strategic assault on the club's invisible racial barrier. According to the *Chicago Daily Tribune*, "A certain coterie, including some of the best known and most progressive, openly declared that the time has arrived to be oblivious to a color line." Henrotin told a reporter that "there is no doubt Mrs. Williams will become a member of the Woman's club." But many club members were less willing than the authors of the resolution to accept a black woman in the club.[77] Barrier Williams later wrote that while "the club motto is *Humani Nihil Alienum Puto* ('Nothing Human is Foreign to Me')," members had never been forced to publicly state their personal views about race and social equality.[78] Discussion of her nomination became so acrimonious that when she was interviewed by a reporter she found herself in the unusual position of defending her right to be a member. "I am very sorry, indeed," she told the reporter, "to be the thorn in anybody's flesh. I did not make the application for membership myself; in fact, had never entertained such an idea until several members asked the privilege of presenting my name. Consent was granted, with the hope I might advance my work as defender of my race from unjust prejudice."[79] She continued:

> For years I have labored to break down the color line. . . . My education consists of a collegiate education in New York and a season at the Boston Conservatory. For a time I taught school in Washington, where I met my husband, who, despite the prejudice against his reception into the Columbian Law School, carried off the prize at the end of his course. Six years ago we came to Chicago where I have interested myself in behalf of colored people and spoken from many pulpits and platforms in the city. Last Sunday, for instance, I made an address at Oak Park and after the meeting several notable women earnestly expressed their gratitude that my talk had overcome their prejudices of a dusky skin. Of course, . . . I would feel better if I thought I should be made perfectly welcome by the Woman's club.[80]

Barrier Williams's defense of herself, her husband, and black people and her refusal to remove her name from consideration probably looked more like defiance and a challenge to those who opposed her nomination. Jenkin Lloyd Jones's passionate defense of her only fueled indignation and anger. "Are they opposing Mrs. Williams' election to the Woman's club?" he asked when a reporter interviewed him. "We'll make it hot for them," he declared. When the reporter asked Jones, "Is Mrs. Williams received into the homes of your parishioners on the same standing with white members?" Jones responded, "To be sure she is, and several times she has presided in my pulpit." He said that Barrier Williams was "as accomplished, intelligent, and philanthropic a little woman as I have in the parish." He added, "Any tendency to draw the color line on her is unqualified narrowness and unmitigated snobbery."[81] However,

Barrier Williams, Henrotin, and Jones could not overcome the opposition. When the membership committee met on the afternoon of November 14, Barrier Williams's nomination was rejected.

Disheartened but undeterred by the first negative vote, the group of women, led by Woolley, decided to focus most of their energies on whether the club's constitution permitted the barring of a black member. For months, they worked to convince the membership to reconsider Barrier Williams's nomination by highlighting the absence of racialized language in the by-laws and by rewording the resolution.[82]

While Woolley was engaged in that battle, Barrier Williams and others waged a publicity campaign of their own. To the chagrin of the CWC, they were aided in their efforts by the local press. And because of the interconnectedness of local, regional, and national publications throughout the country, the national media's interest in the story also grew. Pressure and negative publicity about the CWC mounted. As Barrier Williams noted sometime later, "The Women's Clubs everywhere took up the matter and discussed the question, had lectures upon it, wrote essays on it, and some of them went so far, by way of testing their own feelings, as to vote upon the question of admitting the Chicago colored applicant as an honorary member."[83]

These activities pleased her, but the support did little to diminish the strain she endured as a result of the intense scrutiny from the women in the CWC. When she reflected on the ordeal a decade later, she revealed a more unguarded response than the one she gave the *Tribune* reporter in 1894. Although she still maintained that she had been as surprised by the initial reaction of club members as she had been when she had been asked to leave the music conservatory in Boston a decade earlier, she was much more defiant and unapologetic in hindsight, blaming the debacle on a "determined minority" of racist white members. Their response, she argued, echoed "the whole anti-slavery question . . . with the same arguments." Objections were so strong that there were those who "came to me and frankly told me that they would leave the club, much as they valued their membership, if I persisted in coming in. Their only reason was that they did not think the time had yet come for that sort of equality."[84] She stood by her decision to refuse to withdraw her name: "Since my application was not of my own seeking I refused to recognize their unreasonable prejudices as something that ought to be fostered and perpetuated; beside, I felt that I owed something to the friends who had shown me such unswerving loyalty through all those long and trying months, when every phase of my public and private life was scrutinized and commented upon in a vain effort to find something in proof of my ineligibility."[85]

Barrier Williams insisted that she more than met the qualifications for membership. She had been a member of a number of reform organizations, had worked on behalf of women workers, and had spoken on two occasions at the World's Fair. It was, she contended, her "talent for public speaking and writing" that brought the "recognition" to her. "It, therefore, seemed altogether natural that some of my white friends should ask me to make application for membership in a prominent woman's club on the ground of mutual helpfulness and mutual interest in many things." After all, she concluded, "This progressive club has a membership of over eight hundred women, and its personality fairly represents the wealth, intelligence and culture of the women of the city."[86]

The debate over her nomination dragged on for months during the fall and winter of 1894. During that time she procured a position as one of several state and regional reporters for *The Woman's Era*, a new monthly publication for black women. The assignment was timely, for her work with this aspiring enterprise moved the issue to the forefront of the consciousness of the nation's black women. The monthly excoriated the CWC for the circumstances surrounding the nomination. Reporting that "the modicum of negro blood in her veins out weighed her eminent fitness," the *Era* labeled the situation as blatant racism. The paper reported that a group of black women in Boston were so angered that they confronted Frances Willard, the president of the Women's Christian Temperance Union, a member of the CWC, and a strong advocate of black women's activism at a suffrage fair in Boston in December. In response to their charge of racism, Willard vowed that "if, upon investigation, she finds that her club has, as reported, 'rejected an able, refined highly culture woman solely on account of her color,' then she, Mrs. Willard, will place her light face beside that darker one and walk out of the club with her."[87]

As the pressure mounted on the CWC, Barrier Williams capitalized on the local and national interest in the drama surrounding her nomination. By then she had already served as the chair of the Committee on Dependent Children of the IWA and had established a strong record as a reformer, a lecturer, and a club woman. She parlayed her successful voluntary efforts and her ordeal with the CWC into more work as a public speaker. Invitations to give lectures throughout the area began pouring in. For example, on Sunday evening, December 16, she spoke to an audience at Kenwood Evangelical Church on Greenwood Avenue and Forty-Sixth Street. The overwhelmingly white gathering welcomed her. She gave her speech on "The Intellectual and Religious Advancement of Colored Women since Emancipation."[88] That summer she appeared in Batavia, Illinois, where she gave her presentation on "The Intellectual Progress of Colored Women."[89] To end her tour, she presented a lecture at All Souls, her home church, on Sunday, August 25, 1895, on "The Strength and Weakness of Religious Teaching in the South."[90]

Speaking engagements throughout the nation increased as well, enhancing her visibility and extending her connection to a broader audience. *The Woman's*

Era promoted her. In the spring of 1895, the monthly announced that she would "deliver a series of lectures in New England in April."[91] In November 1895, she participated in a gala held for suffragist Elizabeth Cady Stanton's eightieth birthday at the Metropolitan Opera House in New York, an event that thousands attended. She was the only black woman to speak in a roster that included suffrage luminaries such as Susan B. Anthony, Matilda Joselyn Gage, Clara Barton, Mary Lowe Dickinson, Anna Shaw, Julia Ward Howe, Emily Blackwell, and Emeline Burlingame Cheney. The event was in many ways an extension of organized women's work at the World's Fair and showcased their growing and prominent role in the public arena. Women spoke from the podium on a wide range of topics that included suffrage, religion, education, temperance, medicine, and local, national, and international club activity. Barrier Williams's speech, "The Progress of Colored Women," suggested that interest in black women's activism was growing in the national community of white women.[92]

While Barrier Williams was busy speaking, traveling, and promoting her own agenda, a powerful alliance of women in the Chicago Woman's Club joined forces with Woolley and began to lobby for a constitutional change in the CWC. When Woolley introduced a second resolution on January 23, 1895—"Resolved, That it is the sentiment of the Chicago Women's Club that no one can be excluded from membership on race or color lines"—Dr. Sarah Hackett Stevenson, who could not attend the meeting, sent a telegram declaring, "Justice is eternal, expediency is temporal. Be just and fear not." The membership followed her lead, voting to accept the amendment. A new article was added to the by-laws mandated that "the qualifications for membership shall be character, intelligence and the reciprocal advantage of membership to the Club and the individual, without regard to race, color, religion or politics," effectively ending the debate about the eligibility of black women. Barrier Williams's hometown newspaper noted the occasion: "Mrs. Williams will enjoy the very pleasant honor in history of having been the lady over which this important question was settled."[93]

A triumphant Woolley either wrote or most certainly contributed to a trenchant description of the CWC membership's change of heart. The January 1895 issue of *Unity* editorialized that "the Woman's Club, after much parliamentary sparring, social agitation and private heart-burnings, has found the first American consolation to an abused conscience,—it has passed a resolution saying in effect that merit and not color is the condition of membership in the club. This is but an attempt to refine pure gold, to explain the constitution which needed no explanation, casting thereby an insinuation upon the founders of the club, which is to be regretted, for the club by its motto and its high articles of organization was already committed to that which the resolution tardily recognizes, leaving the painful implication that this club has been working all these years under a document the implication of which they did not understand or the application of which they were not prepared for."[94]

Four months later, Susan C. Barber Jones, the wife Jenkin Lloyd Jones and a member of the club since 1888, told a reporter for the *Chicago Tribune* that "it is the only logical outcome" for Barrier Williams to be admitted to the CWC. But more pressing for her was the continuation of racial attacks against Barrier Williams by a member of the CWC. Angry and indignant, she noted that "a woman who strenuously maintained she was not 'anti-color' said there were reasons other than color why the colored woman proposed for membership was rejected. Now, my hearing is not perfect and I sat in the back of the room, so there is a possibility, of course that I may be mistaken. I went to this woman after adjournment and asked her if I had understood her correctly. She became indignant and denied the charge. Tomorrow I am going to see some of the women who were present and if I find my ears did not deceive me I shall bring the matter publicly before the club, possibly Wednesday. Other women besides myself are determined to have a thorough investigation."[95]

But even with the constitutional change and a strong contingent of support, Barrier Williams's membership was uncertain. An ordeal that had lasted for a year and a half finally came down to whether Barrier Williams would willingly resubmit her application to an organization that had denied her admission in the first place. By then there seemed to be little doubt that she would. As was the case the first time, she had to wait for a final decision while the membership committee deliberated on her second nomination. But this time she had the support of the constitutional amendment and the aid of a broader range of members. Pressure from those such as Catharine McCulloch, a member of the 1895–1896 membership committee who had aligned with Woolley, certainly helped her case.[96] In January 1896, Barrier Williams was among the more than eighty new members who were admitted to the CWC.[97] The organization had made one of the most monumental decisions in the club's history. A black woman had finally been admitted to the club.

The end to the ordeal did not come quickly. The publicity surrounding the debate continued to swirl in the local media. The *Chicago Tribune* applauded Barrier Williams for "Breaking Down the Color Line." The article suggested that "the most logical course for those who entertain prejudices which cannot be removed would be to resign from the club, which already is perhaps so large as to be cumbersome in its movements."[98] The *Chicago Times-Herald* praised Woolley, Bagley, and Stevenson, who "stood unflinchingly by a woman whom nothing could be truthfully suggested except the hue of her skin" and insisted that "Mrs. Williams, having borne for the sake of principle the slings and arrows of outrageous delay, must now stand her ground."[99]

The case even received attention in the national media. The *San Francisco Chronicle* led its coverage with the provocative heading "A Colored Woman Wins." "While the majority of the club have welcomed the intellectual colored lecturer to their sisterhood," the paper reported, "a few members have threatened to resign unless Mrs. Williams does. When the cause of the contention heard their threats she positively announced her intention to remain in the club regardless of the actions of a minority, whom she designated as 'prejudiced, mean and hopeless.'"[100] The *Globe-Republican* in Dodge City, Kansas, succinctly noted that "after fighting over a woman's complexion for fourteen months, the Chicago Woman's club has eliminated the color line, and elected Mrs. Fannie Barrier Williams, a well known colored woman, to full membership at an executive session of the club."[101]

In the end, the ordeal revealed an uncomfortable truth: the vision of a utopian interracial society remained elusive. Living north of Jim Crow and virulent racism did not necessarily bring about equality or acceptance. Boundaries, whether they were regional, gendered, or religious, could not mask the national antipathy toward blacks, regardless of class status. Aristocracy once again failed to produce the cross-racial ideal that Barrier Williams had longed for since leaving Brockport. Even in the Midwest, race was used to socially ostracize talented people. But Barrier Williams was not ready to concede or accept that educated and intellectual blacks and whites could not find common ground, and she continued to seek opportunities for interracial cooperation. However, she also increased her reform activities in the black community and with the black women who had come to her aid during one of the most difficult times in her life.

5. A Distinctive Generation

"The Colored Woman's Era"

In January 1893, Barrier Williams went to Washington to present the paper "The Opportunities of Western Women" to the Bethel Literary Association. She was there to celebrate the installation of Mary Church Terrell as president and to raise awareness about the activism of women in the rapidly growing western industrial corridor of the country. It was not the first time that she had returned to the city since her move to Chicago. She still had a strong tie to Washington and often visited her sister Ella there. But the invitation to speak at the Association in honor of Terrell's presidency was more professional than personal and signaled that Barrier Williams had become a leading representative and promoter of women's activism in the West/Midwest.[1]

Terrell, who had been elected in the fall of 1892, had become the first woman to lead the association. Concern about her leadership capabilities surfaced immediately after her election; some members questioned whether a woman should lead the organization. In spite of the doubts, Terrell was successful. During her presidency, weekly presentations highlighted the major issues of the period and encouraged some of the most prominent blacks in the country to participate. Kelly Miller, a Howard University mathematics professor focused on "Higher Education"; Pinckney. B. S. Pinchback discussed "Reconstruction"; Irvine Garland Penn, a newspaper editor and journalist, examined the question "Race Flattery or Race Importunity, Which?"; and Ella Somerville Lynch, wife of former Mississippi congressman John R. Lynch, presented "The Spiritual Element of Reform."[2]

Barrier Williams joined the elite group. She told the audience gathered at Fifteenth Street Presbyterian Church that "every sentiment concerning women has changed in the last fifty years and changed for the better. . . . The men and

women who at one time talked so confidently about woman's inherent weak-
nesses as arguments conclusive against her claims to equality with men have
begun to recognize that strength may differ in kind as well as degree, and that the
character and strength of women in human society may be quite as efficient as
necessary to the completeness of the social state as the strength of men." Women's
advancement was most apparent in the West because of industrialization. The
economic demands of industry in the region made it possible for women to be
"a decided factor" as employees and to demonstrate "active interest and assertion on the thought side of every debatable question." Eighty percent of goods
manufactured and produced in the region involved the skills of women. As a
result, "the economic questions of supply and demand, capital and labor, co-
operations, wages and wealth are affected more or less decidedly by woman's
increasing contributions to the forces of intelligence, labor and wealth."[3]

More important, Barrier Williams argued that the significant changes that
had occurred for women in the West grew out of their organized efforts and
their devotion to "the humane spirit." Because "every woman's organization of
any prominence and influence is inspired by a motive to help society to correct
its evils and to prevent its menacing dangers," their "redemptive power" over
"the evil tendencies of American life is admittedly the greatest hope of our times
and it is nowhere felt more emphatically than in the west." She pointed to the
protest of the Chicago branch of the WCTU "against the sin of inebriety" and
the Illinois Woman's Alliance's campaign "in righting wrongs, correcting abuses
and the forcing of officials to a complete and full performance of their duties."
The alliance was unique in both location and purpose. "I believe," she noted,
"that this organization has no counterpart in any eastern city."

> It in no way resembles a club of leisure women who engage in reform work as a
> fad. They are mostly women of family and business, and are not distinguished by
> wealth or social position. The alliance gives no receptions or charity balls. It takes
> no vacations. Its season for work is from January to January. Its motto is never lost
> sight of, for it is: "Loyalty to Women and Justice to Children." The unfailing motive
> of all its efforts is to put conscience into the official life of the city.[4]

Barrier Williams's focus on the alliance highlighted a distinctive difference between the West/Midwest and the South. It was an interracial organization that
embraced black women and their concerns about their community. Women in
Washington had no comparable association. But black women in Washington
had done something that black women in the West/Midwest had not. They had
built a cohesive coalition that attracted attention from other women interested
in forming clubs.

Six months before the Barrier William's presentation to the Bethel Literary
and Historical Association, the Colored Women's League had been established

in the city, ushering in what Barrier Williams later referred to as the beginnings of "a reformatory movement" that was "wholly the creation of women." Organized with the specific purpose of developing services for "the improvement of the condition of colored women," the club sought "remedies" to the myriad problems that black women faced in the last decade of the nineteenth century. The league created a fund of $5,000 in its first year for the purpose of building a headquarters and providing space for their educational and industrial reform efforts among women. Within a year, interest in the club's work had grown so significantly that affiliated branches had been formed in the South, the Midwest, and the West.[5]

Several members of the league were members of the black aristocratic society to which Barrier Williams had belonged when she lived in Washington. The president of the club, Helen Appo Cook, was the wife of John F. Cook Jr., a wealthy member of the well-established John Francis Cook family. A native of New York, Helen Cook was, according to Barrier Williams, "a woman of culture, refinement and financial independence" who was "a noted example and inspiration to women of her own social standing, in the serious work of social reform."[6] Charlotte Forten Grimké, the wife of Presbyterian minister Francis Grimké; Josephine Willson Bruce, the wife of Senator Blanche K. Bruce; and Barrier Williams's sister Ella were also members.[7]

A new generation that had migrated to the city just as Barrier Williams was leaving for Chicago were also members. Two of the most notable were Mary Church Terrell and Anna J. Cooper. Terrell, a native of Tennessee, was born in 1863 to wealthy parents. She graduated from Oberlin College in Ohio in 1884. She taught at Wilberforce University in Ohio for a while, then found work at M Street High School in Washington. After leaving the city for two years to study art, music, and languages in Europe, she returned to marry Robert Terrell, a Harvard graduate who worked in the Pension Division of the U.S. Treasury, in October 1891.[8] Cooper was born in North Carolina to a slave woman and her master. She attended St. Augustine's Normal School and Collegiate Institute in Raleigh. She then entered Oberlin College, from which she graduated in 1884, where her classmate was Mary Church. She initially found employment at Wilberforce University but was pulled back to her alma mater, St. Augustine's College, for professional and personal reasons. In 1887 she accepted a teaching post in the public school system in Washington at M Street. The intellectual Cooper found the literary tradition of the Bethel Literary and Historical Association exciting and enriching. An avid reader and writer, she actively participated in the organization, where she presented several lectures. She was also the author of *A Voice from the South* (1892).[9]

Southern black women were not the only cohort that was part of the "reformatory movement." The development of this movement in the Northeast

had begun as early as 1892, when Victoria Earle Matthews and her colleague
Maritcha Lyons of New York organized a tribute for anti-lynching crusader Ida
B. Wells. They held one of the largest gatherings of black women to date at Lyric
Hall on October 5, 1892 to honor the *New York Age* reporter. Prominent black
women from several northeastern states attended, including Gertrude Mossell
of Philadelphia and Josephine St. Pierre Ruffin of Boston. "It was," according to
Wells, "the most brilliantly interesting affair of its kind ever attempted in these
United States." More than $400 was raised as a result of the event, providing
Wells with sufficient funds to publish her anti-lynching editorials in the pam-
phlet *Southern Horrors*.[10]

Victoria Earle Matthews, who was known as an intellectual and as a me-
ticulous researcher and writer, established the Women's Loyal Union shortly
after the successful event. According to her supporters, the goals of the union
reflected her goal "of doing what she can for her race" and "banding together well
thinking women" who "might in their generation pave the way for the success
of the futurity of the race." The union's middle-class members were "conscientious conservative, thinking people" who were committed to Matthews's vision
of reform and uplift in the black community. More than 100 women became
members and helped Matthews shape the direction and development of the
black female club movement in the city.[11]

Boston was also the site of increased interest in organizing among black
women. The Women's New Era Club, which was led by Barrier Williams's friend
Josephine St. Pierre Ruffin, became central to the advancement of black women
in Boston. Ruffin, who was born in 1842 in that city, and her husband George
Lewis Ruffin helped recruit black soldiers during the Civil War. After the war,
Josephine became an active club woman. Aided by her daughter Florida Ridley and her friend Maria Baldwin, she organized the Women's New Era Club
in February 1893. One of the most significant endeavors of the club was the
monthly magazine *Woman's Era*, which began publication in 1894. Edited by
Ruffin, the monthly disseminated news for and about black women nationally.
Barrier Williams was impressed with the publication and wrote four months
after its debut that "the good women of Boston are deserving of much praise
for the largeness of heart and outlook so happily shown in the creation and
publication of the WOMAN'S ERA. At the very time when race interest seems
at such a low ebb, when our leaders seem tongue-tied, dazed and stupidly inac-
tive in the presence of unchecked lawlessness, and violent resistance to Negro
advancement, it is especially fortunate and reassuring to see and feel the rallying
spirit of our women voicing itself in words of hope, courage and high resolves
in a journal that seems to spring out of the very heart and peculiar needs of our
women."[12] By the fall of 1894, when Ruffin added a "New Departments" sec-

tion for the purpose of soliciting and printing news from black women around the country, Barrier Williams had joined the publication staff as the reporter from Chicago. Other regional reporters included Victoria E. Mathews in New York, Mary Church Terrell in Washington, Josephine Silone Yates in Kansas City, Elizabeth P. Ensley in Denver, and Alice Ruth Moore in New Orleans.[13] In a relatively short period of time the monthly had a circulation that covered much of the territorial United States, bridging, at least through rhetoric, the geographical gulf between the North, the South, the East, and the Midwest/ West that hindered a universal association and providing a vehicle that spoke to the needs and aspirations of black women around the country. Catering to the "women of the refined and educated classes," the publication united a broad social network of women by highlighting many common concerns.[14]

* * *

Chicago women also demonstrated interest in creating a local alliance and joining the national reform movement, and in January 1894 they created the Woman's Club.[15] An outgrowth of "ladies' day" meetings of the Tourgee Club, a black men's association, the club initially began as a space for women to listen to prominent speakers and discuss issues of importance to them. It quickly became an organized and proactive body of reformers. Its primary purpose, "the elevation and protection of women and the home," highlighted black women's growing concern over the faltering status of women and their families. The club came to represent the best and most actively engaged black elite women in the city.

Ida B. Wells spearheaded the development of the club. Her interest in Chicago and black women's activism peaked when she was invited to be a guest speaker at the Thursday meeting after the World's Fair ended. Finding common ground and a keen willingness to serve among the group's members, she decided to relocate from New York and move to the city permanently. She took a job at the *Chicago Conservator*, which was operated by Ferdinand Barnett, and focused attention on how black women could bring about change. Wells enlisted the assistance of Mary Jones, the matriarch of Chicago's black aristocratic society, guaranteeing the stature and credibility she needed to attract the members who would ensure the success of the club. Wells later recounted that she calculated that this strategic move "would lend prestige" because Jones was "such a genteel, high-bred old lady of the race." Jones chaired the organization but because she "knew that she had no experience along those lines," she agreed to take the position of "honorary chairman to please me, after I told her that I would do the work."[16] Jones subsequently resigned her position, pushing Wells to take the helm. When Wells left the country to promote her anti-lynching campaign in England, Rosie E. Moore became president. Under her leadership, the club adopted a constitution and by-laws and was incorporated. The club eventually adopted the name Ida B. Wells Club.[17]

The club grew quickly and so did its activism. Nearly 200 women had joined by March 1894, and at its peak at least 300 women were members.[18] Many more attended the club's weekly public lectures and discussions about the welfare of the black community and ways to fight discrimination. The women in these audiences crossed professional and generational lines. According to Wells, "prominent women in church and secret society, school teachers and housewives and high-school girls" attended the meetings.[19] They committed their energy and money to plans to remedy some of the problems their communities faced. When they learned that the husband of a black woman with two children had been killed by the police, they found housing for the widow and her children and paid two months' advance rent. They also raised funds to contribute to the prosecution of the police officer for the death of the widow's wage-earning husband.[20] They also acted as social workers, coming to the aid of a fourteen-year-old girl who was homeless and so desperate "that she was found carrying a revolver, living in hovels and associating with the most degraded." The members effectively adopted her as she was "under complete charge of the Woman's Club." In their ultimate goal of "train[ing] her to become a useful member of society," the club sent her to school and saw to her needs until she was eighteen.[21]

The rapid spread of industrialization in Chicago during the last decade of the nineteenth century exacerbated many of the social problems club women encountered. As more blacks migrated to the city there was a spike in homelessness and in the number of children mired in poverty. Most were not as lucky as the fourteen-year-old aided by the Woman's Club. They remained adrift or became dependent on the state. For Barrier Williams this was one of the most disturbing problems of the industrial age—the ineptness of state policy and the failure of state-run institutions, which were dominated by men, to meet the challenges facing women and children. Promoting a separate spheres ideology, she argued that women's nurturing qualities and social skills meant that they had to either share in the responsibility of providing aid or, if necessary, take the lead and work around government-sponsored programs and facilities. She noted that in Chicago, "the most aggressive forces in the reform movements of the day are those that are outside of, and in many cases, in spite of the institutions and established conservators of human society. It is not the church, nor the school house, nor the political organization, nor the purely social establishments that are aggressively engaged in much of the best reform work of the city." She added, "If it be asked who it is that protects the minor children from the cruelties of store-keepers and factories, who it is that protects the unfortunate women of the slums from the blackmailing of the police force," then "the answer is that that protection comes from the women's clubs of the city—voluntary organizations of noble women, whose culture is so broad and hearts so touched with the divine spirit of altruism, that their nobility is increased by every effort to reach down the helping hand to lift up the helpless and 'disinherited.'"[22]

Barrier Williams was not alone in her belief that women were central to remedying social problems. In her keynote address at the National Council of Women's conference in February 1895, which met in Washington, prominent Rhode Island club woman Fanny Purdy Palmer said that "the correctional work of the future promises to be, not as in the past, the work of sects or classes, nor yet of one sex to the exclusion of the other. The future co-operation of men and women is an assured fact." Barrier Williams reiterated this theme in her speech at the conference. [23] In May 1895 she published a version of her address to the National Women's Council in the *Woman's Era*. "Are there so many dependent, homeless and undisciplined children that institutions must be built to house, sustain and protect them through their minority?" she asked.

> Then send to them as instructors not men or women, but men and women of the best hearts and the finest minds and accomplishments. Women believe that the best that humanity has is none too good to be used in making good men and women out of what are called bad children. The best that woman can offer stands ready to be joined with the best that man can offer in lifting all correctional institutions of the country to a position of greater usefulness in developing character on the ethical side.[24]

She blamed male-run administrations for the poor quality of care given to those "whom fortune and nature have illy favored." Because "man alone has been the stern master ... correctional work has been a matter of business, a policy of hard necessity, of punishment, of discipline, of appropriations and of salaries." Only with the addition of women's "warmer heart and finer instincts" would "the lives of the children of men" be improved. By decoupling correctional work in the public arena from male leadership, Barrier Williams promoted women's role as mothers and guardians in the home and their interests in "the deeper and tenderer side of human life."[25]

Nursing certainly fit her idea of expanding opportunities for women in public institutions. The profession held the promise of illustrating how successful co-operation between male doctors and female nurses could be. The nurses' training school at Provident Hospital was one of the few in the country that trained black women. As the demand for adequate health care in the black community increased, black nurses became important agents of the effort to provide better medical care. These nursing schools elevated nursing from a menial occupation that was associated with poorly educated women who lacked adequate training to a profession that black women could enter.[26] Barrier Williams took great pride in the success of the training school and its symbolism of collaboration and cooperation between regions and races. In a "happy illustration" of the achievement, she highlighted the career of M. W. Dillard, who had been educated at Provident and had moved south to Birmingham. "Her scientific training . . . won the confidence of the entire medical fraternity," she noted. "Prejudice yields wherever she goes," she reported, and "wherever she is associated with white nurses in any important case Miss Dillard is always senior in management and responsibilities."[27] That kind of social and professional achievement encouraged Barrier Williams to continue to promote Provident as a route to professional opportunities for black women. She participated in fund-raising efforts for the school and became secretary of the Auxiliary Committee in 1896.[28]

Like social reform and employment issues, the push for political equality tied club women in Chicago to black club women across the country. Women in the West and Midwest made significant progress toward the goal of universal suffrage during the last decade of the nineteenth century. By 1893, the state of Colorado and the territory of Wyoming had granted women the right to vote. But as in the majority of states, the battle for suffrage in Illinois was more difficult and protracted. Women gained only incremental inroads to the vote. Those small victories were the result of the creation of groups such the Equal Suffrage Association and the Cook County Suffrage Association and labor and reform organizations such as the IWA. Caroline Huling, the president of the Cook County Equal Suffrage Association, who became president of the IWA in 1888, and Catharine McCulloch convened a number of groups throughout the state under the auspices of the Equal Suffrage Association in the period 1888 to 1891. That agitation led in 1891 to a law that granted women voting privileges on school-related issues, including school board elections.[29] Barrier Williams viewed the passage as a national call to arms for women. She jubilantly predicted that this "fragmentary suffrage, now possessed by women in nearly all the states of the union," was a forerunner to an "extension to complete and national suffrage." But she tempered her jubilation with the caution that "just how soon the complete enfranchisement of women will be realized depends largely upon the use we make of our present gains."[30]

Barrier Williams particularly implored black women to fully engage and "prepare themselves, by the best lessons of citizenship, to exert a wholesome influence in the politics of the future."[31] One of the first major tests in the state came on November 6, 1894, when women voted for the nominees for the Board of Trustees for the University of Illinois. This was no ordinary election. For the first time, the names of four women were on the ballot.[32] Barrier Williams was concerned about over how politically uneducated women would use their vote. She pointed to the growing social and political tension between black men and women because of the few results black male suffrage had produced for the community since they had gained the franchise in 1870 and the distinctive raced and gendered characteristics of black women. "Must we begin our political duties with no better or higher conceptions of our citizenship than that shown by our men when they were first enfranchised?" she asked. "Are we to bring any refinement of individuality to the ballot box? Shall we learn our politics from spoilsmen and bigoted partisans, or shall we learn it from the school of patriotism and an enlightened self-interest? If our enfranchisement means only a few more votes added to the republican and democratic sides, respectively, of political issues, there certainly has been no gain for the cause of principle in American politics."[33] This wasn't simply espousing the views of the broader community of progressive and reform-minded women, black and white, about the inherent difference between men and women that argued that women's entrance into the realm of politics would "purify" it, as a prominent black club woman in Colorado suggested.[34] Black women, Barrier Williams insisted, were claiming supremacy as leaders in the black community, and they had to use their voting ability differently because of the multiple forces that shaped and limited their lives.

She recognized that racism divided black and white women. Arguing that white female voters did not have nearly as much at stake as black women, did little to assist black women, and ultimately often oppressed black women, she wrote that "the sincerity of white women, who have heretofore so scorned our ambitions and held themselves aloof from us in all our struggles for advancement, should be, to a degree, questioned." To her, the female candidates didn't seem that different from the male candidates in the campaign, for the men also encouraged female voters, white and black, to vote as Democrats and Republicans instead of voting in the best interest of women. "Without wishing to discredit the good motives of our women, or to criticize captiously their conduct in the campaign," she noted, "I believe this new opportunity for self-help and advancement ought not be lost sight of in our thirst for public favors, or in our eagerness to help any grand old 'party.' We ought not to put ourselves in the humiliating position of being loved only for the votes we have."[35]

To that end Barrier Williams refused to endorse any particular party, choosing instead to cast her vote for the candidate with the platform that best appealed to black women's issues. The stance pitted her against other black women in the Chicago community. Some, including those in the Ida B. Wells Club, who insisted on maintaining their loyalty to the party of Lincoln, believed that the Republican candidates offered the best possibilities for community elevation and success.[36] But Barrier Williams found that the demand for party loyalty restricted black voters and retarded their progress. She argued that the freedom to choose candidates who represented the interests of black women was the primary vehicle for gaining economic opportunity and reaffirming black civil rights. "It would be," she wrote, "much more to our credit if we would seek, by all possible uses of our franchise, to force these ambitious women candidates and women party managers to relent their cruel opposition to our [black] girls and women in the matter of employment and the enjoyment of civil privileges. We should never forget that the exclusion of colored women and girls from nearly all places of respectable employment is due mostly to the meanness of American women, and in every way that we can check this unkindness by the force of our franchise should be religiously done."[37] The reference to "ambitious women candidates" and "cruel opposition" to "civil privileges" was probably directed at two of the most high-profile candidates, Lucy Flower, a Republican, and Julia Holms Smith, a Democrat. Both were longtime members of the CWC: Flower had joined in 1883 and been elected president in 1890, and Smith had worked with the organization since joining in 1877. The CWC supported women candidates, endorsed the election of a woman as a trustee, and effectively urged the membership to assist the two women. But the organization did not have any black women members at the time of the election.[38]

In this racialized context, Barrier Williams viewed the ballot as a means of maintaining and improving the constitutional rights of black women. Too much was at stake for the black community in Illinois for black women to blindly ally themselves with white political candidates simply because they were female or were members of a particular party. The issues of education, the juvenile court system, child labor, police brutality, temperance, and poverty demanded the attention of reform-minded women.[39] And while black aristocratic women may have intentionally separated themselves from the masses, these were issues that united elite black women and poor black women in a shared understanding of the "peculiar" needs of their community. Barrier Williams concluded that if black women did not recognize the unique raced and gendered meaning of their vote and only replicated the political status quo, then "we shall be guilty of the same folly and neglect of self-interest that have made colored men for the past twenty years vote persistently more for the special interest of white men than for the peculiar interest of the colored race."[40]

Barrier Williams's focus on race and how it shaped political engagement was timely. By 1890, antipathy toward the social, economic, and political advancement of blacks had spread to nearly every region of the country. One of the first indications of that retrenchment was in Mississippi, which amended its constitution to disenfranchise black men at its constitutional convention that year.[41] Other southern states soon followed. North of Jim Crow, race relations were also deteriorating. Chicago had become racially divided. Although the black population of Chicago numbered only 30,000 by the turn of the century the limitations to black social and economic equality were already visible. Segregation limited interactions between blacks and whites as more blacks were confined to specific neighborhoods; at the turn of the century, the beginnings of the ghetto were already visible.[42] Blacks were relegated to racially defined jobs and were hired in jobs designated white only when whites went on strike. Barrier Williams framed the assault in national terms when she wrote that "the negroes in the south have learned from the experiences of those who have already come north that there is a distressing scarcity of the milk and honey which they dreamed of. They have begun to learn that the prejudice from which they would flee has been here all the time, and is ready to confront them in this rose colored haven of liberty and equality. They have begun to learn that race prejudice is omnipresent, and as an interference with one's rights to be free, to live and to be happy is quite as decided in one part of the country as another."[43] While the problems blacks faced in Chicago may have stemmed in large part from the uniqueness of the city's industrialization, the racism and discrimination they experienced linked them to the national black community, and the reform efforts of Chicago's black women resonated with the concerns of black women's groups in other regions of the country.

*   *   *

"The colored women of America are becoming conscious of their importance in all things that can make for the social betterment of the Negro race," Barrier Williams declared in 1897.[44] She was referring to the rapid coalescence of black activist women across the nation and her belief in black women's role in guiding the progress of the race at the dawn of the new century. The source of black women's ascendance, she felt, was two concurrent and intersecting developments. The first was national awareness and interest in black women's reform activism. "Colored women are fortunate to live in this era of freedom and interest in womankind," she wrote. "Public interest in us has grown to such an extent that the press is as eager for every item of news concerning our work and achievement as they are for that of more favored races." The second was more gendered and, as historian Deborah Gray White suggests, provided "evidence that black men and women were in conflict" over the role women should play in the black community. Barrier Williams highlighted the tension that had been building for some time in her statement that "the relentlessness of prejudice seems more likely to yield to the winsome voice of our women than to the effort of many of our more or less pretentious brothers." While she argued that "it is not in a spirit of boastfulness" that black women's efforts inspired more "encouragement" than that of men, she declared that if "this is 'woman's era,'" then "with just as much distinctiveness is it the colored woman's era." Barrier Williams was not the first black woman to suggest that it was the "woman's era," but her articulation of black women's centrality in the reform and progress of the black community played a critical role in shaping the activities, policies, and politics of what became a national call to arms.[45]

Black women had been activists long before the creation of the Colored Women's League, the Women's Loyal Union, the Women's New Era Club, or the Ida B. Wells Club.[46] But the increase in activity and the coalescence of local and regional clubs in the early 1890s was unprecedented. Harnessing the energy of the increasing interest in black women's clubs across the nation, the *Woman's Era* called for black women to convene to discuss the possibility and benefits of a national organization. In the May 1894 edition, the paper opined that "The WOMAN'S ERA believes that the time is ripe for a convention of the colored women of the country to agitate the subject." The editor asked readers to respond to three questions: "1. Do you favor a convention of the colored women's clubs, [l]eagues and societies? 2. What in your opinion is the most available place and time for such a congress? 3. State why you do or do not favor a convention."[47] Responses poured in from clubs all over the country. Most were enthusiastic about the idea of convention, although there was disagreement about where it should be held. One of the first printed replies was that of Rosie Moore of Chicago. "In response to your question regarding the holding of a congress of the colored women's leagues I heartily approve of the suggestion. I am of the opinion that great good would result from an interchange of ideas as to how we could best accomplish the more lasting results of the work each league is engaged in," she wrote. She heartily agreed with the suggestion that the first meeting be held in Chicago and suggested that August would be the best time. "You will pardon me for naming Chicago, however, I am convinced there is not another place in the United States that affords as good facilities for the meeting as the great convention city of America." Moreover, she continued, "I think the ladies would gain inspiration by breathing the free air, mingling with the broad-minded women of Chicago."[48] Victoria Earle Matthews agreed that a convention should be held and said, "I believe it would arouse the interest and center the attention of our women in common, which will lead to not only an interest generally but a deeply rooted local pride in the matter of organization and this practical support of the same." While Matthews also suggested that August would be the best time to hold the convention, she felt that Philadelphia was the most convenient and central location.[49] Maria Baldwin, vice president of the Woman's Era Club, concurred with Moore and Matthews about the need for a convention but she believed that Boston was the most viable site because "I know of no other city where the attitude of the press and that of the general public would be as respectful."[50]

Barrier Williams's response, however, received considerable attention. In contrast to the enthusiasm of Moore, Matthews, and Baldwin she was cautious about what she perceived as the "mere spectacular demonstration of our enthusiasm for good works." "It must readily occur to the more thoughtful readers of the WOMAN'S ERA," she wrote, "that large conferences of women inexperienced in the functions of deliberative bodies and without well defined and settled policies of action would be fraught with as many possibilities of evil as of good." Arguing that black women's issues were fundamentally different from those of black men and white women, she was concerned that without careful thought, a women's convention would have little meaning beyond the meeting and would not significantly add to the lives of women attendees and those in the community who needed the most assistance. "We should be careful to avoid the examples of our colored men, whose innumerable Conventions, Councils and Conferences during the last twenty-five years have all begun in talk and ended in talk," she wrote. In addition, her familiarity with white women's organizations in Chicago led her to argue that the racialized context and the gendered construct of race mandated that black women's organization be different from other women's clubs. "We should not degrade our own high purposes into what as yet must be a mere imitation of the methods and work of long established Woman's Clubs." Although she was cautious, in the end, she supported the idea of convening a national forum. "I believe that it is possible for us to work out, define and pursue a kind of club work that will be original, peculiarly suitable to our peculiar needs and that will distinguish our work essentially from the white women's clubs," she noted.[51] But she believed that that kind of planning required a number of years to develop and that the convention should not be held for "two or three years, or until we are able to make such a conference impressive and grandly significant by a display of thoughtfulness, definiteness or purpose, and the presentation of facts and figures relative to work done and planned to be done."[52]

The editors gave serious thought to Barrier Williams's opinion. This was due in part because she had lived in Washington, Boston, and Chicago and had intimate ties to all three regions. In addition, she gained national attention as a result of her performance at the World's Fair. Because of their respect for her, for her ideas, and for her work as a public speaker, club woman, and activist, the editors of *The Woman's Era* sought her counsel. "Mrs. Williams' mind and ability," the paper opined, "are well-known in Washington and Boston, where she formerly lived and her letter will have great weight with the people of those cities as well as with those of the West, with whom she has lived of late years." The editorial noted that she "advises us not to be in a hurry and the advice is timely."[53]

As thoughts about a convention swirled over the next few months, Barrier Williams and the readers of *The Woman's Era* continued to pursue their club work. For example, in February 1895, Barrier Williams was in Washington to participate in the National Council of Women's conference. The major themes of the conference included seeking ways to eradicate problems in public schools, the need for better gendered care for women and girls in the penal system and in asylums, and the need for cooperation between female and male reformers. But her participation in the discussion about women and girls in state care was interrupted by the news of the death of her friend Frederick Douglass. He had just attended the council meeting the previous day. She was so distraught over his demise that she told a reporter that "she could hardly speak."[54] His death had in many ways brought the two friends full circle. She had known him since childhood when he lived in nearby Rochester, New York, and was traveling the country giving antislavery speeches, she had participated with him in the Monday Night Literary Society meetings when she relocated to Washington in 1877, she had hosted him in her home in Chicago when he was there on business, and she was in Washington with him, crusading for women's rights, when he died. In one of her last letters to him, she had invited him to spend time with her and S. Laing as he traveled across the country to attend a fair in California.[55]

After the death of her father nearly five years earlier, Douglass had become her confidant. She trusted him implicitly and at times had confessed her personal failings to him. For example, when she had not heard from him in quite some time, she wrote him a letter that demonstrated her angst. She wrote, "It is an old weakness of mine to have no faith in a friendship that does not express itself; and when friends take no notice of me for a long time I am apt to nurse the belief that they have become indifferent or begun to dislike me."[56] It was a rare demonstration of a fault and one of the few glimpses we have of her private emotions. Clearly, his passing was a painful and devastating personal loss for her.

In April she paid tribute to Douglass in her column for *The Woman's Era*. "Like so many readers of the ERA, I sustained a personal relationship to Mr. Douglass that will remain always as an inspiration and grateful remembrance. But, without intruding myself and my own personal emotions, I feel like blessing Mr. Douglass' name forever because of his always honorable and chivalric regard for womankind," she began. She praised his ability to "tolerate no limitations based on sex lines," concluding that "he so lived not only that men might be free and equal and exalted, but that women, too, by the same emancipating forces, might come equally into the estate of freedom." She concluded that ultimately, "his life was a compliment to women."[57]

There were those who were far less respectful of black women. These included John Jacks, the president of the Missouri Press Association, who had written a letter to Florence Balgarnie of the London Anti-Slavery Society in March in which he stated his belief that black women "were prostitutes and all are natural liars and thieves." While the letter might not have been in direct response to Ida B. Wells's anti-lynching crusade in England, Wells nevertheless viewed it as an "insult to Negro womanhood as well as to myself." When Josephine Ruffin sent copies of the letter to women across to the country, they too viewed it as an affront to black womanhood and renewed their calls for national unity among black women. With less than two months' preparation, Ruffin and a team of women set aside Barrier Williams's early warning about convening too soon and called on black women to assemble in Boston to defend themselves and discuss issues important to them and to the black community.[58]

It was evident from the beginning that despite Barrier Williams's earlier hesitation, her good friend Ruffin wanted her there. When invitations were sent, Ruffin noted under "Conference Notes" that "Mrs. Fannie Barrier Williams of the Chicago Women's Club will lend interest by her presence."[59] But it is unclear whether Barrier Williams actually attended the three-day event, which was held from Monday, July 29, to Wednesday, July 31, at Berkeley Hall in Boston. Nearly 100 women representing more than twenty clubs and at least ten states attended. Among them were Barrier Williams's sister Ella, who joined a contingent from Washington that included Helen Cook and Anna Julia Cooper.[60] Presentations included topics such as "Woman and the Higher Education," Industrial Training," "Individual Work for Moral Elevation," "Political Equality," and "Social Purity."[61] After the events of the last day of the conference, attendees held a business meeting to address important issues facing the black community, particularly in the South. They publicly endorsed Ida B. Wells's anti-lynching work and appointed a committee to write a resolution condemning lynching, the convict system in Georgia, and the enforced legal segregation of black and white children in Florida schools.[62]

It was clear from the beginning of the conference that Ruffin, her colleagues, and several of the women in attendance expected this to be the beginning of a national federation. The coalition deliberated on the best way to create a national organization. Of concern was the relationship between this first national conference and the Washington-based Colored Women's League. However, the group agreed to organize and elected Margaret Murray Washington, the wife of Booker T. Washington, as president; F. Y. Ridley of Boston as corresponding secretary; L. C. Carter of Brooklyn, New York, as recording

thousands of people from around the world. Several meetings and congresses of African Americans were held during the final month of the exposition. One of the most significant speeches was Booker T. Washington's "Atlanta Compromise" speech on the opening day of the exposition. While his speech received praise and publicity for its conciliatory and accommodationist rhetoric from whites and a mixture of approval and derision from blacks, his presence was not the most important aspect of the exposition for black club women. That event was the first national Colored Woman's Congress at Bethel African Methodist Episcopal Church on December 28.

The congress brought together one of the largest contingents of black southern women of the period and attracted 150 women from twenty-five states, including many of those from the northern and midwestern states who had attended the Boston conference. One of the most enlightening presentations, "How Can the Interests of Northern and Southern Colored Women Be More Strongly Related?," illuminated the lingering regional tensions between the women and highlighted the difficulties of bridging geographical, regional, and cultural divisions.[69] Barrier Williams represented Chicago and played important roles at the conference. She, Margaret Murray Washington, and Mary V. Cook "attracted especial attention."[70] *The Atlanta Constitution* highlighted her presence by calling her "one of the best informed of the women who are in attendance." She presented "The Opportunities and Possibilities of the 'Negro Woman,'" which the paper opined "was carefully prepared and showed that she had full knowledge of the responsibilities devolving upon her sex in the development of her people."[71] The congress elected her to the Committee on Courtesies along with Frances Ellen Watkins Harper of Pennsylvania, J. W. E. Bowen of Atlanta, J. C. Napier of Tennessee, Frances Preston of Michigan, and W. B. Derrick of New York.[72]

Barrier Williams felt that the Boston conference and the Atlanta congress demonstrated momentum in the national organization of black club women. "Linked with the Boston Conference of last August, the Woman's Congress in Atlanta can scarcely be less than a historical landmark in the development of the fraternal spirit among the colored women of America," she wrote.[73] And, indeed, as at the conference in Boston, the women at the Atlanta congress displayed considerable concern about the black community, demonstrated the broad reach of their organizational and reform skills, and passed a number of resolutions about lynching, the convict lease system, and other atrocities. But one element of the congress stood out because of its regional distinctiveness. The group pointed to the demeaning Jim Crow rail system that had made their travel to the conference unpleasant.[74] Certainly their awareness of the Homer Plessy case, which had originated in New Orleans in 1892 and was proceeding to a Supreme Court decision, influenced the resolution they passed.

WHEREAS, many women of this Congress, coming from points remote, have had experience with the separate car system prevailing in many states of the south, of a brutal, inhuman and degrading nature, and

WHEREAS, the separate car system is contrary, not only to the law of contract but to the genius of our liberal institutions, tending to accentuate unduly discriminations on account of color and condition, and

WHEREAS, it is the proud boast of Southern white men that the ennobling of womanhood is the basis of all chivalric manhood,

RESOLVED, That we call upon the Southern legislators, in the name of the common womanhood, to adopt a first and second class fare, so that the womanhood of the race may be protected from every outrage and insult. We trust that the white men of the South now in power will heed this just position.[75]

This was not the first time that black women had complained about the rail cars. When Ida B. Wells was forcibly removed from a train in Memphis, Tennessee, for refusing to move to the segregated car, she sued the company. After an initial favorable verdict, she lost when the company appealed the decision to a higher court.[76] Margaret Washington also complained, but she argued that the source of the problem was not rail officials at the corporate level. Instead, she posited that it was a regionalized cultural phenomenon that had been generated and was maintained by "the southern people" who "make these laws." For her, change would come "only as the sentiment of the Southern white man is changed." She believed that "the southern women keep up this thing" because "they are behind the men because their education is more limited—they have little to do except to nurse their predjuices [sic]."[77]

Washington noted that it wasn't just southern black women who were affected by the Jim Crow cars. "The women who live north object to coming south to hold a meeting because of the travel," she wrote in 1896.[78] Barrier Williams certainly was one of the northern visitors she had in mind. As she traveled in Georgia and Alabama, for example, Barrier Williams was both impressed with southern black women's activism and dismayed by the segregated rail cars. Southern women, she observed, were "alert, accomplished and sufficient women" who demonstrated such a "fraternal spirit" and displayed "a variety of talents and fibre of character." She praised them "for noble activities" and for being led "by the better spiritual and social forces of our day." They were "a nucleus of womanly excellence—women who are wide awake to the opportunities and responsibilities of the hour and eager for a larger co-operation of hand and heart in the work of regeneration." She especially recognized the efforts of "Mrs. Washington of Tuskegee, Mrs. Davenport of Montgomery, Mrs. M. A. Dillard of Selma, Mrs. S. A. Childs of Marion, Mrs. S. A. Christian of Greensboro, [and] Mrs. Ross of Birmingham" and concluded that if they "and their associates are a type of our southern sister, then those of us living north of the Ohio will need to bestir ourselves to keep pace with their advancing influence for good."[79]

But traveling through the region for her was a nightmare. "Fortunately, since my marriage I have had but little experience south of the Mason Dixon's line," she wrote. But "some time ago I was induced by several clubs in different States and cities of the South to make a kind of lecture tour through that section." She continued, "I knew, of course, of the miserable separations, 'Jim Crow' cars, and other offensive restrictions," but when actually faced with the injustice of them she recoiled. "The 'Jim Crow' cars were almost intolerable to me," she remembered. Determined to defy the constraint, she used the advantages of her light skin and her economic status to circumvent the injustice; she wrote that she was "fortunate enough to escape them in every instance." She reported that "conductors are very often deceived" because they were unsure of their ability to determine who was black or white. "Beside[s]," she wrote, "they know that an insult can scarcely go further than to ask the wrong person if he or she be colored."[80] The uncertainty of racial demarcations certainly played a primary role in her successful circumvention of the unjust rules, but it was also possible because she had the financial means to ride in the first class car with whites. "I made it a rule always to take my seat in the first-class car to which I felt I was entitled by virtue of my first-class ticket," she boasted. At one stop, she used both resources to evade detection of her black identity.

> I remember that at a certain place I was too late to procure my ticket at the station, and the conductor told me that I would have to go out at the next station and buy my ticket, and then, despite my English book, which I was very ostentatiously reading, he stepped back and quickly asked me, "Madame, are you colored?" I as quickly replied, "Je suis Français." "Français?" he repeated. I said "Oui." He then called to the brakeman and said, "Take this lady's money and go out at the next station and buy her ticket for her," which he kindly did, and I as kindly replied as he handed me the ticket, "Merci." Fortunately their knowledge of French ended before mine did or there might have been some embarrassments as to my further unfamiliarity with my mother tongue. However, I quieted my conscience by recalling that there was quite a strain of French blood in my ancestry, and too that their barbarous laws did not allow a lady to be both comfortable and honest.[81]

She was not the only black aristocrat who passed. Others included Mary Church Terrell and Victoria Earle Matthews. Although this practice may have been a contradiction for lighter-skinned women who battled racism on the one hand but seemed to cooperate with the racist system by passing, it nevertheless mocked the certainty of white southerners that they could determine racial identity and the laws that bound and constrained the lives of blacks because of color.[82] Barrier Williams pointed to this topic in her article "Perils of the

White Negro." "The term 'White Negro' suggests one of the most interesting paradoxes of American life. The people to whom this term is applied are not Negroes according to the principles of ethnology and are not white according to understanding and usage of that term in the United States," she began. "There seem to be but two courses open to these so-called 'white Negroes', one is to remain where American prejudice forces them and heroically share the fate of their darker kindred, the other course is to establish themselves in communities, where their identity is not known, and quietly take their places in the ranks of the white people exclusively. Thousands of them, weary with the ceaseless struggle against American prejudice pursue this latter course and successfully 'pass for white.'" In the South in particular, she argued, the "white Negro" posed a difficult problem. "Railroad conductors in the South" acted as gatekeepers and were "required to be experts in order to save [the] 'Jim Crow' car law." This, however, proved nearly impossible, as she knew from her own experience and as had occurred in the case of a black man "in Texas [who] boarded a train and took a seat in the 'Jim Crow' car, where by their own legal classification he belonged." But what the conductor saw was a white man making a gross social error by taking a seat in the segregated and inferior black car. "He was promptly told by the conductor that white people were not allowed to ride in the Negro car and that he must go into the white car." When the man refused, "He was threatened with arrest." In the end, Barrier Williams concluded that race was indeed, as historian Evelyn Brooks Higginbotham notes, a "double-voiced discourse." And because of that, she opined, "Thus it is that right or wrong, the Negro is carried into the very heart life of the proud Anglo-Saxon, in spite of laws and hatreds of all kinds, which are not of his own making. In thousands of places, safeguarded by every possible social restriction, the Negro is undetected and unsuspected. From this secret blending the chivalric South is as insecure as staid New England."[83]

Jim Crow laws obscured class distinctions among blacks, and sometimes whites inaccurately judged the color of a person's skin. But Barrier Williams's empathy toward and acceptance of those like her who were forced to pass did not detract from her elitism. Her disdain for the "repressive and unjust laws" originated in her "abiding heartache for the refined and helpless colored women" forced to abide by them. While she certainly did not condone the universal oppression of black people, it was public humiliation of the "refined" rather than contempt for the impact of the laws on both the elite and the black masses. Such reluctance led her to suggest that the most odious aspect of the laws was that "this hateful interpretation of these laws is to make no distinction between the educated and refined and the ignorant and depraved negro."[84] Clearly her class consciousness complicated certain aspects of her race consciousness when the demarcations of elitism were threatened.

Though Barrier Williams's race consciousness was ambiguous at times, it remained intact because she could never forget that regardless of skin complexion and trappings of class she was subject to the same injustices as all black women. When asked to "address a club of very aristocratic white women" in the South, for example, she found that "although it had been announced in all the papers as a public meeting, not a colored person was present except myself." On another occasion, she feared for her life because "I noticed while on my way to the church where I was advertised to speak to a colored audience, that we were being followed by a half dozen of what seemed to me the typical Southern 'cracker,' red shirt and all. I was not thinking of moonshiners, but of Ku-Klux clans, mid-night lynching parties, etc." She calmed down only after discovering that the group of men who sat near the stage where she was speaking included "the deputy sheriff," who "remained to the close of the lecture" along with several other "fierce"-looking men.[85]

While living north of Jim Crow failed to ensure complete freedom for her, she much preferred it over the South. She was permitted to travel relatively freely, and she was unencumbered for the most part by the laws and cultural and gendered norms that limited the lives of blacks in the South. Her geographical location enabled her to continue her personal and professional missions of battling the racism and discrimination that marked black women's lives. Black club women certainly encouraged her. For example, the Woman's Era Club in Boston invited her and several other women to celebrate a week of New England anniversaries in 1896. That week, she spoke before a group of suffragists, at a banquet, and at the Era Club. *The Woman's Era* reported that she attracted a "fine sized audience," and afterward the club held a reception to honor the guests at the home of Josephine St. Pierre Ruffin. By all accounts that too was a "delightful success." The guests were so interested in the speakers and the event that a "throng . . . filled the house from chamber to basement, and overflowed on to the porch for air."[86]

Many of the "throng" who attended the Boston festivities had probably already made plans for the first official conference of the now one-year-old National Federation of Afro-American Women in Washington the following month. What had begun as an urgent and rather hastily called meeting in the summer of 1895 had become a national organization that had the support of women across the country. But, the federation, which consisted of eighty-five clubs by 1896, was not the only national organization for black women. The Colored Women's League in Washington, led by Helen Cook, continued to compete for national primacy. It had been organized three years earlier than the federation and had at least 113 affiliated branches by 1896. An awareness of these competing groups had been articulated at the Colored Woman's Congress in Atlanta, which had recommended to "the various organizations here represented, local, state and national, the wisdom of uniting for the establishment of one national organization of women."[87] The women from the federation and the women from the league ultimately heeded the recommendation in 1896, the year that both groups held their conventions in Washington. The league held its convention from July 14 to 16 at the Fifteenth Street Presbyterian Church. The federation, headed by Margaret Murray Washington, convened on July 20 to 22 at the Nineteenth Street Baptist Church. After much deliberation, the organizations merged and became known as The National Association of Colored Women (NACW). Mary Church Terrell was elected the first president. Shortly after the new organization was formed, Barrier Williams praised the group, noting that "the organization of the 'National Association of Colored Women' in this country [who are] bent upon making their goodness felt wherever good influences are needed, is an event of extraordinary importance, because the best elements of womanhood are behind and a part of the movement. Our women, thus organized, have it in their power to supplement the blessed influences of the churches, the moulding forces of the schools, and all the restraining powers of the official forces of our cities, to such an extent as to link their efforts with the best results of woman's work in these latter days of the nineteenth century."[88] In the summer of 1898, the NACW held its first biennial conference in Nashville, Tennessee. At that conference the women of Chicago made a successful bid to hold the second NACW conference in their city.[89]

*   *   *

In November 1898, as president of the state-based "Federation of Afro-American Womens' Clubs," Barrier Williams issued a call for a "mass meeting for women only" that was to be held on December 8 at Bethel Church in Chicago.[90] She headed a contingent of organized club women that had been steadily growing since the Ida B. Wells Club had been formed in 1894. By 1897 the number of black women's clubs in the city had increased significantly. They included the Phyllis Wheatley Club, the Woman's Civic League, the Progressive Circle of Kings Daughters, the Ideal Woman's Club, the G. O. P. Elephant Club, the Julia Gaston Club, and an umbrella group called the Women's Conference that was an alliance of organizations charged with organizing and hosting the NACW conference that was to be held in Chicago in the summer of 1899.

For much of the first half of 1899, Barrier Williams promoted the organization and the conference by advertising in the local media and going on a speaking tour. In February, she and the federation's secretary, Fannie Hall Clint, stated the objectives of the coalition:

(1)   To fraternize the Afro-Ameri[can] state of Illinois
(2)   To encourage the organization of clubs where such organizations do not exist, and where the helpfulness of womens' organizations are needed

(3) To hold joint meetings of all the clubs as often as practicable for subjects of special interest to women and their relation to home and society in general.
(4) To aid the clubs in becoming more thoroughly acquainted with the various kinds of work that properly come within the scope of womens' clubs.
(5) To interest the Afro-American women of Chicago and the state of Afro-American Women to be held in 1899.

"The hour has come," Barrier Williams and Clint ultimately concluded, "when it behooves us to make an impressive showing of our strength and our intelligence and we believe this meeting can do much to affect public opinion more favorably as to our worth as women. A juster estimate, more humane treatment and a kindlier interest will certainly result from this concourse of intelligent and earnest women, if we but do our part."[91]

In March and April, Barrier Williams traveled south to present at least three lectures to promote the conference in Chicago. She spoke at the Woman's Day program at Bethel Church in Baltimore, at the Bethel Literary and Historical Society at Metropolitan A.M.E. Church in Washington, and at the Woman's League at Plymouth Congregational Church in Washington.[92]

She also led a local committee consisting of Agnes Moody, Anna Douglass, Mary Davenport, Mrs. Albert Hall, Rosie Moore, Mrs. Taylor, and Birdie Evans that implemented a logistical plan for hosting the NACW in the Midwest for the first time.[93] Elizabeth Lindsay Davis, the state organizer, canvassed the state and was the liaison between the NACW and the federation. Invitations, notifications, and public announcements were sent to a number of black and white women's organizations locally, throughout the state, and across the nation that provided specific information about conference events. They secured Quinn Chapel African Methodist Episcopal Church, one of the oldest black facilities and most prominent religious institutions in the city, as their headquarters.[94]

The advertisement campaign was supported by the local press. One newspaper announced that the convention would "be largely attended by the most notable and prominent women of our race in the United States." That list included Mary Church Terrell, Josephine Bruce, Margaret Murray Washington, Josephine St. Pierre Ruffin, Imogene Howard, Josephine Yates, and local club women Fannie Barrier Williams and Elizabeth Lindsay Davis.[95] Barrier Williams's sister Ella arrived from Washington in late July and remained throughout the summer, and her sister-in law Delia Pelham Barrier came from Detroit to report on the activities of the Willing Workers Club in that city.[96] They were joined by women all over the country. Participants attended sessions about domestic science, moral standards, kindergartens, the convict lease system, lynching, temperance, and Jim Crow cars.[97]

In a judicious push for the NACW to be recognized by the largest national organization of white women in the country, the General Federation of Women's

Clubs (GFWC), and to demonstrate the interracial activities that she had been
engaged in for more than a decade, Barrier Williams solicited the services of
several white women. Ellen Henrotin, who had supported her nomination to
the CWC and had just stepped down from serving two terms as president of
the GFWC (1894–1898), delivered the evening address on the first day of the
conference.[98] Henrotin's presence and the GFWC's close ties to the Chicago
Woman's Club certainly signaled white club women's awareness of the question
of race within their own ranks. The CWC had been one of the founding clubs
of the GFWC in 1890, had hosted the second biennial of the GFWC in Chicago
in May 1892, and had entertained members of the GFWC during the World's
Fair.[99] Barrier Williams's membership in the CWC demonstrated the complex
relationship between individual clubs, state federations, and the national federation. Her individual membership in the CWC included a membership in
the GFWC and the state federation, but black clubs as organized bodies were
excluded from membership in the GFWC.

While Henrotin was the most prominent white woman to attend the NACW
conference, other white women also attended. Corrine Brown, former president of the now-defunct Illinois Woman's Alliance, and Mary McDowell, who
headed the University of Chicago Settlement, also attended.[100] And Belle M.
Stoutenborough, who had been president of the Nebraska Federation from 1897
to 1898 and was visiting in the city at the time, attended sessions.[101]

A number of others attended who were committed to black women's reform.
Booker T. Washington accompanied his wife Margaret to the conference. Bishop
Henry McNeal Turner of the African Methodist Episcopal Church, who was
in town for the Afro-American Council meeting that began on August 17, after
the NACW meeting ended, was present as well. Ida B. Wells-Barnett, who was
busy with her duties as secretary of the council, was not present at any of the
NACW sessions on Monday or Tuesday. She did, however, attend the Wednesday morning general session and delivered two invitations. One was from Jane
Addams of Hull House and the other was from the Afro-American Council.[102]
Several women heeded the invitations and visited Hull House and attended the
council meeting. Timothy Thomas Fortune and W. E. B. Du Bois gave public
addresses to council participants, as did Barrier Williams.[103]

When the festivities ended, the women of Chicago could certainly claim
success. Nearly 150 delegates from fifty clubs and sixteen states had attended.[104]
They had found amenable hosts in the city and had demonstrated the ties of the
secular NACW to the religious community by visiting many of the churches in
the area. The connection to religious institutions was not unusual. Methodists,
Baptists, and other denominations had sent delegates to the first national conference of black women in Boston in 1895 and in various ways had demonstrated
their support for the mission of the group.[105] But the level of participation by

NACW leaders attending the Chicago convention in Chicago's religious community was unprecedented. At the beginning of the conference, several NACW women appeared in Sunday morning pulpits at some of the most distinguished churches in the city. As she had on numerous occasions, Barrier Williams spoke to the congregation at All Souls. Mary Church Terrell, Josephine Bruce, and Josephine Yates spoke at Bethel A.M.E. Church, Quinn Chapel A.M.E. and Olivet Baptist. Anna Julia Cooper spoke at Grace Presbyterian Church.[106] Barrier Williams, who had been lecturing and writing about the important role of religious leaders in elevating the black community since her appearance at the Parliament of Religions in 1893, had to have been involved in the coordination of this particular event. That ministers and congregants so willingly cooperated confirmed how integrated she and other club women were in nearly every aspect of black community life.

The conference generated numerous comments from local newspapers. While *The Broad Ax* disapproved of the behavior of some of the women, noting that they "were as unruly as a crowd of politicians in convention," and pointed to some of the tensions among NACW members over the election of new officers, it reported that "many excellent papers were read and the sentiments which they contained will leave a favorable impression upon the minds of those who heard them."[107]

In the end, Chicago women had successfully positioned themselves and the Midwest as a formidable group within the club movement. One Chicago woman was elected to the executive board of the NACW. Connie Curl became recording secretary. Barrier Williams was nominated for the position of corresponding secretary but lost out to Mary Lynch of North Carolina.[108] More important, the Woman's Conference and the federation that Barrier Williams headed had determined to become a permanent organization with the goal of uniting black club women across the state. In October 1899, the group met at Institutional Church, created the Illinois Federation of Colored Women's Clubs, and joined the NACW. Barrier Williams left her mark there as well. The organization highlighted her passion for helping women and children and endorsed the motto of "Justice to Children—Loyalty to Women" that the now-defunct IWA had adopted when it began in 1888. The group adopted the motto "Loyalty to Women and Justice to Children," which seemed to bind together Barrier Williams's vision and the quest of national black club women to protect both underserved groups.[109]

By the dawn of the twentieth century, Barrier Williams had become a transitional figure between an old century and a new one; and between the geographically distinct regions of the North, the South, and the Midwest. She had participated in the transition from a loosely allied group of black women to a powerful network of club women that constituted one of the largest black organizations in the country. She connected aristocratic black elite women and working class black female laborers with her campaigns to increase employment opportunities for black women in an industrial economy. She was firmly entrenched in local and national debates and discussions about how to best develop, implement, and sustain programs to assist the black community and was recognized as one of the foremost authorities on race, gender, and reform.

6. The New Century

North and South Meet

In 1899, the *Washington Post* called Barrier Williams "one of the best known colored women on the continent."[1] Her appeal was local, regional, and national, it reached into the black and white club women's movements, and it extended to leading black male educators and intellectuals. Her work as a journalist connected her to communities across the country and provided opportunities to discuss race, labor, and gender issues. She was an invited contributor to several black and white publications, opportunities that increased her visibility as she elucidated the important role of black women.[2] She was recognized for her integrative activism with white women and her membership in one of the largest and most powerful white female clubs in the country; in this role, she became both an intermediary and the conduit through which white women learned of black women's achievements. Because of her intellectual analysis of how industrialization and urbanization were transforming the Midwest and reshaping the lives of women, she was often a principal speaker at local and national conferences about the intersectionality of gender and labor. She was an advocate of the southern industrial model of education and one of the leading authorities to articulate how the black working class could benefit from the development of industrial schools in the North. Her place among a group *The Colored American Magazine* called "the greatest thinkers of the black race" was assured.[3]

This visibility came at the same time that white hostility and animosity became more visible and the black community became polarized. As the white women's club movement sought to create a national network by merging northern and southern associations in the last decade of the nineteenth and the first decade of the twentieth centuries, Barrier Williams found far less racial tolerance than she expected, even among northern women. This was a time when southern, mostly rural and uneducated black migrants were pushed out of the South by white aggression and pulled to Chicago for social, political, and economic opportunities. As these migrants began to flood into the city, she found that her approach to assisting them with their economic and social misfortunes drew a great deal of interest from southern white supremacy theorists and prominent black Chicagoans. For white supremacists, her writings and speeches seemed to reinforce their own ideas about black inferiority. Her association with Booker T. Washington and her commitment to his idea of black industrial education pitted her against prominent blacks in Chicago who found Washington's acquiescence to the interests of southern whites offensive and dangerous. She, her husband, and her friends became a target of their anger.

*   *   *

On the heels of the success of the biennial NACW convention in Chicago, the editors of *The Club Woman*, the monthly journal of the General Federation of Women's Club that reached an audience of nearly 150,000 women, published an article about the formation and purpose of the NACW in the October 1899 issue. The article was located under the heading "other state federation news" and was marketed as being "interesting to the Club Women of the country." They chose the lead organizer and host of the event to write the article. Fannie Barrier Williams thus became both the public relations voice for the national community of black women and a critical link between black and white club women. This was the first time that the NACW had been covered in a predominantly white female publication.

The article gave her a chance to boast about the achievements of black women and assess their importance. She told her audience that "the convention of the National Association of Colored Women, recently held in Chicago, is by far the most interesting and helpful demonstration of the progressive social life of the race yet witnessed in this country." One hundred fifty delegates had attended the conference, including many from "eight of the ex-slave-holding states" as well as those from the North, the Midwest, and the District of Columbia. Such a remarkable achievement only a few short years after the founding of the association, she told readers, spoke to an "earnestness and a spirit of heroism in their renewed pledges to concentrate the best heart, the best culture and the most unstinted sacrifice to every problem that fittingly comes within [t]he scope of woman's influence and women's power of co-operation."[4]

While she conceded that "our women have, of course, caught their suggestions and inspirations from the greater and more perfect organizations of the women of the other race" and had even used white women's organizational methods as a model, she stressed two significant differences in the formation of black women's clubs. The first was related to the unique ways that race shaped the movement. Black women operated under "peculiar conditions," and it was those circumstances that "give club work among us a character and interest peculiarly its own."[5] The second reflected on the origins of self-help. She pointed out that the creation of the NACW was the culmination, not the beginning, of black women's activism. Years before the birth of the NACW, formal associations had already been formed and welfare work had been implemented in both the North and the South. She highlighted the two "more progressive clubs along social lines," the Colored Woman's League in Washington and the Woman's Era Club in Boston, which she referred to as the New Era Club or the Era Club. Both groups had formed within three years of the founding of the GFWC and commanded the largest audience of black women in the South and the North, respectively. She described the president of the Colored Women's League, Helen A. Cook, as "a woman of wealth, who has lent herself to this work with untiring devotion and zeal," and she noted that the league was a broad-based coalition of southern organizations that were meeting the needs of the poor. She noted that Josephine St. Pierre Ruffin, the president of the Woman's Era Club, was "known all over the country for her uncompromising denunciation of all wrongs perpetrated against her race" and that the club was connected to black and white organizations throughout the northern states. Both of these groups, Barrier Williams wrote, had a strong sense of community consciousness and social responsibility that made them particularly important "in social and reform movements." They had successfully organized "kindergartens, sewing schools, Mothers' meetings, day nurseries, orphans' homes, etc." "Their efforts," she wrote, "were soon imitated throughout the South and North wherever there were teachers or other women of sufficient intelligence to appreciate the value of organized effort."[6]

Barrier Williams emphasized Ruffin's skills as a mediator and an organizer. She wrote that "she was a striking figure in the Chicago Convention and will be remembered with pride for her fearless condemnation of certain unfortunate efforts, born of thirst for power, which seriously threatened the life of the association" and argued that the national coalition owed its success to Ruffin. It was Ruffin, she recalled, who arranged a conference after "a thoroughly libelous article against the character worth of colored women" was published, and this conference ultimately led to the formation of the NACW.[7] Her glowing assessment of Ruffin's role in the development of a black women's national organization on the surface seemed to have been a simple narrative that praised a particular black woman's activism and was designed to familiarize a national white audience with the specifics of black women's reform work. In reality, it was a cleverly orchestrated effort to test the racial policy of the GFWC. Along with more than 160 individual and state federation applicants seeking membership in the federation that year, Ruffin had taken the bold step of submitting the necessary paperwork and dues for the Woman's Era Club of Boston. The club, which was identified as the New Era Club in the handwritten board minutes, didn't particularly stand out among the other applicants for admission.[8] But, it was different, as Barrier Williams so meticulously pointed out in *The Club Woman*. And it was that difference that set off a chain of events that sharpened tensions between black and white women and nearly shattered the fragile GFWC coalition.

In the spring of 1900, just as the decade-old GFWC was preparing for the upcoming biennial in Milwaukee, the president, Rebecca Douglas Lowe, sent a letter to the Woman's Era Club to announce the club's admission to the federation. "It is with great pride," she wrote, "that I write to extend to your club my congratulations, and at the same time assure them of the desire to be helpful to them in any way possible."[9] As the president of the club and its delegate, Ruffin appeared at the June biennial expecting to be seated along with the other delegates. But to her disappointment, her effort to claim her place was thwarted by Lowe, the executive committee, and the membership. Lowe, who by then had learned that the New Era Club "was a club of colored women," sought the counsel of the executive committee about whether Ruffin should be seated. The board, recognizing the significance of the issue, equivocated, deciding ultimately to table the issue.[10]

That equivocation was the product of uncertainty and fear driven by the flurry of activity among the membership about the New Era Club's membership in the federation. An assumption that Ruffin would be seated as a result of the inaction of the board brought vehement objections from southern delegates. The Georgia Federation submitted a resolution that said: "Whereas;—The fact that a club of colored women has been admitted to our body, renders some action upon the question necessary, the delegation from the Georgia Federation of Women's Clubs to the Fifth Biennial Convention of the General Federation of Women's Clubs has the honor to give notice to the Executive Board of the GFWC that Georgia will at the next Biennial Convention of the G.F.W.C. propose to amend the By-Laws of this order by adding to Article II the following words 'Clubs desiring to join the G.F.W.C. must be composed of white women and must show that no sectarian or political test is required for membership.'"[11] Other southern states similarly protested. Club women from Kentucky predicted "that the admission of this club will be a precedent for the admission of colored clubs generally, and that such action will precipitate the disintegration of the federation."[12] Their objections were the primary reason the board ultimately decided to block Ruffin's attendance as a delegate and to deny the New Era Club admission to the conference. This decision reignited the debate about race and social equality in the club women's movement.

An incensed Barrier Williams told a reporter shortly after the decision that she was "astonished at the action of the committee."[13] Angry about the injustice to her friend and about the broader implications for the national community of black club women, she argued that the action ultimately denied access to the "300 Afro-American women's clubs in the United States with a membership of 15,000." Moreover, coming on the heels of the successful NACW conference in Chicago, at which Ellen Henrotin, the second president of the GFWC, had appeared, and the invited article Barrier Williams had written for the GFWC monthly, the action called into question many of the interracial inroads that black and white women had made in the midwestern region. The rebuff was striking because "in Chicago" alone, she noted, "there are at least four important clubs of Afro-American women: the Phyllis Wheatley, Woman's Conference, Civic Women's League, and the I.B.W. club. Those four have a membership of about 400."[14]

While Barrier Williams focused her outrage on the racism of club women, *The Colored American* argued that the "fuss" over Ruffin had much broader implications. Racial hostility had increased to such a degree by the turn of the century that black women and men in every region of the country and in every economic class were as affected by it as blacks living in the Jim Crow South were. The Supreme Court's "separate but equal" decision in *Plessy v. Ferguson* in 1896 had upheld the constitutionality of Jim Crow legislation and in many ways had broadened the scope of segregation and dashed any hope for black equality for even the best-educated aristocrats in the black community. "The nation's 'Old man of the sea' is the color question" the publication opined. It noted that "although the Negro is theoretically an American citizen, and the law says he is entitled to equal protection with all others in the enjoyment of his natural rights, when he appears and puts in claim for them, there is invariable a row of the most aggravating proportions."[15] It was in this climate that the GFWC closed its door to black women.

In spite of the hardening of racial lines, elite northern black women had emerged as a powerful force in the last decade of the nineteenth century, and their relationships with liberal-minded groups of northern white women before the rise of the national coalescence of white women's organizations beckoned their white allies to address the issue of racism in the organizations they joined. That is what happened in the GFWC. After the conference, regional animosity over the "color question" festered to the point that the federation was compelled to provide a public forum for members to debate the issue. *The Club Woman* became that vehicle.[16] Many northern groups argued that admission to the federation should not be based on race. The Executive Board of the Medford Women's Club of Massachusetts was so incensed that the group withdrew its membership from the GFWC, noting that "if the delegate of the Woman's Era

Club had been a white woman, representing a club of white women, it is probably true that she would not have been rejected."[17] Few other clubs demonstrated such forceful action, but many were clearly angry about the decision to exclude Ruffin. A vice-president of the Massachusetts Federation wrote that "any one having knowledge of the undercurrent of feeling that is sweeping through her clubs, can foresee that it will be impossible for them to retain membership in the General Federation under the conditions prescribed by Georgia, as the Southern clubs declare it will be for them to remain in the organization if colored clubs are admitted."[18]

Southern women staunchly adhered to their tradition of racial segregation. Anne Johnson, president of the Georgia Federation, discussed the sincerity of southern women's views, her anger over the suggestion that Lowe's administrative interference was suspicious because she was a southerner, and the fundamental reason for the rejection of admission for the Woman's Era Club. She noted that while "Georgia's position on the admission of colored clubs into the G.F.W.C. is too well known to require repetition," she was offended by the idea that the question about black female membership was perceived to be "of a much lighter nature, much smaller import than is really true." She argued that when members were "voting to admit or not to admit the colored clubs that they are voting for or against a large body of their own race, are voting for the continuation or disruption of the G.F.W.C." Moreover, they should "well understand once for all the position of the southern women was not taken in a moment of excitement, but with the cool determination; that this stand was not held through caprice but from knowledge of surrounding circumstances, not from sentiment but from conviction." Johnson also disagreed with the claim that Lowe had "used extraordinary means to prevent the withdrawal of the South." Ultimately, the objection to admitting black women was based on notions of "social equality." "For paradoxical as it may seem," she concluded, "the very people who are most urgent for 'social equality' knows [sic] but little of the negro and his particular needs, while those who are the most determinedly opposed to social equality are the very ones who are now and have been for years the most active in the bettering of the condition of the race. As a northerner of many years residence in the South I want emphatically to remark that while 'social equality' is now and always will be impossible at the South, yet history does not record a parallel example where a superior race with extremely limited means has done more for the moral, religious and educational training of an inferior race than have the people of the South for the negro."[19]

The southern women prevailed, in part because even northern members who were uncomfortable about discriminating against elite black women shared the beliefs of southerners about social equality. A physician from Illinois, for ex ample, noted that although she had "a strong personal abhorrence for the social equality of the African race" she ultimately believed that black women should be integrated into the GFWC because "their clubs should stand for something larger than social functions." She demanded that members set aside their "childish" objections and be the "loyal American" who understood that "a club has larger issues than personal prejudices." Essentially her remarks transformed the GFWC from a private, white social space to what she likened to a "Republic" of soldiers determined to direct progressive reform and social welfare. In that venue black women were welcome. But the loss of the once private space of the club did not mean that lines demarcating class and race should be dissolved. She reminded members that they could still "draw narrow lines in the hospitality of our homes."[20]

The GFWC membership remained polarized for several years. It was not until 1902 that the answer to the question about the status or place of black women in the organization was decided. Pledging "Unity in Diversity," the GFWC passed a resolution stating that membership for black women was based on their "membership in their state or territorial federation," essentially adhering to states' rights.[21] The changes did little to allay the anger of women like Barrier Williams and Ruffin who had spent much of their lives interacting with white women in intimate social spaces and engaging with them in their clubs and reform activities. Two years later Barrier Williams recognized the intransigent nature of racism: "the whole matter seems that whether I live in the North or the South, I cannot be counted for my full value, be that much or little."[22]

*   *   *

After the GFWC debacle Barrier Williams shifted her sights from a national push to integrate with white women to an effort to more clearly define her place in the CWC, chronicle the successful ascendency of black women in the public arena, and fashion a long-term career as a public intellectual. Her presence in the CWC at the height of racial polarization seemed incongruous. But regional residency, elitism, and a long history of social integration with white women made it possible. Her membership was celebrated by other blacks. For example, in December 1900, *The Broad Ax* noted that she "has the distinction of being the only Afro-American woman in Chicago belonging to the Chicago Woman's Club or any other white club."[23] The newspaper noted that she was "treated with much deference by the best members of the Chicago Woman's Club."[24] Even at a time when white hostility in Chicago had escalated, segregation had become more commonplace, and black leaders had begun to exhibit a more combative stance in their interactions with whites, Barrier Williams's presence in the exclusive women's organization still represented the integrationist dream of equality that the old guard had once preached. Like other CWC members, she gave public presentations, wrote articles, and served on committees. Her topics varied from the development of benevolent associations to the ethical and moral issues women and the country faced at the turn of the century.[25]

Barrier Williams's presence in the CWC gave her prestige and set her apart from other black women. Her membership and active participation were driven by her personal ambition and elitism. But the CWC also gave her something that black female organizations could not. Membership in the CWC gave her access to financial backing from wealthy women who were committed to supporting various projects Williams was closely tied to. The club offered one of the largest and most attentive audiences in the country, an efficient means of circulating literature, and a politicized machine that could mobilize its forces to shape government policy. Moreover, the CWC was an efficient and well-organized entity. There were monthly and annual meetings for the entire membership as well as separate meetings and activities for six departments: the Home Department, the Education Department, the Philanthropy Department, the Reform Department, the Art and Literature Department, and the Philosophy and Science Department. Each department operated like and independent group that engaged in numerous projects related to education, politics, and labor issues. The club was so successful that over the first forty years of its existence (1876–1916) it contributed more than $352,000 to nearly 100 causes, clubs, and organizations.[26] By the turn of the century, it had grown so much that it became necessary to limit the membership to 1,000.[27]

As the only black member, Barrier Williams educated white women about black club women by chronicling black women's activities and publicly recording their biographies. In the December 1908 edition of *The Club Record*, the CWC's monthly magazine, she highlighted black women's reform activism, as she had been doing for more than decade. A portion of her lecture on "Philanthropic Work among Colored Women" was published in the designated space of the Reform Department. In it she equated black women's reform activism with the work of white women.[28] She also helped obtain financial support for causes important to the black community. In May 1903, during Ellen Henrotin's tenure as president of the CWC (1903–1904), Booker T. Washington gave a presentation on Tuskegee and Hampton and was the guest of honor at the reception afterward.[29] One of the reasons for his visit was to ensure the continuation of the funding that had already begun to arrive at the school. The Home Department contributed $35 to help support a cottage on the school grounds that the CWC was sponsoring.[30]

While her involvement with the CWC had a functional purpose, her work with black women was motivated by her desire to expand their opportunities and to offer pragmatic services and solutions to the black community. From 1890 to 1910, the black population of Chicago increased from 1.3 to 2 percent of the total population. In a glowing assessment of the potential this growth made possible, Barrier Williams noted that "the Census reports show that Chicago will soon stand next to Washington in the size of its colored population." Black migrants, pushed out of the South by its "repressive laws," had been arriving in Chicago for more than a decade. Most came from the Upper South states of Kentucky, Missouri, Tennessee, and Virginia. Deep South states such as Mississippi, Alabama, Arkansas, and Georgia also contributed to that number, albeit in smaller proportions.[31] The escalation of the exodus from the South drew a great deal of attention. When the magazine *Charities* devoted a special issue to "the negro problem" in September 1905, Barrier Williams was among the guest contributors. The group included a cross-section of reformers and educators. Some of the most noted were scholars such as Thomas Jesse Jones, a white researcher at Hampton Institute; Columbia University anthropologist Franz Boas; sociologist W. E. B. Du Bois of Atlanta University; and activists such as Cornell Law School graduate Frances Kellor. "This increase of the Negro population," Barrier Williams wrote, "has brought with it problems that directly affect the social and economic life of the newcomers. Prevented from mingling easily and generally with the rest of the city's population, according to their needs and deservings, but with no preparation made for segregation, their life in a great city has been irregular and shifting, with result that they have been subject to more social ills than any other nationally amongst us." Restricted mobility forced blacks into designated and confined spaces in Wards 2 and 3, where they constituted 25 and 24 percent of the population, respectively. These conditions, she posited, constituted a "Black Belt" that by the time of World War I would become a black ghetto.[32]

Barrier Williams argued that although Chicago blacks were plagued by an increase in "demoralizing conditions," "the colored people of Chicago have shown in their efforts for self-help and self-advancement a determination that is altogether creditable." She pointed to the establishment of a host of reform and welfare organizations and institutions, the strength of black churches, and cross-racial alliances as evidence of uplift efforts.[33] Black women's clubs were some of the most impressive and active groups. The correlation between the intensification of black migration, the increase in poverty rates, and the formation and growth of black female clubs and organizations was underscored by the fervor with which black women tackled the issues. The number of clubs specifically focused on benevolence and philanthropy increased rapidly. In the mid-1890s, only a few existed, but by 1906 at least fifteen clubs with no denominational ties existed. They included the Ida B. Wells Club, the Phyllis Wheatley

Club, the Woman's Civic League, the Frederick Douglass Center Woman's Club, the Necessity Club, the Mothers' Union, the Cornell Charity Club, Julia Gaston Club, the Volunteer Workers Charity Club, the North Side Women's Club, the Ladies Labor of Love Club, the Imperial Art Club, and the Progressive Circle of Kings Daughters. All of them included a charitable component that addressed the increasing needs for such services. For example, the Volunteer Workers Club was established in December 1904 specifically to serve the Home of Aged and Infirm Colored People. By 1911 it had broadened its mission and had become the Volunteer Workers Charity Club.[34] The demand for social welfare and charitable services grew so fast that in March 1906 the presidents of the existing fifteen clubs met to create an umbrella organization. The City Federation of Colored Women's Clubs was born as a result. Cordelia West was the first president.[35]

Many of these charitable clubs were formed in the fifteen-year period of 1895 to 1910. Many of the women who were attracted to them were of a different generation of club woman than those in the Prudence Crandall Club. Chicago's ruling black elite of the 1880s and its singular focus on the superiority of those with an aristocratic legacy gave way to a new form of leadership that had been shaped by the needs of the community. Barrier Williams noted the exceptional shift in the character of black women involved in activism: "The young colored women of this generation are emerging from obscurity in many interesting ways that will happily surprise those who have never known them by their womanly qualities and graceful accomplishments. Such women seem to have no relationship to the slavery conditions of the yesterday of history. In a surprisingly brief period of time they have been completely lifted out of the past by the Americanism which transforms and moulds into higher forms all who come under the spell of American free institutions."[36]

In addition, black women in Chicago were serving in a number of new capacities in the fields of business, medicine, and law. Barrier Williams pointed to Ida Platt, who was perhaps the most professionally accomplished of the group. Born in Chicago in 1863, she had graduated from high school at the age of sixteen. She had a "mental versatility" that made her exceptional. She was a student of music, but she was also proficient in several languages. She took advantage of the lucrative clerical field that the expansion of industrialization had created for women. From 1883 to 1892, she was employed as a secretary and stenographer in an insurance office. Seeking new opportunities, Platt transferred those skills to a law office. After developing an intense interest in the profession she enrolled in the Chicago College of Law, from which she graduated in 1894. Soon after that, she became the first black woman in the state to be admitted to the bar. In the 1906 *Colored People's Blue Book of Chicago*, she was still the only woman listed in a field of nearly forty black lawyers.[37]

Others made their mark in business. Alberta Moore Smith, who became a probation officer, established the Colored Women's Business Club. She calculated that more than 250 women held membership in the six business organizations that existed in Chicago. While the number of black women "actively engaged in business" remained small compared to white women, the clubs had great "influence" on the success of black women by "encouraging our women in opening establishments of their own, no matter how small the start may be."[38]

Some women devoted equal energy to their professional advancement and social welfare activities. Fannie Emanuel, who became the recording secretary for the Illinois Federation of Colored Women's Clubs (IFCWC) in 1901, attended classes at the Chicago School of Civics and Philanthropy. She organized a number of settlement communities and went on to earn an MD.[39] Like Emanuel, Fannie Hall Clint, the secretary of the federation that hosted the NACW in 1899, blended activism and professional employment. Clint, who had been born in Mississippi in 1871, settled in Chicago after graduating from college. She was an elocutionist who traveled quite often and found some success on the Chautauqua circuit. But it was her club work that brought her the most notoriety and success. In 1904, she became the president of the Illinois Federation of Colored Women's Clubs.[40]

Some of the women seemed to have created a full-time career in reform work. These included Barrier Williams's colleagues and friends Florence Lewis Bentley, Agnes Moody, and Elizabeth Lindsay Davis. Florence Bentley, the second wife of prominent dentist Charles Bentley, devoted much of her time to Provident Hospital by lecturing and raising funds.[41] Agnes Moody, a member of the committee that hosted the NACW in 1899 and the aunt of Fannie Hall Clint, was the president of the Ida B. Wells Club and was actively engaged in the NACW; she was elected the second vice-president of the NACW at the biennial meeting in Buffalo, New York, in July 1901. By the time Moody died at the age of sixty-five in April 1903, she had played a significant role in propelling the club movement in Illinois forward.[42]

Perhaps one of the most important friendships that Barrier Williams developed with a black woman was with Elizabeth Lindsay Davis. Born in Peoria, Illinois in 1855, Elizabeth Lindsay Davis came to Chicago in 1893 after teaching in Louisville, Kentucky; New Albany, Indiana; and Quincy, Illinois. The strong bond between the two women dated back to Davis's service as the first secretary of the Ida B. Wells Club. It deepened when she and Barrier Williams joined other black Chicago women in calling for the creation of the NACW in 1896. And it solidified when Davis helped ensure that the NACW came to Chicago in 1899. She organized the Phyllis Wheatley Club in 1896 and served as its president for twenty-one years. In 1908, she spearheaded the creation of the Phyllis Wheatley Home, whose purpose was to "solve the problem of the colored girl or woman of good character who come to Chicago for the purpose of advancement, often without relative, friends or money."[43] She later became the national organizer of the NACW and the president of the Illinois Federation of Colored Women's Clubs. More important, her commitment to the national and state organizations made her one of the most significant members of both. She published histories of the NACW and the IFCWC, which provided the earliest biographies of members, details about meetings, and descriptions of affiliated groups.[44]

This generation of women also found expanded opportunities in other venues. They enjoyed positions as commentators in the black press, as presenters at conferences, and as members and officers in predominantly male-led organizations. Barrier Williams was the most successful. Capitalizing on her skills as an orator and author, she built such an impressive résumé that she became one of the most notable black women in the early twentieth century. She provided expert commentary on gender, race, and labor at conferences; served as liaison for Chicago with the National Negro Business League; and was elected an officer in the Afro-American Council. By 1905, she had embraced her success as a writer, advertising it as her profession. The nation recognized it as well. One newspaper called her "one of the ablest and most caustic writers we have when defending her race."[45]

She wrote on various topics and for a variety of audiences. She chronicled the activities of the club movement and presented critical analyses on race. She wrote commentary on the importance of art and leisure and fictional pieces that delved into the crisis of the mulatto. For example, in 1902 she published "After Many Days: A Christmas Story" in *The Colored American* that explored her fascination with and distress about the race and gender peculiarities of the South and her own views about interracial liaisons and the children born of them. The fictional account chronicled the painful discovery by a woman who had been designated as white all of her life that she was actually mixed raced. Told by an elderly black woman during a Christmas celebration on a former plantation that she was in fact the child of her black daughter and the white master's son, the woman had to confront the reality of what it now meant to be identified with a "despised" race. Her fate was further complicated by the fact that she was engaged to a northern-born white lawyer. The woman vacillated between keeping her secret and telling it. Both the grandmother and the white mistress of the plantation home advised her never to reveal her racial identity. The plot was guided by Barrier Williams's own experiences as a mixed-raced woman, and the truth won out: the woman told her fiancé of her heritage. He found her confession so incredulous that he responded, "You do not expect me to believe such a wild, unthinkable story as this!" Insisting that they leave the house immediately, he also confessed that he did "not love the South or a southerner, with my whole heart, in spite of this 'united country' nonsense." Although touched by the "violence of his indignation," she told him that the story was true, that she was indeed of mixed race. As the realization of the truth struck him, "suddenly his calm face whitened and an expression terrible to see swept over it." Understanding the implication of his plight, she asked him to think about the situation, then meet her later in the evening. Although still unsure at the beginning of the meeting, the white fiancé eventually declared his continued commitment to her.[46]

While her fictional account ended happily, her more critical analysis of racial identity in *The Southern Workman* in 1904 summed up the anxieties of a number of old guard mixed-raced aristocrats about the question of assimilation. In "Do We Need Another Name?" she pointed to the ideological and generational shift that had occurred at the turn of the new century. She wrote of "the present generation of Negro scholars and writers" who "have succeeded in making the people feel and believe that all the designations by which the American descendants of Africans are known and described are hopelessly and discouragingly associated with all the miseries of bondage and race prejudice; that the existing names are hindrances to progress and persistently suggest inferiority to the educated young men and women of the race." The question of whether a new name was needed had some validity for the "new Negro" in the new century. She argued that the difficulties in deciding how appropriate the terms "Negro," "colored," or "Afro-American" reflected the "new conditions" under which blacks lived. While opinions varied, she, not surprisingly, believed that "colored" was the most useful primarily because of "its lack of essential or deep significance." For the new Negro, the "indefinite" identifier represented the transformational progress of the race that the other labels lacked; it provided the vehicle "towards the full enjoyment of all the blessings of equality in American life." Moreover, the term was so nebulous and included so many different people that its inference as a racial marker "will gradually fade as a term of difference and will finally become a mere term of convenience, having no deeper sense than the name brunette." The quest, she ultimately concluded, should not be about debating racial identity; rather it should be about claiming an American identity.[47]

Barrier Williams's writing also revealed the frustration and anger of an elite black woman struggling to debunk the myth of white supremacy, grappling with the slow process of racial uplift, and fighting heightened racial animosity and rhetoric that maligned the black community. She found a platform for her views in the fledgling literary journal *The Voice of the Negro*, joining an illustrious group that included Howard University professor Kelly Miller, club woman and activist Mary Church Terrell, Harvard scholar W. E. B. Du Bois, Atlanta Baptist College professor John Hope, *Colored American Magazine* editor Pauline Hopkins, novelist Charles W. Chesnutt, vice president of Wilberforce University William Scarborough, and educator and author Booker T. Washington. The new journal, which published its first issue in 1904, was edited by J. Max Barber, among others, who viewed the publication as a strong measure of black progress. He observed that "there is nothing interesting in the launching of a Negro magazine; but to the careful observer, to the philosopher of history, to him who is a reader of the signs of the times it means much. It means that culture is taking a deep hold upon our people. It is an indication that our people are becoming an educated, reading people, and this is a thing of which to be proud."[48]

In the first issue, Barrier Williams tackled the national debate about the "Negro Problem." This article, "The Negro and Public Opinion," was one of the first in a series of indictments against white assumptions about blacks. She argued that the vast majority of whites knew little about blacks yet judged them unfairly. "The average white American," she began "knows the Negro only as he sees him on the street or engaged in some employment that does not permit of association. As this average American sees but little of the Negro and knows but little of him he is at liberty to form any kind of erroneous opinions concerning him."[49] That essay laid the groundwork for her response the following month to an article entitled "To Exclude Negroes" that appeared in the local paper. The perspective, she wrote "is but one of the many evidences of a national habit of endeavoring to make the Negro race in this country an object of apprehension and doubt, if not contempt." She continued, "If the people of the world are to form an opinion of the condition and character of the Negro people only from what they may read of them in the articles, speeches and books, that are given the widest circulation because of their extreme and sometimes wicked sensationalism," then "it will not be long before the public will be ready to accept as just any proposition that will place them beyond the pale of 'Christian civilization.'" Suggestions that the only solution to the race problem was the removal of blacks from the country were ludicrous. "The colored people cannot be deported, they cannot be excluded from every place in deference to 'white ruffians,' and their advancement by means of education has put to shame all false theories concerning their mental and spiritual capacity," she declared. "As poor as he is," she argued, "the Negro has a way of haunting the American conscience for every wrong done to him." She concluded, "There is nothing noble or gainful in a great nation, so abundant in opportunities, in trying to force down and under a part of its citizenship."[50]

*   *   *

By the summer of 1904 Barrier Williams had made an indelible mark as one of the leading intellectuals of the turn of the century. She was one of two women to participate in a group of articles that were published on industrial education in the *Colored American*. This article solidified her career as a writer and critic, linked her to the most powerful black figures of the era, and transformed her life. Barrier Williams presented the last in a series of essays on the question "Industrial Education—Will It Solve the Negro Problem?" Like the other authors in the series, T. Thomas Fortune, John Edward Bruce, Booker T. Washington, Kelly Miller, Nannie H. Burroughs, William Lloyd Garrison, W. E. B. Du Bois, and Edward Horton, she had strong opinions about the merit of the model of industrial education. She found the teaching method to be efficient and successful and argued that Washington's implementation of the model in the South was nothing short of a "heroic" endeavor. Her loyalty unquestionably allied her with him.[51]

Barrier Williams's admiration for Washington was not new. It had been nearly a decade in the making. Initially the connection seemed tangential, primarily cultivated through the Unitarians and her husband S. Laing. The Unitarians had provided financial resources for Washington during the first decade of the establishment of Tuskegee. S. Laing had both a personal and professional relationship with Washington, who invited him to deliver the commencement address at the school in May 1895.[52] The day after Washington's famous presentation at the Cotton Exposition in Atlanta in September 1895, S. Laing congratulated him and exuberantly noted, "In my humble opinion no word uttered by a colored man during the past 20 years will go farther and do more to set us right in public opinion than your eloquently apt and philosophically sound words that have become a part of yesterday[']s remarkable event."[53] But Barrier Williams's respect for Washington was independently cultivated. That same year, she told the Ladies Auxiliary of the Whittier Association, a Memphis group, that Washington was the person "who has done more for practical education of the colored people in all things than any other one man in America."[54] By 1900, when Washington established the National Negro Business League, Barrier Williams had become one of his closest associates. In 1902, she had replaced Alberta Moore Smith as the primary female liaison between the Chicago business community and Washington's league, a position that enabled her to discuss the relevance of black women's work to the success of the black community.

Her position with the National Negro Business League offered her a venue for interacting with a cross-section of business-minded men and women. This activity rekindled the labor activism she had begun with the IWA. In August 1902, at the third convention of the league in Richmond, Virginia, for example, she spoke about the omission of black women in business deliberations. "In all that you do, or may aim to do, the colored woman must be counted in, not only as a factor, but as a necessity," she told the mostly male audience, because "by the necessities of our being and progress we women must work, we cannot be idle and live and grow in the strength and nobility of womanhood."[55] Recognition of the links between women's labor, the meaning of their womanhood, and their indispensable contribution to the survival of the black family highlighted the necessity for dual incomes in the black community, even among the elite. A speech she gave two years later in Indianapolis, "The Woman's Part in a Man's Business," argued forcefully that the married men in the audience owed much of their economic success to their wives. She declared that as a "silent partner" who was "concealed from the public eye," it was the black woman who "often stands between the business man and bankruptcy." The declaration may well have been autobiographical and may have alluded to her own partnership with S. Laing. Since her marriage in 1887, she had consistently generated revenue for the couple as an artist, a speaker, and a writer. The importance of her contribution became more clear as S. Laing's partnership with Ferdinand Barnett ended and the two chose opposing sides in political and intellectual debates. S. Laing failed to secure lucrative political appointments, and his unsuccessful investments in a number of ventures weakened their financial position.[56] Barrier Williams seemed to suggest that in these instances of male ambition and folly, it was the wives who provided the safety net, essentially enabling their husbands to pursue their own aspirations. After extolling the virtues of black women's work and affirming their importance in the economic realm she concluded, "With this kind of woman in your business, you cannot fail, and without her, you have already failed."[57]

While elitism often clouded her judgment, Barrier Williams understood that the vast majority of black female laborers had neither an affluent husband nor formal professional training. The solution, she believed, could be found in the industrial education paradigm. While critics argued that Washington's model raced and regionalized the black labor force, restricting them to Jim Crow jobs and subordinating them to southern whites, Barrier Williams argued that the expansion of the industrial model crossed racial boundaries and brought "a new dignity . . . to the occupations that concern our health, our homes and our happiness." Interest in the "industrial, polytechnic and agricultural schools" had increased to such a degree that a number of them had been constructed "in the North states during the past ten or twelve years," essentially nationalizing the concept. "These schools," she declared "are always over crowded by white students," and the idea "has become so broadened that even the great universities are enlarging their curricula so as to include schools of technology." If whites embraced this type of training and experienced its benefits, then "can it be right or just to urge it as especially suited to the condition of the colored people?"[58]

Barrier Williams believed that the industrial model's heavy emphasis on domestic science would certainly benefit black women. At a Hampton conference in July 1903 she told her audience that "domestic service is the one occupation in which the demand for colored women exceeds the supply" and that there was little competition from "other nationalities" in Chicago employment. The wages were much better than in the South and offered a steady and "respectable" source of income, yet more than 500 positions remained unfilled. That, she believed, was because of the perception that domestic work was "degrading." She complained that many of the women who entered it only did so as a transition to something better, earning them a reputation as "unreliable." To provide legitimacy and "to enable our girls to enter upon this occupation without loss of self-respect and without the danger of ostracism by so-called society," she proposed that domestic service be designated "a profession" that would require training with the same accruements of "dignity, respectability, and honor" as other professions. "We must learn that the girl who cooks our meals and keeps our houses sweet and beautiful deserves just as high a place in our social economy as the girl who makes our gowns and hats, or the one who teaches our children."[59] The following year she observed:

> The time is coming, aye, is now here, when a colored graduate from a school of domestic science will be more honored and better paid than are many white women who now hold the positions colored women cannot enter. The time is coming when there will be no excuse for a colored young woman to remain in soul-destroying idleness, because she cannot obtain a clerkship. She can be trained in an industrial school for positions that she can fill and still be socially eligible among those who make "society." An increasing respect is being shown to the young man or woman who is brave enough to learn a trade and follow it with pride and honor.[60]

Barrier Williams was not the only club woman who espoused this view. Black activists such as Nannie Helen Burroughs were also major proponents. And because of Chicago's multiethnic population and unique industrial characteristics, interest in the professionalization of domestic service resonated across race lines. At a CWC conference on women and industrialism in 1904, for example, the session devoted to domestic service "aroused [attendees] to a high pitch of interest" primarily because, Barrier Williams argued, the "respectability of domestic service" was important to whites as well as blacks. The first solution to the question "How can the servant girl problem be solved?" was "Recognize that they are working at a trade." The CWC's involvement in women's domestic work did not end with the conference. The Philanthropy Department's financial contribution to the School of Domestic Arts and Science in Chicago, which opened in 1901 to professionalize domestic labor and train women in the science of household management, signaled an ongoing interest among CWC members in the intersectionality of women's work, race, and the home.[61]

Barrier Williams found that arguing for the professionalization of a subservient class of laborers posed a dilemma. Encouraging domestic labor among black women was part of her larger argument that northern blacks needed to ensure their own economic viability by laying claim to the same kind of essential work in Chicago as southern blacks had with agricultural labor in the South. This concept attracted the attention of white supremacy theorists. For example, southern economist Alfred Holt Stone pointed to the ideas of a number of black activists, including Barrier Williams, to support his argument that once-promising employment opportunities for blacks in northern cities were in jeopardy because of immigrants and white superiority. Stone argued that only in the South could the black race "obey the command to eat its bread in the sweat of its face, side by side with the white man." In the North, he contended, few prospects existed for black workers primarily because of their "inefficiency, unreliability, and lack of thrift" and the "prejudice upon the part of the white man."[62]

In his examination of several northern centers he noted that Barrier Williams was among the black activists who provided support for his assessment. And indeed, she had expressed concern that there were clear signs of "unfavorable conditions" for black migrants. Although recognizing that it was "race hatreds" in the South that pushed migrants to the North as much as employment opportunity, she advised that "the South affords the best opportunity for young men of first-class ability." It was ultimately, she concluded, "intelligence and self-reliance" that "the negro needs more than a change of habitation."[63]

He also extracted portions from two articles Barrier Williams had written for *The New York Age*. In the first one, she began by noting that "the timely discussion of The Age of our loss of occupations in the Northern cities may well include conditions in Chicago as a further illustration. Here every industrial and economic problem not only exists but takes on an intensity of meaning peculiar to Chicago." Jobs in "barbering, bootblacking, cooking, hotel and restaurant waiting, janitors in office buildings, elevator service, and calcimining," occupations that had been clearly identified with black workers in Chicago, were now controlled by "White men" who "wanted these places and were strong enough to displace the unorganized, thoughtless and easy-going occupants of them." But it was not native-born white men who were leading the transition; it was instead immigrants, including Greeks, Italians, and Swedes who were replacing blacks. As their population increased so did whites' desires for their services.[64] She lamented:

> One occupation after another that the colored people thought was theirs forever by the sort of divine right fell into the hands of these foreign invaders. This loss was

not so much due to prejudice against colored, as to the ability of these foreigners to increase the importance of the places sought and captured. The Swedes have captured the janitor business by organizing and training the men for this work in such a way as to increase the efficiency and reliability of service.

White men have made more of the barber business than did the colored men, and by organization they have driven every Negro barber from the business district. The "shoe polisher" has supplanted the Negro bootblack and does business in finely appointed parlors, with mahogany finish and electric lights. Thus a menial occupation has become a well organized and genteel business with capital and system behind it.[65]

Even the outlook for the black female labor force was alarming. According to Stone, Barrier Williams argued in the second article that "white girls prefer to pass by the clerkship, which colored girls cannot get, and enter schools of domestic science to prepare themselves for trained domestic service, and to fill places scorned by colored girls though open to them."[66]

Barrier Williams's appraisal of the factors contributing to the decline in black employment opportunities certainly seemed to support Stone's argument. Her ideological affinity to Washington's philosophy was heavily predicated on a model that relied on class stratification to maintain black dominance in menial jobs. Blacks had been so "unorganized," "thoughtless" and "easy-going" that they contributed to the problems they faced. And immigrants, seizing the opportunity created by white prejudice and the willingness of employers to replace black workers, moved into employment positions that had been mainstays for the previous generation of blacks.

But Stone failed to provide the context for Barrier Williams's comments, misrepresented her argument, and omitted portions of her statements in the articles regarding the status of black male and female laborers. While she acknowledged that specific categories of jobs had disappeared for blacks, she argued that "there is less idleness among the colored people than among any other class of citizens in the city. There are no Negro beggars on our streets. The landlords all say that Negro tenants pay a larger rent and pay more promptly than any other class of citizens of like grade." Thus, "The question naturally arises as to what our people find to do to make the above statement possible since the old places have been taken away from them." The answer, she concluded, reflected the "versatility and adaptability of the race." Black people had found positions "in a greater variety of occupations and are doing things that they never thought of doing twenty years ago. . . . The ex-waiter and ex-bootblack and would be barber are employed extensively as teamsters, porters, expressmen, foremen and, in some cases, as shipping clerks, and here and there in increasing numbers, as regular clerks in stores and offices."[67] Moreover, there was a history of conflict between employees and employers in the industrialized corridor. Her reference to the "unorganized" included the inexperienced black scabs that had been recruited and imported from the South during some of the worst labor unrest. Employers had used them to break unions in strikes in the stockyards in 1904 and in the garment industry in 1905. The companies would dismiss these employees when they no longer needed their services.[68] With few resources or options, they remained in the city to fend for themselves. The misuse and abuse of their services caused concerns, as did the increase in the poor and uneducated population and their need for the welfare services developed by black women. Though Barrier Williams remained concerned about the status of black migrants, she would come to a guarded but much more hopeful attitude about migrants from the South who found "work in the stock yards and in many other places where everyday plain work is in need of plain workers."[69]

Her critique of the evolution of immigrant whiteness received no attention at all. Immigrants had become an acceptable buffer for native-born whites precisely because they were not black and could assimilate. But to keep them in line, employers pitted poor black workers against them, fostering racial strife and labor conflict. Thus, in Barrier Williams's analysis, the primary culprit in the subjugation of black laborers was white racism rather than the absence of ability or "efficiency" among black workers. She reported in 1907 that "in spite of even organized opposition" black workers were "quietly and unobtrusively doing things that they were never expected to be able to do," including holding middle-class jobs in engineering, accounting, and bookkeeping.[70]

In her discussion of domestic servants Barrier Williams made it clear that the white girls who were eagerly entering the occupation were classed in a way that black girls were not. They came "from good families" and they were "not restricted as to the kind of occupation they may choose" which made it possible for them to "pass by the clerkships which colored girls cannot get." In addition, she maintained, because domestic service was classed differently in the black community and because it lacked the same kind of "respectability" that white girls enjoyed, few young women willingly entered the occupation. "In a thousand ways we convey to them a subtle feeling of scorn for the word 'domestic' or 'servant,'" and while "'our set' may respect [them], in a condescending way," few, if any, would willingly "associate with the girl who 'works out.'" She declared that "all this nonsense must be changed if our girls are to be saved from soul-destroying idleness and trained to skilled service in this new field which domestic science is developing." She called on black club women to "make themselves felt in a constructive way" by "creating a sentiment in favor of our girls who must enter the field of domestic service, so long as a determined prejudice shuts them out of the work they are fitted for and would like to do."[71]

While white theorists viewed the link between Barrier Williams and Washington as positive reinforcement for their own arguments, many blacks in Chicago perceived the connection as a disturbing reminder of Washington's national influence and power. One midwestern newspaper referred to him as the person "who is recognized by white and black men alike as the most effective worker for negro progress along practical lines today."[72] And indeed, when he visited Chicago in the spring of 1904, blacks and whites lined up for blocks to hear him speak.[73] But the opposition to Washington and those who had ties to him had been mounting for some time, revealing divisions among the black elite. Regionalism certainly played a role in the debate. North of Jim Crow, black Chicagoans were less hesitant than their southern colleagues to criticize Washington and the deplorable social, political, and economic circumstances in the South that encouraged so many blacks to flee the region. In nearly every southern state, black men had lost access to the ballot, lynchings had increased, and most blacks were relegated to menial jobs. Meanwhile, Washington seemed to be acquiescing to white supremacy and increasing in influence. He appointed lieutenants in various regions to spy on those critical of him and financed a number of black publications, which ensured that he played a significant role in controlling the types of essays that were published. He also took control of several prominent organizations and orchestrated the election of many of his supporters to offices in them. That was what happened at an Afro-American Council meeting in St. Paul in 1902. Troubling concerns from the membership over Washington's reported manipulation of election procedure surfaced at the meeting. While most of the delegates were absent, a host of officers were elected, including Barrier Williams. One member was so outraged with the procedure that he called the election "illegal"; others threatened to withdraw their membership. When asked what he thought of the incident, W. E. B. Du Bois, who was teaching at Atlanta University in Georgia, told a reporter that he "opposed" the way the election was conducted and "did not approve of it at all." The debate was so acrimonious that it was laid over to the following morning.[74]

Barrier Williams found the press coverage of the meeting misleading and employed her position as a journalist for *The Colored American* to counter the unflattering account. She expressed excitement about the large turnout and about the future of the organization. More important, she downplayed the parliamentary and procedural "shortcomings" of the conference. She wrote that although "there were some dramatic incidents in the St. Paul conventions, the integrity of the Council is still unimpeached."[75]

But she couldn't squelch the increasing anxiety over Washington's growing influence and propensity for maneuvering situations to consolidate his power. After the election of officers the following year, where Barrier Williams was once again elected secretary, *The Broad Ax* acerbically quipped:

> This latest deal shows that the Afro-American Council, the Afro-American Press Association, and the Negro National Business League are all one and the same thing, that they are owned and controlled by Booker T. Washington, old drunken

Tom Fortune and company, that from henceforth they can be of no practical benefit to the Negro race.[76]

The denouncement validated the concerns of those such as Ida B. Wells-Barnett, her husband Ferdinand Barnett, and attorneys John Jones and Edward Morris. Jones, of course, had been an early adversary of Barrier Williams and S. Laing in the struggle over the building of Provident Hospital. In the decade since then, Jones had created a successful political career; in 1900, he won a seat in the Illinois House of Representatives. Morris had been in Chicago politics for a long time and commanded even more power than Jones. Born a slave in Kentucky in 1859, he was educated in Ohio and Illinois and was a successful lawyer. He was also a shrewd politician and businessman who became, according to Harold Gosnell, "the dean of colored lawyers." When he ran for and won a seat in the Illinois House in 1890, he became only the third African American to serve in the state. When he was elected for a second term in 1902, he was one of the most powerful politicians in the city.[77]

The local group was joined by a number of prominent national leaders, including Monroe Trotter, the Harvard-trained editor of the *Boston Guardian*, who used his newspaper to critique and expose Washington's control, and W. E. B. Du Bois.[78] It was the publication of Du Bois's *The Souls of Black Folk* by a Chicago company in 1903 that intensified the debate between the pro- and anti-Washington groups. In the fourteen essays of the book, according to biographer David Levering Lewis, Du Bois "redefined the terms of a three-hundred-year interaction between black and white people and influenced the cultural and political psychology of peoples of African descent throughout the western hemisphere, as well as on the continent of Africa."[79] But it was his essay "Of Mr. Booker T. Washington and Others" that caught the eye of many in Chicago; in it, Du Bois clearly and emphatically stated his opposition to Washington.

A group that included Barrier Williams, S. Laing Williams, Ida B. Wells-Barnett, Ferdinand Barnett, Florence Lewis Bentley, Charles Bentley, Lloyd Wheeler, Monroe Work (then a sociology student at the University of Chicago), Jenkin Lloyd Jones, and several others held an intellectual discussion about *Souls of Black Folk* at a Sunday evening meeting in May 1903 in Celia Parker Woolley's home.[80] The group focused on the essay about Washington. S. Laing and Fannie Barrier Williams strongly disagreed with Du Bois's assessment, as did fellow Unitarian Jenkin Lloyd Jones. Wells-Barnett and her husband Ferdinand, on the other hand, strongly supported Du Bois's position. The Bentleys found that there was no middle ground. They were longtime friends of Barrier Williams and S. Laing but were also on cordial terms with Du Bois and had hosted him in their home.[81]

Woolley saw the debate as a call to arms and an indication that white support was a key ingredient to black success in overcoming the problems that plagued the black community. By the winter of 1903, she had implemented a plan to open a social settlement center. She invited a number of prominent blacks and whites to a meeting, at which she solicited their support for the fledgling center. In the spring of 1904, she presented her model to the Western Unitarian Conference membership. There Woolley publicly declared that a "solution" to "the Negro question" in large cities like Chicago could be found in "the establishment of centers adopted on the plan of social settlements. It would place the race question upon a wise civic basis, and bridge over the differences between the colored race and our own with common sense."[82]

With the backing of the CWC, which named a liaison and provided funding, and a number of prominent blacks and whites, Woolley opened the Frederick Douglass Center in her home on 44th Street.[83] She declared that the center "is based first, in the conviction that, as Professor Du Bois says, 'the problem of the twentieth century is the problem of the color line'; second, in the belief that, however named or to whatever class of suffering or ill-used humanity it is applied, the human problem is always the same."[84] The center's motto was "With Malice Towards None, With Charity For All," and its charter linked her vision of interracial cooperation with the promise of uplift. The center was "organized to promote just and amicable relations between the white and colored people, to remove the disabilities from which the latter suffer in their civil, political, and industrial life; to encourage equal opportunity, irrespective of race, color, or other arbitrary distinctions; to establish a center of friendly helpfulness and influence in which to gather useful information and for mutual cooperation in attaining to right living and higher citizenship."[85] The Executive Board was comprised of Woolley as president, Charles Bentley as secretary, Mary Redfield Plummer as treasurer, and S. Laing Williams and John O'Connor, also a lawyer, as the trustees.[86]

From the beginning, Barrier Williams was a prominent spokesperson for the center. On at least three occasions in the period 1904 to 1906 she described its history and articulated its goals in national black publications. Much of what she wrote praised both her friend Woolley and the activities of the center and reflected her long-term commitment to engaging whites and forcing them to face their own prejudices. The center, she argued in June 1906, "is not organized to do slum work in what may be called the black belt of Chicago, but to be a center of wholesome influences to the end that well-disposed white people may learn to know and respect the ever increasing number of colored people who have earned the right to be believed in and respected."[87] She claimed that the center was unlike any other institution in Chicago; it was "a settlement plus something else." And indeed, it was. By then a project that had begun in Woolley's home was a twelve-room three-story stone building located "on the eastern edge of what is known as the black belt." She and her husband lived there. Like the Unitarian

All Souls Church in the early 1890s, its purpose was to meet the needs of the community. Its many resources included a kindergarten, numerous classes on sociology and literature, and arts and crafts for boys and sewing for girls. True to its mission of racial cooperation it was governed by an interracial board of directors, of which more than half of the members were black, including, by 1906, Barrier Williams's friend Elizabeth Lindsay Davis and Ferdinand Barnett. Both Booker T. Washington and W. E. B. Du Bois were honorary members.[88]

The driving force behind the center was the Frederick Douglass Woman's Club, which was organized in 1905. Nearly two-thirds of the seventy women members and most of the officers were black. Its four departments, the Home Department, the Educational Department, the Philanthropic Department, and the Domestic Science Department, developed numerous projects. Barrier Williams highlighted the activism of the women in the Education Department as a way of demonstrating the success of and need for the center. The department offered a summer "Vacation School" that targeted black children "in neighborhoods where there are no play grounds, and limited house yards" and for "the children of poor people" who "suffer many deprivations." Under the tutelage of women, children engaged in "nature studies, modeling, light manual training, games and plays properly conducted, free excursions into the country once or twice a week and instructions in many things that have proved both a delight and benefit to thousands of children in our hot and congested districts."[89]

The center's broad social and economic programs and its strong interracial emphasis were not without critics. Shortly after the center opened, anger over the fact that blacks and whites met there on an equal footing created quite a stir in the local white press. It may have been a new century and Chicago was north of Jim Crow, but notions of equality between black and white women were still controversial. When a group of black and white women met to discuss meeting the needs of the poor, a portrait of the women sipping tea as social equals touched off a debate in the local white press. Barrier Williams defended the center and her friend Woolley in *The Voice of the Negro*. "It would seem that the surest way to injure a colored person as an individual, or to bring discredit, if not failure to a Negro Institution or enterprise of any kind," she charged, "is to raise against him, her or it, the malignant cry of 'social equality.'" Because the Center was "a new experiment in the work of social justice" the black and white women who met "are neither for or against social equality, but they are for what is right, what is just and what is human, and are willing to go, whenever and wherever these promptings lead them."[90]

The question of racial interaction did not resonate in the same way in the black press as it did in white newspapers. Social equality between the women was never a concern. Instead the central focus was on the inherent racism the center and its administration exhibited. Julius Taylor, the editor of *The Broad Ax*, sharply criticized the institution because he felt that it was "of the slightest benefit to the great mass of the Afro-Americans." Its location in an interracial middle-class neighborhood, he noted, was too far away from the black slums to be of much aid.[91] Taylor also disapproved of Woolley's paternalistic views. Woolley certainly didn't help matters when she patronizingly opined during the first year of operation that the center "was to assist the [h]ordes of colored people coming up from the South, the majority of whom are ignorant, dissolute and idle, falling easily into vicious and criminal ways. The rapid increase of such an element lowers not only the standard of the colored population in our midst, but of our common citizenship, and seriously threatens the well-being of the whole."[92]

Ida Wells-Barnett also raised concerns. She charged Woolley with discrimination when she selected a white woman to be president of the Woman's Club, relegating Wells-Barnett to the secondary position of vice-president. Wells-Barnett felt that black women had invested as much of their time as white women in the creation of the center and the club. Black women contributed financially toward the purchase of the first building, had championed the center, had actively engaged in activities that focused primarily on the black community, and constituted the majority of the members of the Woman's Club.[93] The animosity between the two women came to a head when Wells-Barnett argued, "I came to the conclusion before our relations ended that our white women friends were not willing to treat us on a plane of equality with themselves."[94]

The complaints from Taylor and Wells-Barnett were fueled by more than their concerns about equal representation of blacks in the administration of the center or about how well the center met the needs of the black community. Private bitterness between Barrier Williams and Wells-Barnett and the debate over Washington's leadership also contributed to the disagreement. Woolley became a casualty of these disputes. The animosity that had been festering for some time was clearly visible by the dawn of the new century. Wells-Barnett blamed Barrier Williams, Agnes Moody, and other local black women for the fact that she had not been an integral part of the planning of the NACW meeting in 1899. Angry over the slight, Wells-Barnett did not attend many of the meetings of the association, choosing instead to focus her attention on the Afro-American Council.[95] The ill feeling between Barrier Williams and Wells-Barnett took a nasty turn four years later. Some of the reports made for tabloid-style press coverage, as when *The Broad Ax* commented in October 1903 that "Mrs. Fanny [*sic*] B. Williams and Mrs. Ida B. Wells-Barnett hate each other like two she rattlesnakes and it is said 'their enmity toward each other is so bitter that they never speak when they meet face to face.' This is nothing strange for no doubt both of these high strung ladies who work for the elevation of the Afro-American race for revenue only, have a slight recollection of some unpleasan[t] experience in their lives while residing in Washington, D.C. and Memphis, Tenn."[96]

Some of the attention given to the conflict between the two women was driven by the growing appetite for tabloid journalism and anxiety over the increasing perception that the power of black women was increasing while black male patriarchy was declining. But Barrier Williams's cozy relationship with Washington also contributed to the escalation. On more than one occasion she gave public presentations or wrote editorials that sounded as if Washington had written them for her. For example, at a church in Evanston, Illinois, she told the audience that "the much talked of right to vote is not nearly as important as the right to be educated," and in the *Record-Herald* she noted that the disfranchisement of southern black men "has been a great blessing in disguise; since he is not permitted to vote, he is acquiring land and money" at a time when southern black men, strangled by the choke hold of Jim Crow, had lost their civil and political rights through both violence and legal means.[97] Wells-Barnett, who abhorred Jim Crow, had built a career around highlighting the atrocity of lynching, and believed that the franchise was an essential key to ending the violence, found little reason to hide her disgust.

Barrier Williams benefited from her closeness with Washington. As a writer and public intellectual, access to his publication and organization empire helped her spread her messages about gender, race, and labor. Her commentary in newspapers and even the articles in the CWC publication gave her access to a local audience, but Washington's backing gave her a national platform. By the end of the first decade of the twentieth century, Washington either heavily financed or controlled key publications with a national distribution. These included *The New York Age*, *The Southern Workman*, *The Colored American*, and many other major publications. He also contributed to Barrier Williams's celebrity by featuring her prominently in histories and anthologies. In 1900, he published *A New Negro for a New Century*, which was marketed as "the best selling book of the age." Advertisements for the book featured an image of Barrier Williams positioned next to an image of Washington, almost as if they mirrored each other. Only the subtitle, "An accurate and up-to-date record of the upward struggle of The Negro Race," separated them.[98]

The essays by Barrier Williams and Washington in *The Colored American from Slavery to Honorable Citizenship*, which was produced by J. W. Gibson and W. H. Crogman in 1903, were promoted on the front cover as "Special Features." Barrier Williams chronicled the "Club Movement among Negro Women," while Washington wrote the introduction and reported on the National Negro Business League.[99]

Figure 4. This advertisement for the publication of *A New Negro for a New Century: An Accurate and Up-to-Date Record of the Upward Struggles of the Negro Race* highlights Fannie Barrier Williams's stature as one of the most prominent black women at the dawn of the twentieth century and the strong professional connection she developed with Booker T. Washington. The advertisement appeared in *The Colored American*, June 1, 1901. Courtesy of Chronicling America, Library of Congress, Washington, DC.

In addition, Barrier Williams's support for Washington ensured that S. Laing received the much-coveted references that he needed to gain lucrative positions. He certainly needed her help because many of his aspirations were thwarted by the politicos in Chicago who recognized him as one of Washington's main Midwestern contacts: he brokered deals on Washington's behalf and reported on the activities of anyone perceived to be in the opposing camp.[100] When S. Laing was recommended to lead the black branch of the Republican Party in Chicago by Washington in 1904, a number of rivals, including Ferdinand Barnett, prevented him from obtaining the position. When he sought a federal appointment in 1905, John Jones and Edward Morris blocked that as well.[101]

By late 1905, Washington had successfully neutralized some of the power of these men. S. Laing was offered two consulships. One was at Bahia in South America and another was in Vladivostok, Russia.[102] The first he declined because of finances and the strong desire to be appointed to a federal position in Washington, and the second he declined because of the climate. Washington expressed disappointment in his decisions but continued to write letters for him. In 1908, he finally found a position that did not necessitate a move. In March he was appointed as both assistant attorney in the Northern District of Illinois and as special assistant to the United States Attorney for the Southern District of Illinois. A month later he became the special assistant to the United States Attorney for the Western District of Wisconsin. His compensation was a salary of $2,000 and reimbursement for travel expenses.[103]

These professional and financial benefits played a major role in Barrier Williams's support for Washington, but she also genuinely admired him because she believed he was a progressive leader. Moreover, she knew what few outside his inner circle did, that he complemented his accommodationist public position with a private and secret attack on violence against blacks and the racial restrictions under which black southerners lived. Washington appointed Barrier Williams to collect statistical evidence on the number of lynchings that occurred in the United States.[104] His recognition of Frederick Douglass's stature and of his contribution to the black community and the nation sealed her respect for him. When Washington contracted to write the biography of Douglass, it was to Barrier Williams and S. Laing that he turned for assistance. They ghostwrote the book, which was published in 1906.[105]

Barrier Williams paid a high price for her loyalty. The attacks in the media were so hostile that in many ways they resembled a public flogging. *The Broad Ax*, a paper that had praised her (along with Ruffin) in 1901 for "playing a grand part in assisting to bring around a better feeling and understanding between the two races," turned on her with a vengeance. In the fall of 1904, an article titled "Mrs. Fannie Barrier Booker T. Washington Williams Slops Over on the Negro

Question" married the identities of the two reformers and questioned Barrier Williams's loyalty to the black community. Taking her to task on an article that she had written for the *Record-Herald*, the paper wrote that "to read the article it would appear that Booker Washington formulated it and simply signed Mrs. Williams [*sic*] name to it."[106] Even more disparaging was a resolution that was adopted at a Chicago club meeting:

> Whereas, Mrs. Fannie Barrier Williams, of this city, has from time to time contributed articles for some of the Chicago daily papers in which she is attempting to convince the white people in the Northern states that the colored people are being better treated in the Southern states than they are in the Northern states, and
>
> Whereas, Such unwarranted statements are calculated to do much mischief and thereby create a false impression among thousands and thousands of people who have always been loyal friends to our race; therefore, be it
>
> Resolved, That we, the colored people, and members of the Chicago Club, do enter this, our solemn protest against the unkindly and unwarranted conduct on the part of Mrs. Williams.
>
> Resolved, Further, that we brand each and every statement of Mrs. Williams as being false in every particular, and as done for the purpose of securing financial subsistence and aid for herself backed up and encouraged by the Negro-hating class of white people in the Southern states and their sympathizers in the North.[107]

Branded as a race traitor, she became one of the few black female faces of disloyalty and dishonesty of the decade. As late as 1908, for example, she was referred to as "a warm worshiper of Prof. Booker T. Washington" and was accused of lying to promote his agenda.[108]

The personal cost to her and S. Laing added to the difficulties. Their long-term friendship with Charles Bentley was strained. Bentley didn't simply disagree with them; he joined Du Bois and other prominent men in the Niagara Movement in 1905.[109]

A lucrative writing opportunity also ended. One of the most important vehicles for Barrier Williams for articulating her message of self-help fell victim to the debate between the pro- and anti-Washington camps. *The Voice of the Negro* ended its run in 1907. Even a move from Atlanta to Chicago by editor J. Max Barber in 1906 in the aftermath of the Atlanta race riot could not bridge the gulf that had widened between Barber, a Du Bois supporter, and Washington as they sparred over the content and direction of the publication.[110]

While the public attacks and loss of friends compounded her anxiety, several personal tragedies consumed her near the end of the decade. Her brother George died suddenly in Detroit in the winter of 1907 a few months before his fifty-seventh birthday. By all accounts he was quite prosperous. His marriage to

Delia Pelham had made him a member of one of the most distinguished aristocratic families in the city. The family owned the Detroit *Plaindealer*, a weekly
newspaper, and several members of the family were actively engaged in the
Republican Party. Like his father, George became a barber, then he found several
appointments in the Republican administration of the city. He and Delia had
three children, a girl named Harriet and two sons, Fred P. Barrier, who would
become a dentist and held a position at Howard University Medical School in
Washington, and Robert A. Barrier, an engineering student at the University
of Michigan.[111]

Two years later the family was rocked by more adversity. George's youngest
son Robert drowned while on a class field trip on July 27, 1909. The death, which
the coroner declared accidental, "left a feeling of gloom upon the entire camp,"
reported one of the professors. Although he was the only black student in the
class, he seems to have fared well among his classmates. Barrier's "work in camp
up to the time of his death," the professor noted, "had been such as to steadily
increase our regard for him." In his memory students collected $69. Ten dollars
was spent to purchase flowers and the remainder was sent to his mother. In
addition, the Engineering Society quarterly publication *The Michigan Technic*
printed a memoriam in his honor.[112]

Barrier Williams lost her friend and colleague Mary Jones in 1909. A stalwart
of black Chicago, she seldom interacted with the club women of the new century
because of her age. Few of the modern generation of club women probably knew
who she was or how significant she had been to the development of the club
movement in the city. Jones, one of the last of a generation of black Chicago
elite, died in December at the age of eighty-nine.[113]

*   *   *

As the decade came to close Barrier Williams found herself under intense media
scrutiny and devastated by personal loss. In addition, one of the most atrocious
southern customs had moved to Illinois. The lynchings of black men in Belleville
and Danville in the summer of 1903 paled in comparison to the racially motivated violence in the state capital. The Springfield race riot of 1908 demonstrated
that anger over increasing black migration had escalated into xenophobic intolerance. Joe James, a drifter and vagrant, was reportedly caught in the bedroom
of the sixteen-year-old daughter of a white miner. After an altercation, James
stabbed the miner, who later died of his wounds. Arrested for the crime, James
remained in jail for several weeks. Later in the summer a white woman reported
to authorities that she had been raped by a black man. George Richardson was
arrested and joined James in the same jail. Angry crowds gather around the facility, forcing the sheriff to send the prisoners to Bloomington for their safety. A
crowd of angry citizens turned their rage on the black community. The violence

was so intense that several blacks were killed, including an 80-year-old man, and property worth more than $100,000 was destroyed. Order was restored only after the militia arrived.[114] In the aftermath, a wealthy white former slave owner from Kentucky called together a group of blacks and whites to seek solutions. At that gathering a new organization, the National Association for the Advancement of Colored People (NAACP), was born. Washington refused to attend the conference or join the NAACP citing the radical leanings of some of the members, including Du Bois and Wells-Barnett. So the debate about leadership and the direction of black progress raged on as the *Chicago Defender* featured a drawing of a black man hanging by a rope from a tree on its front page in April 1910. The caption read "Good Friday Was Celebrated Thus in Arkansas—An American Citizen Void of Protection by Our Great Government."[115] In the midst of the turmoil, Barrier Williams looked for a center.

7. A New Era

Duty, Responsibility, and Tension

For Barrier Williams, the center was anchored in the nearly 20-year-old black women's club movement. Her involvement shifted from solidifying a national network to expanding the services of local organizations and increasing black women's engagement with municipal work in Chicago. Responding to both hardening racial attitudes and the explosion of the black population in the second decade of the twentieth century, she joined forces with black and white club women in their attempts to solve the many problems that plagued the black community. The makings of the black ghetto that had begun at the turn of century had solidified by 1910, forcing thousands into cramped spaces on the south side of what would become known as the Black Belt. Restrictive covenants in white neighborhoods and municipal zoning that restricted the mobility of blacks contributed to an unsanitary environment. From 1915 to 1920, when the largest number of southern black migrants arrived in the city, the competition for adequate housing soared and the need for social services grew.

Barrier Williams also renewed her efforts to support programs aimed at addressing the concerns of women and girls. She supported the Phyllis Wheatley Home and the Frederick Douglass Center as both institutions expanded their services. As settlements and employment bureaus, they became training grounds for the graduates of the city's new schools of civic and social work, hosted forums, and promoted the activities of reform-minded club women. In 1913, the Illinois legislature, responding to pressure from suffrage activists, passed a law granting women suffrage in municipal and presidential elections. This success opened new doors for women leaders in the public realm, and black women figured prominently in the discourse about the shape and function of government.

* * *

In 1908, several months before she was to deliver an address at the fifth biennial meeting at the NACW in Brooklyn, New York, Barrier Williams articulated her disappointment about the direction of the national movement in an article titled "Work Attempted and Missed in Organized Club Work." More than a decade after the black women's club movement had begun, her enthusiasm had waned. She worried about the caliber of the new membership and expressed disappointment about the lack of progress in many areas of the country. She believed that many members had become too distracted. They seemed more interested in the "flattery by colored men" that allowed them to "easily persuade themselves that they are really accomplishing something worth while" than in being fully engaged in social welfare work. Because clubs seemed to have moved beyond the original intention of attracting "women whose education and training fit them for successful leadership in making woman's influence positive in the direction of social betterment," the clubs had abandoned their independence and simply become appendages of other institutions. She specifically pointed to women's devotion to traditional religious establishments that had dogmatic ideas about a woman's place as a primary obstacle. Her anxiety about the power of black religious institutions and black ministers in particular had a long history that was rooted in both class and gender consciousness. As she noted in the late 1880s, religious worship for black aristocrats like her who were well educated was more progressive and scientifically based than services for the traditional masses. She complained that the unenlightened black ministers who dominated the vast majority of churches and served the unschooled masses played such a significant role in retarding the race's advancement that their leadership threatened the reform activism of club women. She feared that women's club work had become so entangled and "dominated by church influence" that it hindered the club women's independence and changed the purposes of their clubs.[1]

While noting that there were "encouraging instances of what is possible," she insisted that "the fact still remains that the large majority of our women's clubs are without a definite program of work that can be counted as a part of the essential good of our progressive life."[2] She charged that a number of the clubs "are mere imitators of white women's clubs" and that "their plan of work is not made responsive to the peculiar conditions that surround colored women who organize themselves for club work." A lack of attention to the unique characteristics of geographical regions stifled the growth and success of national women's clubs and led to homogenization: "A woman's club in Chicago will find itself confronted with a very different sort of problem and work than the club in Alabama, Mississippi or in Ohio, where the needs of the colored people are not so obvious," she wrote.[3]

Barrier Williams voiced a legitimate concern about the new conditions and
challenges created by the rapid social and economic transformation of Chicago.
As a seasoned reformer, she had come to understand the vital importance of
women's engagement in public affairs and how their service was closely tied
to the ability to shape policies that determined the success or failure of young
black women. In a 1904 essay entitled "The Colored Girl," she highlighted the
general hardship of black women and discussed the magnitude of the problems
that they faced. Lamenting that "the colored girl is called upon to endure and
overcome more difficulties than confront any other women in our country," she
argued that the young black woman lacked the protection of either black or white
men, was not given equal opportunities, and commanded little respect. Yet "she
is always doing something of merit and credit that is not expected of her. She
is irrepressible." Geography certainly shaped how black women fared. In the
South, black women were much more restricted and limited. Barrier Williams
boasted that in Chicago, however, although segregation remained entrenched,
black girls challenged the discrimination and were "holding positions of high
responsibility" in areas "never intended for them."[4]

Five years later her concern for black girls in Chicago had intensified. In the
context of an increase in the influx of migrants from the South, the growth of
racially defined residential boundaries, and numbers of blacks living in poverty,
she expressed apprehension about "the young colored girl" who "is in need of
advice, inspiration and protection." These girls were "the poor, weak, misguided
daughters of ill-starred mothers and of dissolute and indifferent fathers."[5] The
shift in tone reflected both Barrier Williams's awareness of the environment
black girls inhabited and the emerging interest in black life among social workers and sociologists.

In his critique of elite black leaders at the turn of the century, Kevin Gains
argues that Barrier Williams was not the only reformer who was concerned
about the fate of black girls and the rise of the ghetto or who delivered blister-
ing assessments of the poor. "Among participants in conferences devoted to
the study of the race's social problems," Gaines writes, their "tributes to family,
motherhood, fireside training as bulwarks against sexual degradation, disease,
and crime approached mythical proportions."[6] He argues that elite black progressive reformers who embraced the new field of sociology were so determined to
shape the "morality and behavior" of the masses of blacks that they appeared
to be driven as much "by the racial assumptions of elite whites" as they were by
their own distain for the poor. And indeed, Barrier Williams was an aristocratic
reformer who shared the class consciousness of her contemporaries. She pointed
out that most black children could not escape an environment that "often presents a depressing picture of squalor and neglect; yards untidy and unrelieved

by flower or tree."[7] She was a recurrent speaker at a number of conferences and wrote about the issue in several publications.

These ideas were not new for her. As members of the Prudence Crandall Literary Club, she and Mary Jones had insisted in the late 1880s that many of the problems plaguing the black community began in the home. Barrier Williams's conviction that the environment was only part of the problem pushed her to move beyond the elite culture of the literary club and join forces with the Illinois Woman's Alliance and participate in its campaigns for equitable and adequate employment for women and better access to education for children. What had changed was the maturation of Barrier Williams's thoughts about how the problems could be solved. In the twentieth century, she felt that government intervention was as critical to making significant progress as the organized efforts of club women. One of the most significant arguments of the IWA was that the male-dominated municipal government was failing local citizens because of incompetence and inefficiency. Barrier Williams emphasized the relationship of the black community to the city. "Without adequate police protection" in the community, "evils of all kinds flourish in the face of childhood and decency" she wrote. She argued that those most equipped to intervene were black female reformers who had for more than a decade cultivated the organizational and lobbying skills needed to force change. It was club women who knew how "to bring the proper pressure on the officers of the law to protect the family life in such communities from these destroying influences." And only they were prepared to lead the charge in "creat[ing] a sense of neighborhood pride that shall inspire a whole community to vie with each other in making attractive home surrounding so that no longer shall uncleanliness, shiftlessness advertise the color of certain neighborhoods."[8]

Barrier Williams's view of club women's political engagement had shifted from her concern in 1894 about black women's readiness to vote to a concerted effort to create a political platform that embraced black women and catered to their ideas about remedying the problems in their community. To achieve her goal she adopted a two-pronged strategy. The first involved increasing the resources of institutions devoted to the welfare of black women. The second involved engaging in the statewide movement for the expansion of female suffrage.

For many girls, the Phyllis Wheatley Home, which Barrier Williams characterized as "the most important undertaking among colored women," was an available, safe, and reliable temporary shelter.[9] The home, which opened in May 1908, was an outgrowth of the Phyllis Wheatley Woman's Club that had been organized in March 1896. Elizabeth Lindsay Davis was the first president and remained in the post for much of the club's history. From the beginning, the club was rooted in the community and devoted to the welfare of children. Members provided training in sewing and supported a day nursery at Trinity A.M.E. Mission. The club also acted as a protective agency by pushing for the closure of drinking establishments that were near public schools. As the migration from the South progressed, the number of women and girls without adequate housing or employment increased. Club members created a building fund so they could establish a facility to assist the "alarming proportions . . . of colored women coming into the city, many of them from the best families in other States, [who find] it impossible to secure a congenial environment in which to live or desirable employment by which to support themselves."[10] The club paid $3,400 for a nine-room house and moved several girls "who had been temporarily sheltered in the homes of the club[']s members" into the institution. Within six months, the home had boarded twenty-three women and girls and helped almost 100 find jobs. Many of those jobs were as domestic servants, work Barrier Williams had been championing for nearly a decade.[11] These migrants were, Barrier Williams wrote, "a class of women" who "cannot be ignored"; they were the women workers she had in mind when she promoted the professionalization of domestic service for black women. These were "the women who work with their hands in the humbler walks of life, as cooks, housecleaners, laundresses, caretakers, and domestics" because so few opportunities were open to them.[12] However, the needs of female migrants overwhelmed the home and the limited resources of the club, so club members sought the assistance of other women's organizations. They created a coalition, the Phyllis Wheatley Home Association.[13]

Barrier Williams became a charter member of the Phyllis Wheatley Club and worked closely with Davis, the home, and the association.[14] She was elected an officer of the club, spoke often at meetings at the club, and used her influence in black and white aristocratic communities to raise funds for the home. Her efforts highlighted how important the success of the home was to "the leaders of the four hundred" who "were out in full force" to raise "a nice sum of money" for the home in 1911.[15] Barrier Williams also acted a liaison between the home and the CWC, reporting to club members on the institution's activities. As a result, two CWC departments, the Philosophy Department and Philanthropy Department, donated money to the home. The CWC also appointed three representatives to assist the Phyllis Wheatley Club with paying off the mortgage of the home. Members of the club also appeared as invited guests, as did representatives from other white organizations. For example, Harriet Taylor, the former president of the Chicago Political Equality League, gave a presentation at one of the meetings.[16]

The home had strong ties to the new field of professional social work. Barrier Williams viewed such work, which was based on scientific methodology, as necessary for legitimizing the reform work of club women. Chicago was one of the primary centers of the shift from women's voluntary benevolence to formal training in social science methods. Led by white women such as Sophonisba Breckinridge, the Chicago School of Civics and Philanthropy had developed a rigorous curriculum that had become a national model of how to train women to tackle urban problems. The Phyllis Wheatley Home hired Jennie Lawrence, one of several black female graduates of the program. Under the leadership of Lawrence, a former North Carolina school teacher, the home earned a reputation as an efficiently run and professionally sound institution.[17]

Barrier Williams also viewed the Frederick Douglass Center as an important part of the fight to increase women's economic opportunities. Like the Phyllis Wheatley Home, the center had an employment center for black women.[18] Barrier Williams welcomed the center as a vehicle through which she could help integrate black women into a professional workforce. Acting on a desire that had begun nearly two decades earlier, she focused most of her attention at the center on training black clerical workers and locating jobs for them. In the early 1890s, she had sponsored "a bright young woman to a well-known bank president of Chicago who was in need of a thoroughly competent stenographer and typewriter." But she met stiff racial resistance, and the woman was rejected.[19] It was so difficult for black women to gain office employment in the city that the number of black clerical workers made up only between 0.1 and 0.4 percent of the total in the decade between 1890 and 1900. In contrast, native-born white females constituted between 30.4 and 31.2 percent of the clerical workforce, and native-born white females of foreign or mixed parentage made up between 52.4 and 53.8 percent in the city. The remaining jobs in the field went to white females of foreign origin, who constituted 17.1 percent of clerical workers in 1890 and 14.6 percent in 1900. Barrier Williams was fully aware of how difficult it was to create a professional track for black women in the world of business. She declared in 1897 that "it is next to impossible for colored young women to obtain such employment in this free America. In nothing is the color-line so relentlessly drawn as it is against the employment of accomplished young colored women in the higher grades of occupations."[20]

Nearly two decades later the changing female workforce and the center's resources offered a more seasoned Barrier Williams a way to revisit her campaign for black clerical positions. By 1910, the industrial economy in Chicago had advanced to such a degree that stenography or typing positions made up nearly a quarter of the clerical jobs and clerical work had become professionalized field.[21] Although business schools dotted the community, race remained an impediment: few of the schools admitted black women. Indeed, in 1910 black women still only made up 0.4 percent of the clerical work force.[22] Barrier Williams fought to change that. She called on employers to hire black women, developed classes to train clerical workers, and acted as a broker between employers and black female laborers. By 1913, she was accepting applications at her home on Lawrence Avenue and teaching classes in stenography and typewriting at the Frederick Douglass Center.[23]

She was equally devoted to increasing opportunities for black women in other professional fields. The employment success of the nurses who graduated from the Provident Hospital program continued to be important to her. When these nurses encountered discrimination in hiring practices at local hospitals, Barrier Williams was among the women who fought back. For example, Cook County Hospital refused to hire black graduates of the program because of race. In response, Barrier Williams and others enlisted the help of prominent white women such as Celia Parker Woolley to help bring an end to the discrimination. Woolley gladly cooperated, chastising the administration in a letter that noted that the hospital was "supported by public funds, gathered in the form of taxes from every class of citizens, no one of which can be properly deprived of any of its benefits either in the wards or in any department of practice, study and instruction." Woolley also pressured prominent white philanthropists to use their influence to ensure that graduates of Provident were fairly treated.[24]

Barrier Williams singled out graduates of Tuskegee for their contributions to Chicago's black community. In a 1914 article, for example, she proudly noted that "more than one hundred" graduates of Tuskegee lived in Chicago and that "none of them is out of employment." In what seemed to be a response to her early critics, she highlighted the successful outcomes of the program by arguing that most of these new residents were employed in professional positions. The women graduates held jobs as dressmakers, nurses, and clerks.[25] This emphasis on middle-class professions highlighted the success of the industrial model of education. It provided a pathway to upward mobility just as much as it assisted women with employment in domestic labor. Barrier Williams's comments also reveal that the population of migrants, particularly before 1915, exhibited diversity in terms of class and education.

The professionalization of the black female labor force remained a priority for Barrier Williams primarily because she believed that it contributed to "the enlargement and improvement of the home life of the Negro people." Blacks who had previously lived "in districts of the city bordering on what may be called the 'slums'" where "vices of all kinds menaced the morals and health conditions of their families" had witnessed "great improvement in this respect."[26] She attributed the change to "better economic conditions" that "have enabled them to purchase and occupy residences on some of the finest avenues and boulevards of the city." A new class of women had entered many jobs that had previously not been open to them, such as teachers in interracial schools, clerical workers, department store workers, probation officers, attorneys, doctors, and nurses.[27] Barrier Williams attributed the vast majority of the gains to the women who "seem to be confident of their own worth."[28]

*   *   *

In December 1904, the Chicago Woman's Club supported the adoption of a resolution in support of "granting women the right to vote for Presidential electors and certain other officers." The club also recognized the importance of women's engagement in municipal politics by contributing funds to support the effort to grant women municipal suffrage.[29] Scholar Maureen Flanagan argues that this was a change in a strategy that had emerged in the 1880s. In the twentieth century, the earlier argument for women's equal rights became "suffrage as a woman's political need in the city."[30] What women's historians refer to as "public housekeeping" in municipalities became the dominion of women, enabling them to participate in discussions with city officials and ultimately demand improvements in housing and increased access to public amenities such as libraries and playgrounds and education. But it wasn't just local organizations that supported the platform. The National American Woman Suffrage Association promoted the idea of public housekeeping as well. At its February 1907 convention in Chicago, one of the main topics was municipal suffrage.[31]

Barrier Williams's espousal of women's participation in municipal politics was defined as much by race as it was by gender. Racism and discrimination contributed to the lack of adequate housing, poor garbage service, inadequate transportation, inadequate education, and police brutality in densely populated segregated neighborhoods and undermined the social and economic success of blacks as a group as much as gender inequality limited women's access to civic affairs. She believed that the only possibility for real change was through the combination of interracial cooperative efforts and in black women's access to the ballot. So at the CWC meeting in December 1913, where the topic was "Colored People in Chicago," she joined prominent white activists, educators and philanthropists Louise deKoven Bowen, Sophonisba Breckinridge, Mary McDowell, and Mary Wilmarth to consider the impact of discrimination on the black community.[32]

But Barrier Williams recognized the fragility and limits of interracial cooperation. For example, the Chicago Political Equality League, which Celia Parker Woolley had created under the auspices of the CWC in 1894, excluded black women from its ranks at a time when its influence and membership had significantly increased. Under the CWC member Catherine Waugh McCulloch, the organization had claimed an important position among the groups fighting for the enfranchisement of women within ten years of its founding. By 1914, interest in the organization and its platform had grown so significantly that it had nearly 1,400 members.[33] Barrier Williams and two of her colleagues saw an opportunity to harness the organization's power and influence, and they challenged the discrimination. Barrier Williams, Elizabeth Lindsay Davis, and Mrs. George Hall applied for membership in the league in 1912. The applications were rejected. Refusing to retreat, the women sought the assistance of Woolley and members of the Frederick Douglass Center. Letters of complaint poured in concerning the treatment of the three applicants, and eventually they were admitted to the league.[34] The *Defender* championed the decision, noting that "the League by that action has evidently decided that the color line has no place in a suffrage organization."[35]

The interest that Barrier Williams, Davis, and Hall expressed in the franchise was matched by black women statewide. At the 1912 conference of the Illinois Federation of Colored Women's Clubs, the main speaker's presentation was "Why Women Should Vote."[36] Some black women created their own suffrage organizations. The first was organized by Ida B. Wells-Barnett with assistance from Belle Squire, a white woman who was a member of the No-Vote-No-Tax League. They established the Alpha Suffrage Club in January 1913.[37] At a well-attended organizational meeting in January 1913, Squire argued that the importance of the organization crossed race lines. She acknowledged the similarities in the desires of black and white women, telling the audience that "the Negro woman has exactly the same interest at stake as her white sister. She has property and her children to protect. She has the same vital interest in the creation and enforcement of laws." By the end of the year, the club had at least 100 members. The club invited numerous guest speakers, including white suffragists such as Jane Addams of Hull House and Grace Wilbur Trout of the Illinois Equal Suffrage Association. Perhaps the most important mission of the organization was teaching women how to use voting machines.[38]

In 1913, the passage of an Illinois bill granting women the right to vote in presidential and municipal elections transformed how the state's women engaged in the public arena. Illinois women had held positions on school boards and in some cases on state university boards for more than two decades. But women's impact in local and state government was still limited. As women created national political alliances, formed state and local political organizations, and entered the professional field of social welfare they pushed for greater access to the ballot. The National American Woman Suffrage Association facilitated regional and interregional networks among women. The national group strategized with local groups about how to gain full citizenship rights with a constitutional amendment. That did not happen until 1920, when the

Nineteenth Amendment was ratified. In Chicago, affiliation with NAWSA increased the opportunities for local women's groups to develop political goals that sought to restructure city services to meet the needs of the increasingly diverse population.

The new ability of women to vote in Illinois highlighted different attitudes of men and women about the meaning of suffrage. Most male voters viewed their ballot as a way to maintain their position and hegemony within political parties. Black men especially sought to win recognition from white political bosses by gaining lucrative municipal appointments and positions within the party, positions that had long been closed to them. In contrast, women saw the ballot as the capital they needed to expand their reform efforts. *The Chicago Defender* illuminated the difference: for black women the key municipal concerns were "the garbage question," "the welfare of children," and "transportation."[39] Barrier Williams and Davis illustrated this gendered understanding of the meaning of the ballot. Davis saw it as a bulwark against the instability of the family, a tool for helping homeless children, and a defense against poverty. It was, she declared, a means of assisting "the abandoned wife, the wage earning girl, the dependent and delinquent child, or the countless hordes of the unemployed." Barrier Williams perceived the vote more broadly. She argued that it provided the weapon black women needed "to combat prejudice and discrimination of all kinds."[40]

A number of black women aligned themselves with white female reformers who were seeking municipal positions. For example, Barrier Williams and Ida B. Wells-Barnett were members of the political committee that supported the campaigns of two women candidates, Harriet Vittum and Mary McDowell, for positions on the Cook County Board of Commissioners in 1914. Other members of the committee included Grace Abbott, Jane Addams, Sophonisba Breckinridge, Anna Wilmarth Ickes, and Agnes Nestor.[41] Although the women were not elected, their campaigns demonstrated women's willingness to run against party insiders and promote their own platform.

Black women also attempted to influence how black men engaged in politics. Black men had built a strong Republican Party coalition in the first decade of the twentieth century, but they had not been able to loosen the firm grip of the white officeholders in majority black wards. That changed in 1910 and 1912, when Edward Wright ran for the post of alderman of the Second Ward. Although he was unable to garner enough white votes to defeat the white candidates backed by the party machine, his candidacy and respectable showing drew attention from both the black community and the Republican Party machine. By the time that the bill granting women the right to vote in municipal elections was passed, black women were primed to participate in a campaign to elect a black man to the city council. While some men were concerned that this new public role for black women might compromise or dilute their power, the majority viewed it as an opportunity for success. In the year after the new law was passed, black women and men mobilized their forces. A number of suffrage clubs were created, joining the ranks of the Alpha Suffrage Club, and mass meetings were held. Most important, black women registered in droves. In 1914, real estate agent William Randolph Cowan ran as an independent candidate. Although Cowan, like Wright, lost to the machine-supported candidate, his strong showing in the election was partly attributable to the commitment of black women to transforming politics.[42]

The increasing political activity of women garnered much attention in the black community. Barrier Williams told an audience at the Progressive Negro League that "the subject of woman suffrage was at one time a thing to be ridiculed and sneered at and many women timidly turned away from it as something unworthy of their womanhood. But thanks to the inherent power of organized 'Woman's Suffrage' it is now the biggest question in the public mind today."[43] Yet the interest remained mired in a narrowly defined racial context. She argued that "the Colored women as citizens have been and still are handicapped on all sides. Who they are, what they have done for themselves and even what they deserve has not been of interest to the average American. It has been and still is our lot to bear the burdens of suspicion, mistrust and race hatred." She envisioned the franchise as the most powerful means of lifting the veil of black women's invisibility. She predicted that "when Colored women as well as white women begin to realize the real significance and power of the ballot, respect for the race will wonderfully increase."[44]

She praised black women for their political ambitions and for educating themselves about the political process. Revealing the continuing tensions between black male and female leaders, Barrier Williams noted that "it must also be remembered that Colored women have been trained in schools, church life and in their clubs and organizations to such an extent that they are much better qualified for suffrage than were the Colored men when they were first enfranchised."[45] In her view, black women still led the direction of black progress. She didn't differentiate along race lines when she told the women in the audience that "it is possible by those in official power to keep you out of your rights." Women had to be steadfast in their resolve because so much was at stake. In particular "the dependent and delinquent Colored children in the state of Illinois" who "have been most cruelly neglected for lack of suitable homes or institutions for them" required women's commitment. Young black girls were especially prone to being "absolutely shut out" of the county and state homes "according to complexion." Ultimately, she declared, black women "will find a way to right this great injustice" because they understood "that voting is not only a right but a duty."[46]

Barrier Williams certainly wasn't the only person to sound the alarm about the discrimination that limited black children's access to state facilities or to suggest that black women use the ballot as a tool to bring about change. But she was leading the charge. A year after her resounding condemnation of discrimination against needy black children, the Illinois Federation of Colored Women's Clubs formed a committee for the purpose of lobbying the state legislature to "build suitable housing quarters for girls who had become wards of the State." This action at the federation's convention in Champaign in 1915 reflected both awareness of women's political power and recognition of the ongoing struggle for race and gender equality.[47]

In 1915, Oscar Stanton DePriest became the first black to be elected as an alderman in Chicago. His success was made possible because of the overwhelming support he received from black men and the press, the Republican Party's endorsement of him as a candidate in the Second Ward, and the politicized culture black women created. DePriest had been born in Alabama in 1871. His family became part of the migration of exodusters who moved to Kansas in 1878. He had lived in Chicago since 1889, two years after Barrier Williams and S. Laing moved to the city. A onetime painter and decorator, he opened a real estate business in 1906. He developed an interest in politics and began cultivating ties to both black Republicans and white party bosses. He was elected county commissioner in 1904 and 1906. During the years between the end of his term as commissioner and the passage of the female suffrage bill he had straddled the fence between his black cohorts and the white Republican Party machine. After Wright and Cowan were defeated, he saw an opportunity to blend the two groups. He sought the endorsements of white party bosses and many black groups, including women's organizations. By December 1914 he had secured enough support to become the top black candidate.[48] In January 1915, he launched his candidacy at Olivet Baptist Church, the largest black Baptist Church in the city. Speakers such as Ferdinand Barnett, J. T. Jenifer, state senator Samuel Ettelson, and S. Laing urged voters in an overflowing crowd to elect him.

When DePriest spoke, he seemed to direct his comments to the issues that were of paramount concern to women, including education and discrimination. He pledged to "secure the naming of some Colored person as a member of the board of education in order to stop such damnable discrimination as has existed at the Wendell Phillips High School" and "the passage of an ordinance that will require the mayor to revoke the license of any person upon conviction of discriminating against citizens on account of their color." In February he won the primary, and in April he became the first black alderman in the city, partly because, he noted, women "cast as intelligent a vote as men."[49] DePriest's triumph provided leverage for black women by ensuring that the Republican Party machine would no longer ignore the black community. Historian Allan Spear argues that blacks were so integral to the city's electoral process that "by 1920, Negroes had more political power in Chicago than anywhere else in the country." More black men won seats on the city council, and they took over leadership of the Republican Party in the Second Ward. Moreover, because of the cooperative efforts between politicized black male and female citizens in the early twentieth century, the state strengthened the civil rights legislation that had been engineered by black leaders in the late nineteenth century. In 1920 the state adopted a constitutional clause that made it illegal to discriminate on the basis of race in schools, housing, and places of public accommodation.[50]

But on the municipal issues that were important to women, power did not always translate into real reform. Corruption, political machinery, and the patriarchal structure of city politics meant that politicians like DePriest devoted more rhetoric than substance to the issues women cared about. He was embroiled in his own legal battles for much of his administration and had little time to champion their causes. The alliances he made with corrupt white politicians produced few universal gains. The ghetto remained, poverty rates escalated, and the red light district flourished. In addition, black men failed to endorse a black woman for any significant political leadership positions, demonstrating their continuing anxiety about women's place in the world of politics.

Still, black women continued to display enthusiasm for the franchise. The suffrage bill of 1913 gave them the ability to vote in presidential elections for the first time. For the most part, black Chicago women's party affiliations at the national level were the same as they were at the local level. So when the Republican Party held its convention in Chicago in the summer of 1916 to endorse its nominee, Supreme Court Justice Charles Evan Hughes, black women were eager to participate. Barrier Williams quickly joined the Colored Women's Hughes Republican group and served as the chair of publicity.[51]

Her support of Hughes was driven as much by her frustration with the national escalation of racism and discrimination as it was by her disgust with Woodrow Wilson's administration. The Ku Klux Klan that had terrorized black southerners in the late nineteenth century had reawakened and spread to the Midwest and the North. By the end of the decade, the group had become a well-organized and powerful force with the goal of uniting native-born whites against blacks and immigrants. Fueled by the national release of the film *Birth of a Nation* in 1915, which was based on a racist novel by Thomas Dixon that depicted blacks as villainous aggressors who wreaked havoc on the South and violated white women during Reconstruction, and increasing xenophobia and anti-foreign sentiments, the group gained much support. With the help of the city's mayor, blacks in Chicago successfully blocked the showing of the film, but the enthusiastic reception across the country revealed an ominous note about race relations. And President Wilson demonstrated little interest in their plight in part because he harbored some of the same white supremacist views as many southerners. He appointed white southerners to his cabinet who insisted on segregating black and white employees and rarely consulted with black leaders.

Barrier Williams also may have had a more personal motive for her enthusiastic engagement in national politics. S. Laing, who had been thwarted in many of his political ambitions, found himself in a precarious position at the dawn of the new decade. As financial resources decreased and philosophical differences increased, the Republican Party split, and the Progressive Party was created in 1912. The balance of political power at the national level shifted from Republicans who viewed Booker T. Washington as a power broker and favored many of his recommendations to government posts to Democrats who neither deferred to Washington nor provided a guarantee of designated black jobs. One of the casualties was S. Laing.

In 1909, during the administration of Republican William Howard Taft, the Bureau of Naturalization was moved from the Department of Justice and became part of the Department of Commerce and Labor. This happened at the same time that S. Laing's federal appointment as assistant attorney in the Northern District of Illinois was expiring. For two years he sought a permanent post. Booker T. Washington came to his aid by including him, along with several other prominent black men, in his successful tour of Arkansas in the late summer of 1911. He also wrote letters of recommendation for him.[52] But shortly after the tour, a tightening budget and questions about his eligibility to work in either the Department of Justice or the Department of Commerce and Labor put his employment prospects into jeopardy. Attorney General George Wickersham told Secretary of Commerce and Labor Charles Nagel in October 1911 that after the naturalization cases were transferred to the Department of Commerce, S. Laing "was left in the District Attorney's office." Correspondence from James H. Wilkerson, the U.S. attorney for the northern district of Illinois, demonstrated that because "there is really nothing in that office which he can very well do," perhaps S. Laing could find a home in the Commerce and Labor Department.[53] But that was not to be. On October 12, Charles Nagel wrote to George Wickersham that

> I have your letter of the 9th instant in regard to Assistant U. S. Attorney Williams, and wish I were in a position to suggest something to you. It is learned, however, upon informal inquiry of the Civil Service Commission, that Mr. Williams was given an appointment without examination, under Schedule A of the Civil Service

Rules, in September, 1909, and that there appears to be no way in which he may be transferred to, or appointed in, the Naturalization Service or any other branch of the competitive classified service, except by means of an Executive Order. The Commission but recently established a register of eligibles for naturalization examiner as the result of a special competitive examination, and we would hardly be justified in asking for an Executive Order.[54]

In response, Wickersham wrote, "From this it would appear that the suggested transfer is impracticable, which I greatly regret."[55]

However, through the maneuverings of Booker T. Washington, S. Laing's employment contract was extended. The reprieve, however, was short lived. He was soon asked to resign. He contacted Washington for help, but Washington's response in January 13 was tepid. He wrote that he had learned "that nothing can be done except through the initiative and leadership of the District Attorney in Chicago. If you can bring any influence to bear through U. S. Senators or your local people in Chicago on Mr. Wilkerson it will help, but matters are in such shape that the Attorney General does not feel warranted in going over the head of Mr. Wilkerson."[56] By then Washington had apparently come to the conclusion that S. Laing was indeed inept. On the same day he responded to S. Laing, he also wrote a letter to a cohort demonstrating his irritation. "It is pretty hard to help a man who has no ability to help himself," he complained.[57]

Desperate for help, S. Laing sent a letter to President Taft on February 1, 1913. "I am taking the liberty of writing this letter to assure you that any representations to the effect that I was not loyal to you at all times is wholly untrue," he began. "Throughout the entire presidential campaign I kept in close touch with the 'Taft Headquarters' at Chicago freely tendering my services as speaker or organizer and did in fact assist in organizing and promoting, among the colored people, the largest and most important meetings of the campaign. These facts can be, at any time fully verified."[58] But according to Wickersham, S. Laing's loyalty was never in question. The request for his resignation was made for a much more serious reason. The United States Attorney at Chicago "found, after trying out Mr. Williams in almost every branch of the work in his office, that he was not competent in any particular line" and that he "was really of no use to him." He was told to reapply for the position of Assistant United States Attorney for the Northern District of Illinois at Chicago. But neither his April 1913 application letter nor the recommendation letters from Jenkin Lloyd Jones, several judges (including Louis Brandeis of Boston), and a member of Congress, were enough to prevent the end of his career as a federal employee.[59]

His employment troubles were compounded by a sudden illness in November 1913, when he was rushed to Provident Hospital shortly after boarding a trolley car. He was diagnosed with a strangulated hernia. After physician George Hall performed surgery, S. Laing was hospitalized for three weeks. A black weekly reported that he was fully recovered by Christmas.[60]

With his federal appointments exhausted and his relationship with Washington frayed, S. Laing shored up his law practice. He cast himself as one of the most vociferous champions of black rights in the Midwest by defending a number of civil rights cases and becoming the vice-president of the Chicago branch of the NAACP. He devoted a considerable amount of his energy to providing legal advice for that organization.[61]

*   *   *

Chicago had become a mecca for blacks in the second decade of the new century. It had one of the largest proportions of blacks in the country and it was the nation's second largest city. So the commemorations of Abraham Lincoln's birth and the fifty-year celebration of the end of slavery were momentous occasions. The preparations for these events attracted an illustrious group of black and white community leaders. Committee members included Barrier Williams and S. Laing, Charles Bentley, Ida B. Wells-Barnett, and Celia Parker Woolley. The all-day event enveloped the whole city. A prominent list of speakers included local residents such as Jane Addams and national figures such as W. E. B. Du Bois. Schools were closed so that children could attend the festivities and celebrate the life of the great emancipator.[62]

The Lincoln commemoration was the precursor to the grand celebration of fifty years of black freedom. A month-long Chicago Illinois National Half-Century Exposition was held two years later in August 1915. The event was endorsed by President Wilson, the governor of the state, and dignitaries from around the world. Thousands of dollars were pledged, and numerous committees were appointed.[63] Barrier Williams and many of the black club women with whom she had worked for decades had positions on various committees. Theresa G. Macon, the president of the Illinois Federation of Colored Women's Clubs and a member of the Board of Directors of the Phyllis Wheatley Home, headed the Department of Social Progress. Barrier Williams served under her guidance on the Bureau of Literature.[64] Dr. Mary F. Waring, who chaired the Health and Hygiene Committee for the NACW, was elected national commissioner to represent the IFCWC for the celebration. She was also the vice-chair of the Department of Education.[65] Elizabeth Lindsay Davis assisted Eva T. Jenifer, a member of the IFCWC and the Frederick Douglass Woman's Club, who served as vice-chair of the Department of Industry.[66] Black women around the nation expressed interest in participating. Among the list of honorary vice presidents and advisory board members were Margaret Washington, the president of NACW, and Nannie Burroughs, an NACW member and a strong supporter of black women's rights.[67]

The exposition was to feature an array of activities. It included a number of congresses that focused on religion, education, sociology, industry, and agriculture. Perhaps the most attractive was an "International Interracial Congress" that sought to move "toward the establishment of a permanent peace between the two races." Also, there were to be over 800 exhibits that included artifacts and information related to tailoring, baking, literature, painting, historical collections, broom making, social settlement work, and domestic science and the 250 patents obtained by blacks for their inventions.[68]

An anticipated 372,000 visitors residing outside the state and nearly half a million residence of Illinois were expected to join in the festivities before the exposition closed.[69] By all accounts the event was a resounding success. Residence of Cook County demonstrated great enthusiasm. *The Broad Ax* reported that on "Chicago Day" alone, 10,000 showed up to support the exposition.[70] Others came from as far away as the South. Barrier Williams's nephew Fred Barrier and his wife traveled from Alexandria, Virginia. He was there to attend the National Medical Association convention and to enjoy the exposition during the final week. Barrier Williams' niece Harriet Barrier and brother-in-law Robert Pelham of Detroit, Michigan, accompanied the couple on their trip to Chicago.[71]

The commemorations designed to chart the progress of the black community also revealed the unprecedented demographic mobility of black people since slavery ended. Over that period, an ever-increasing number of blacks moved long distances to unfamiliar regions. Chicago was a major destination. An unprecedented influx of black migrants from the South arrived in the city from 1915 to 1920. By 1920 the number of black residents of Chicago had nearly tripled to 109,458 from the 1910 census count. They increased the black proportion of the city's population to 4.1 percent.[72] Lured by the jobs created by the war that erupted in Europe in 1914, they transformed the economic climate. Buoyed by the drastic reduction in the number of immigrants arriving in the United States, which eliminated much of the competition for jobs, they gained access to employment in areas that had previously been closed to them.[73] Social institutions were transformed as well. Scholar James R. Grossman argues that churches benefited more than any other established institution from the influx. Olivet Baptist Church, which "claimed to be the largest Baptist church in the world, added more than five thousand new members between 1916 and 1919."[74] Migrants also added to the political strength of the black belt by ensuring the election of blacks to political positions throughout the remainder of the decade.

But the sheer numbers of migrants and their increasing needs strained the charitable resources of black club women. In an effort to keep up with the demand, black women developed more clubs to provide charitable assistance. Some committees within the clubs were forced to shift from their initial mission of a purely consultative role to one where members actively engaged in finding resources to sustain institutions and their operations. For example, although the Clara Jessamine Club was established in 1912 to act as an advisory board to the Phyllis Wheatley Home, just one year later, members of the club were raising money to help pay the mortgage and contribute to the purchase of electrical supplies.[75] But even with such additional support, the demand was greater than the available resources. That was why a number of black club women found it expedient to attend an organizational meeting to discuss the creation of a branch of the Urban League in the city in December 1916. Jennie Lawrence, Joanna Snowden-Porter, and Irene Goins of the Chicago Federation of Colored Women's Clubs were among those who championed the development of the organization and its commitment to labor, housing, and child welfare issues. Once the league was established, club women like those in the Clara Jessamine Club contributed funds "towards the feeding and clothing of the unemployed."[76]

Migrants also exposed the growing divide between the educated and the uneducated, the elite and the poor, and the southern newcomers and the city's established black residents. Those who had lived in Chicago for many years welcomed the prospect of increasing economic and political power, but they worried about how the influx would "disrupt the community and embarrass the race."[77] There were public discussions and concerns about the crude behavior and the moral code of southern migrants. Even the *Chicago Defender*, which had played such a significant role in luring migrants to the city, admonished migrants for their unsophisticated conduct. It often published advice about how migrants should act in public settings and how they should conduct their lives.[78]

The actions of established residents such as Barrier Williams who lived in wards with heavy concentrations of blacks betrayed the anxiety and unease of even those who organized and supported organizations and institutions to assist the newcomers. Elite blacks found the behavior of a large number of migrants so disconcerting that they made a determined effort to insulate themselves. Things came to a head less than two months after the exposition, when Barrier Williams wrote about the creation of the Douglass Neighborhood Association: "a most commendable enterprise has been inaugurated by the residents and property owners in the second and third wards of Chicago." The new association illuminated the fierce battle to control and define the spatial boundaries of the neighborhood. Using the language of warfare, Barrier Williams argued that the notion of respectability was under attack. She likened the newcomers to amoral invaders and explained that in other to defeat this aggressive assault, the elites had to fortify their defenses. The primary purpose of the association was "to protect the resident of the district against the invasion of bad characters, saloons, disorderly pool rooms, disorderly and neglected appearance of property, unnecessary noise and other things of an objectionable character."[79]

The creation of the association also reflected the fear of longtime residents of encroachments on their class privilege. Barrier Williams and many of her colleagues had always been as conscious of class distinctions as they were about race distinctions. They abhorred racial segregation but maintained a strict adherence to upper- and middle-class rules that excluded the poor, the unrefined, and the uneducated. For example, in 1906, when white residents in Hyde Park had instituted a plan that was initially designed to limit the number of black servants in the neighborhood, the plan transformed into an effort to rid the neighborhood of not just black servants but also the few elite blacks who lived nearby as well. The Hyde Park Improvement Protective Club had such great success that servants and many upper-class blacks were forced out of the neighborhood. Barrier Williams, who had lived there for many years, complained that whites had deliberately pushed "Negroes of the better class" out of their homes and community.[80] More than a decade later, neighborhoods such as Hyde Park continued to symbolize the ongoing battle about racialized space that had engulfed Chicago. From 1916 to 1920, lured by real estate agents and declining property values, hundreds of blacks purchased property in the neighborhood as whites fled the area. The whites who remained became more determined to remove black residents and to deter others from moving into the community. Protective associations organized in a number of communities such as Hyde Park to intimidate blacks, and real estate agencies claimed that the presence of black residents decreased property values.[81]

Black elites such as Barrier Williams also worried about declining property values. But unlike the racially charged objections of white Hyde Park residents, they conflated race and class in their analysis. Racially restricted neighborhoods had made it difficult if not impossible for even the wealthiest blacks to avoid engaging with the poorest blacks in some capacity. But because of their status they had managed to maintain some kind of perimeter between themselves and the masses. They lived on the edges of white communities or in a particular section or block of the black neighborhood and successfully avoided living in the ghettos that had become all too common in the city. But the influx of migrants and the growth of white covenants threatened their perimeter as the need for housing increased and red light districts expanded. The distress of the elites and their concern over the ways that whites perceived them forced Barrier Williams to declare that the Douglass Neighborhood Association was also created "to overcome the prevailing impression that the presence of colored people in high class resident districts depreciates the value of property" and "that the offensive thing known as 'segregation' will cease to be when it becomes known that colored people will demand the best conditions and surroundings for themselves and their families."[82] In the end, the association and groups like it engaged in a long and protracted battle to maintain the sanctity of residential conclaves that divided along class lines, but its members never succeeded in blurring race lines.

In the face of the alarming and escalating racial divide, several black organizations began to look for ways to institute preventive measures to maintain distance between themselves and the black working class. But even organizations like the NAACP, the Chicago Protective League, or the Urban League could not halt the growing tide of white xenophobia.[83] The bombings of black homes that began in 1917 escalated to such a degree that in 1919 alone fourteen bombs were set off and a six-year-old girl was killed.[84] Black anger over competition for housing, inadequate municipal services, and continued discrimination as well as distrust of the police, all of which had been concerns for reform-minded women, came to a head in the Red Summer of 1919, when the city erupted in violence. The riot was sparked by the July drowning of Eugene Williams, a young black boy, in an area unofficially designated for white beach goers at Lake Michigan. Blacks and whites battled for nearly a week. People were shot, stabbed, and beaten and homes and businesses were destroyed. When calm finally returned, twenty-three blacks and fifteen whites had been killed, hundreds had been injured, and the property damage was enormous. In addition, there was little doubt that racial segregation would remain intact and that any hope for an integrated city was dead. The black community became more insulated and isolated than ever before.[85]

* * *

For Barrier Williams, the riots were only part of the end of a difficult and challenging decade. In 1915 she lost two of the most significant figures in her life. Her mother Harriet died on April 16, 1915, at the age of eighty. She had lingered for some time, finally succumbing to "starvation" with a contributing factor of "cardiac spasm." She was remembered as a "prominent social and religious worker" and was the second family member to be buried in the Brockport cemetery.[86] Booker T. Washington's death seven months later in November 1915 left a leadership vacuum nationally and in many ways was a transition for black leaders in Chicago. Attacks on him and his supporters had certainly abated as Washington's power had diminished under the Democratic administration of Wilson and more pressing issues took center stage in urban centers. One of the most telling signs of change was that the year before his death, the local Tuskegee Club hosted S. Laing who was then the vice-president of the local chapter of the NAACP.[87]

The sudden and unexpected loss of Celia Parker Woolley on March 9, 1918, left another vacuum. At her memorial service on April 7 in the Abraham Lincoln Center, Barrier Williams told the audience that "Mrs. Woolley belonged to that choice group of men and women who could not be happy so long as unrighteousness had sway over this country. She conceived it to be part of her mission in life to help to correct public opinion that is now either indifferent to or actively hostile against the present generation of colored people." Even when "she knew she would be misunderstood, criticized, and even maligned," she followed her heart and "established the Frederick Douglass Center." In many ways the institution symbolized her commitment to "prodding the American conscience to be just to the Negro and to enlarge the term citizenship so as to include all men."[88]

Beyond her professional admiration of Woolley, Barrier Williams admitted that she felt a profound and devastating loss. "I cannot refrain from voicing a sense of personal bereavement in the death of Mrs. Woolley for she was my personal friend," she told the mourners. "There are few in this city who could have left behind so many who could say 'She was my personal friend.' She could always be seen and heard by any one of us and her wholesome advice, her inspiring optimism, and her generous spirit of comradeship will make her name and memory a sacred heritage."[89]

The Frederick Douglass Center died along with Woolley. The Chicago Urban League, which had initially shared space with the center, began using the entire building upon Woolley's death. The agency centralized many of the programs that the center and club women had been doing for more than a decade. The league encouraged interracial cooperation and provided assistance with housing, employment, and health care. It became one of the premier welfare organizations in the city.[90] The closing of the center meant that Barrier Williams lost access to a place that had rooted her in the club women's reform movement, highlighted interracial cooperation, and illuminated her labor activism. Moreover, the building was also Woolley's home and its familiarity, like her friend, had offered a respite from the indignation of racial discrimination. The loss signaled the end of an era in the club movement and pointed to the waning of Barrier Williams's public activism.

Within six months of Woolley's death, Jenkin Lloyd Jones died, the man who had played a major role in introducing Barrier Williams to Unitarian ideology, nurtured her quest for social justice, and spearheaded the building of the interracial Abraham Lincoln Center in 1905. While in Tower Hill, Wisconsin, in September 1918 he suffered a strangulated hernia. The subsequent surgery proved too difficult for him, and he never recovered. Most newspapers highlighted his pacifism and views against the war, but Barrier Williams would remember him for his unwavering support of her.[91]

The greatest loss, however, came when S. Laing died at home on December 21, 1921, at the age of sixty-three. One newspaper reported that he had suffered for nearly a year after being injured in an automobile accident. He was so incapacitated that he found even the work he had done all of his life to be too taxing. He retired from his law practice and languished at home.[92] For Barrier Williams his death marked an end to a partnership that had lasted thirty-four years. It was because of him that she had migrated to the Midwest and made Chicago home, and it was, in part, because of his unwavering commitment to her and her aspirations that she had become one of the most recognized women in the country.

The location of his funeral service at Abraham Lincoln Center represented both his and Barrier Williams's commitment to Unitarianism and their vision of a utopian dream of racial justice and equality. A commentator for *The Broad Ax* called him "a real leader in all of the good that can be ascribed to men—a real gentleman: honest, honorable and fit to be copied by any of the living today." The *Chicago Defender* remembered him as a "brilliant jurist" who "was in the forefront of all movements for civic betterment and social service." Another paper referred to him as a man who "was regarded by members of his race as one of its most brilliant orators."[93]

Nearly sixty-six, widowed, and without the aid of her most ardent white friends and benefactors, Barrier Williams was adrift. She tried to rally by continuing to participate in women's clubs in the city. She worked with the Phyllis Wheatley Club and made history by becoming the first black woman to serve on the city's Library Board in 1924.[94] But age weighed her down and she had lost too much. Chicago had become a much more hostile place and had drifted too far from the promise of racial tolerance and reconciliation. So she sought refuge. Completing the migration circle, she returned to her roots in Brockport.

Conclusion

Revealing that she had cut her ties to Chicago, Barrier Williams wrote to Francis Grimké in January 1927 that "my sister and I very much appreciated your kind words of approbation for the rather radical change we have made in our surroundings and life." The burden of trying to inhabit "two places at once" had become too difficult and had forced her to make the decision to leave the city she had worked in for almost four decades. She didn't regret the move but did express some unease, primarily because "it is a change of course and one which calls for constant adjustment." One of those changes included the fact that many of her family, friends, and classmates had died and she and Ella faced the travails and uncertainty of "making new friends."[1]

Delighted to be back in the place that had offered her so much opportunity in her youth and so many fond memories in adulthood, she told Grimké that she and Ella were "well and happy" and that Brockport remained the "pleasant and peaceful" place that it had always been. She felt that it had been a good decision to return to the village and that they were "content." That contentment lasted nearly twenty years and was fulfilled by their ability to frequent the "fine library" in the village, attend "occasional lectures," and read letters from friends.[2]

The bond between the sisters greatly contributed to the pleasure of returning home. Barrier Williams and Ella had been close all of their lives, although they spent much of their adulthood living in different regions of the country. Ella, who never married, was a professional educator and had lived in Washington for more than forty years. She had an illustrious career as a teacher, a principal, and an activist. She played a major role in the development of the Washington branch of the Young Women's Christian Association (YWCA). She was also an international traveler who promoted the reform activities of black women;

she represented Washington at the Paris Exposition in the summer of 1900. Among her most prominent colleagues at that event were Anna Julia Cooper of Washington, Agnes Moody of Chicago, Imogene Howard of New York, and W. E. B. Du Bois of Atlanta, Georgia. The sisters' connection remained strong throughout the decades. Barrier Williams traveled to Washington so often that she continued to be listed in the city directory long after she had left in 1887. Ella in turn traveled to Chicago, staying for long periods of time and engaging in club activities. She was a regular at Phyllis Wheatley Club meetings, where she often reported on her work in the development of the YWCA.[3] The pair also vacationed together, as they did in 1911 when they visited Toronto.[4]

Of course Barrier Williams's achievements eclipsed Ella's on the national stage. There were numerous accolades. *The Broad Ax* noted that she was "doubtless one of our ablest women, and although modest and unassuming she has made a host of friends and acquaintances of the people who enjoy the larger life, and who engage in the larger activities." She was "a forcible speaker, with a trenchant pen" who was revered for her oratory and writing skills. Others championed her reform work. For example, a group of black women in the coal-mining town of Buxton, Iowa, established the Fannie Barrier Williams Club sometime before 1911 to demonstrate their reform activism, tie themselves to the national black club women's movement, and honor Barrier Williams.[5]

She was also praised by the Brockport community. The local newspaper often highlighted her visits to the village and reported on her activities. Local women's groups celebrated and honored her success in the reform movement by inviting her to speak to their constituents. In July 1898 she spoke to a small gathering of women at a local residence. That presentation was a precursor to a much larger event sponsored by the Woman's Christian Temperance Union at First Baptist Church. At a cost of ten cents per ticket, the audience listened to Barrier Williams discuss her "very practical" views on women's activism.[6]

By the time Barrier Williams returned to Brockport nearly three decades later, she led a much quieter life. One of the few reports about her appeared in *The Brockport Republic* in 1932, which noted that she was "very ill."[7] She seems to have recovered from that illness, but declining health probably played a central role in her decision to craft her last will and testament five years later. She bequeathed her possessions to the people she genuinely cared for and respected and the organizations and institutions in the two regions of the country where she felt most comfortable and where people had embraced her and her activism. Ella was to receive all assets unless she died first. Then her estate and proceeds were to be divided among a number of people and entities including the Phyllis Wheatley Home of Chicago and Brockport institutions such as First Baptist Church and the public library. The artistic craft she had fought so hard to attain and had developed into a profitable and rewarding career remained dear to her. To ensure that it continued to be part of her legacy, she willed her "hand painted oil paintings" to her niece Harriet Barrier.[8]

Barrier Williams died seven years after she made her will, on March 4, 1944, at the age of eighty-nine. She was buried alongside her parents in the village cemetery.[9] She had been such an iconic figure that newspapers across the country paid tribute. *The Brockport Republic* was one of the first to report on her demise. The detailed obituary recognized the regional context of her life while also emphasizing her permanence as a villager. She had been "born in Brockport," the paper noted, and even "after residing in other parts of the country returned here in 1926." The notice recounted that her father had owned a barbershop and that she had been highly educated. She had taught school, had been a member of a number of organizations, had been a lecturer, and had actively engaged in "social service work." Had it not been for the bold headline "Negro Leader Dies at Local Residence" and the mention that her husband S. Laing was "the first Negro admitted to the Chicago Bar Association," the obituary might well have been that of a prominent white citizen.[10]

While the local newspaper emphasized her class-based accomplishments and her connection to the village, the national press emphasized her race status and her ties to the black community. The *New York Times* noted that she was an "89 year-old Negro, who devoted a lifetime to furthering the lot of her race." The *Chicago Daily Tribune* commented that she was "a Negro woman leader in Chicago for many years" and called attention to the fact that she was "the first and only Negro member of the Chicago Woman's club" and "the first Negro to be appointed to the Chicago public library board."[11]

Only the *Chicago Defender* remembered her as "a figure of national prominence." Editor Lucius C. Harper argued that her "Death Tells a Story of Early Chicago Prejudice." His front-page tribute described in detail Barrier Williams's triumphant admission to the CWC because "ordinarily, the white press pays scant attention to the passing of a respected colored person, unless there is some very unusual angle attached to his or her career." And, indeed, "it was over her that the race issue among the most aristocratic women of Chicago was waged back in 1894." Centering her in the struggle against discrimination, he recounted the hostility and difficulties she had faced and the gratifying triumph of victory when she was admitted.

> Certain it is that no more interesting contribution to the literature of the color question in this country can be found than that growing out of this discussion whose main actor rang the curtain on its final chapter when she passed into dreamless sleep this week in the little village of Brockport, her childhood home. So ends the story of the battle of prejudice and discrimination among the wealthy, intellectual

and cultured of Chicago exactly 50 years ago—1894 to 1944—and we wonder if the mental status is any better among this same class after a lapse of a half century.[12]

Barrier Williams was as much a symbol of privilege, resilience, and defiance during the budding years of the modern-day civil rights movement as she had been in the late nineteenth century during the nadir of race relations. Her struggle was also a reminder of how racism and discrimination had steadily evolved and become an entrenched institutionalized system a half-century later.

By the late twentieth century, few people knew who Barrier Williams was. She became a victim of history, a casualty of a gendered narrative that marginalized women, and a martyr to history's penchant for celebrating heroic figures who waged public, aggressive, and often protracted battles against individuals, institutions, and government. When Carter G. Woodson wrote his essay "Honor to Booker T. Washington" three years after Barrier Williams died, the only woman he mentioned was Ida B. Wells-Barnett. Woodson's lists of Washington supporters did not include a single woman, although Barrier Williams's fellow Chicago resident George Cleveland Hall appeared.[13] Even when Barrier Williams was rediscovered by scholars of women's and African American history and was embraced by the Unitarians as one of their strong advocates, she remained part of a supporting cast of reformers and club women rather than the iconic celebrity, noteworthy intellectual, and labor activist that she was.

Barrier Williams gained fame because she was smart and driven and developed and implemented a strategy that helped shape the reforms of the Progressive Era. She had the type of crossover appeal that resonated nationally and reached into both black and white communities and organizations. She was a privileged northern-born mixed-raced educated woman who was one of the most socially, politically, and economically engaged women of the late nineteenth and early twentieth centuries. Although neither a light complexion nor a life in the Midwest could release her from the tentacles of Jim Crow, she refused to bow to its relentless onslaught. She used her pen, her oratory, and her own class ideals to challenge white racism and seek solutions for the black community. Brockport, a place that was both her home and a representation of who she became, rewarded her fortitude, made her a symbol of the village, and erected a historical marker in front of her home on Erie Street.

Notes

Introduction

1. "Cupid's Captives: A Fashionable Colored Wedding," *National Republican* (Washington, D.C.), April 29, 1881, 4; Grimké, *The Journals of Charlotte Forten Grimké*; Woodson, "The Wormley Family," 75; Preston, "William Syphax," 448–476. See also Gatewood, *Aristocrats of Color*; and Moore, *Leading the Race*. The compromise between Democrats and Republicans that officially ended congressional Reconstruction occurred at a meeting at the Wormley Hotel.

2. "People Talked About," *The Morning Call* (San Francisco), December 7, 1894, 6.

3. Williams, "A Northern Negro's Autobiography," 92.

4. See Deegan, *The Collected Writings of Fannie Barrier Williams*, for a compilation of many of her essays.

5. "The Negro Business League: A Fine Gathering," *Richmond Planet* (Richmond, Va.), August 30, 1902, 1; "The Voice of the Negro," *The Appeal* (St. Paul, Minn.), March 4, 1905, 3.

6. "Women in Politics," *The Woman's Era*, November 1894, 13; "In Honor of Mrs. E. C. Stanton," *New York Times*, November 12, 1895.

7. See Fortune, "Industrial Education: Will It Solve the Negro Problem?," 13; and advertisement for the new monthly magazine *Voice of the Negro* in *The Appeal* (St. Paul, Minn.), August 5, 1905, 3.

8. Williams, "Club Movement among Negro Women," 197–232.

9. See, for example, Williams, "A Northern Negro's Autobiography," 94; "Color Line in a Club," *Chicago Daily Tribune*, November 14, 1894, 2; "Primed for a Tilt," *Chicago Daily Tribune*, May 21, 1895, 8; A Colored Woman Wins," *San Francisco Chronicle*, January 24, 1896, 2; No title, *Globe-Republican* (Dodge City, Kans.), January 30, 1896, 6; "Our Daily Mail," *Daily Public Ledger* (Maysville, Ky.), January 20, 1896, 4; "Frederick Douglass Center," *Chicago Defender*, June 27, 1914, 5.

10. Anderson, *The Education of Blacks in the South*, 80.

Chapter 1. North of Slavery: Brockport

1. "Lynch Law and Riot in Ohio," 580, 586.

2. Williams, "A Northern Negro's Autobiography," 91; "The Race Problem—An Autobiography," *The Independent* (March 17, 1904): 586–589; "Experiences of the Race Problem," 590–594; "Observations of the Southern Race Feeling," 594–599.

3. Williams, "A Northern Negro's Autobiography," 91.

4. Ibid.

5. Ibid.

6. United States Department of State, "Aggregate Amount of Each Description of Persons within the Northern District of New York—Continued," in *Fifth Census; or Enumeration of the Inhabitants of the United States*, 40.

7. Ibid., 40–41.

8. Tuttle, *The Village of Brockport*, 1–2; Martin, *The Story of Brockport for One-Hundred Years*, 4–8; Bush, *Hiel Brockway*, 22–25; William Andrews, "Black Families Prospered in Early Centuries," *The Brockport Post*, February 19, 1998, newspaper clipping, Eunice Chestnut File Collection, Western Monroe Historical Society, Brockport, New York.

9. See Walker, *The Statistics of the Population of the United States . . . Compiled from the Original Returns of the Ninth Census (June 1, 1870)*, 51–52; Tuttle, *The Village of Brockport*, 1–2; Martin, *The Story of Brockport for One-Hundred Years*, 4–8; Andrews, "Black Families Prospered in Early Centuries."

10. For a discussion of the development of the region and the changes the building of the canal brought, see Johnson, *A Shopkeeper's Millennium*; and Dedman, *Cherishing This Heritage*. By 1830 a school had opened in the nearby town of Clarkson. Seven years later it had a mixed-gender student body of 127.

11. Williams, "A Northern Negro's Autobiography," 91; Edward C. Lehman, "The Barrier Family," unpublished essay, Eunice Chestnut File Collection; Fannie Barrier Williams (1855–1944), Eunice Chestnut File Collection. Anthony Barrier's birth year is listed on his cemetery headstone as 1824. In the 1850 census he is listed as twenty-four years old, giving him a birth year of 1826. This agrees with the 1880 census record, which also lists his birth year as 1826. See Anthony J. Barrier, in Schedule I: Free Inhabitants of Town of Sweden, Monroe County, New York, 89, federal manuscript census for 1850; Anthony J. Barrier, in Schedule 1: Inhabitants of Brockport, Sweden, Monroe County, New York, 28, federal manuscript census for 1880, both available at Ancestry.com.

12. United States Department of State, "Aggregate Amount of Each Description of Persons within the Northern District of New York—Continued," in *Fifth Census; or Enumeration of the Inhabitants of the United States*, 40–41; United States, Census Office, Department of State, "Aggregate Amount of Each Description of Persons within the Northern District of New York," in *Sixth Census or Enumeration of the Inhabitants of the United States as Corrected at the Department of State in 1840*, 94.

13. Dedman, *Cherishing This Heritage*, 6–9; Tuttle, *The Village of Brockport*, 1–3; United States Bureau of the Census, "Population by Subdivision of Counties," in *The Seventh Census of the United States: 1850*, 101. In 1850 the village continued to cling to its separate identity, although the census subsumed it under the larger town of Sweden. The 1840 census is the last one in which the village was treated as a separate entity.

14. United States, Census Office, "Aggregate Amount of Each Description of Persons within the Northern District of New York," in *Sixth Census or Enumeration of the Inhabitants of the United States as Corrected at the Department of State in 1840*, 94–95. See also Dedman, *Cherishing This Heritage*, 6.

15. Smith and Husted, *We Remember Brockport*, 30–32.

16. *Brockport State Normal School Semicentennial* (Brockport, New York: 1917), 22, RG 30/4, SUNY Brockport College Archives; Dedman, *Cherishing This Heritage*, 12–13; *History of Monroe County*, 160; Cross, *The Burned-Over District*, 93–98.

17. *Brockport State Normal School Semicentennial*, 22; Dedman, *Cherishing This Heritage*, 12–13; *History of Monroe County*, 160.

18. Martin, *The Story of Brockport for One-Hundred Years*, 28–29; *Brockport State Normal School Semicentennial*, 22; Dedman, *Cherishing This Heritage*, 12–13; *History of Monroe County*, 160; Somerville, "Homesick in Upstate New York," 181–182.

19. United States, Census Office, "Aggregate Amount of Each Description of Persons within the Northern District of New York," in *Sixth Census or Enumeration of the Inhabitants of the United States as Corrected at the Department of State in 1840*, 94–95.

20. *History of Monroe County*, 34, 158–160; Bush, *Hiel Brockway*, 22–25; United States, Bureau of the Census, "Professions, Occupations, and Trades of the Male Population," in *The Seventh Census of the United States: 1850*, 119.

21. William Andrews, "Village's Early Blacks Ruled Barber Trade," *The Brockport Post*, February 12, 1998; Smith and Husted, *We Remember Brockport*, 31; Anthony J. Barrier, in Schedule I: Free Inhabitants of Town of Sweden, Monroe County, New York, 89, federal manuscript census for 1850, available at Ancestry.com.

22. Bristol, "From Outposts to Enclaves," 10–11, 102–105; William Andrews, "Brockport Family Was Influential on Race Issues," *The Brockport Post*, February 26, 1998; "Business Cards," *The Brockport Republic*, July 7, 1859; Smith and Husted, *We Remember Brockport*, 31.

23. Williams, "A Northern Negro's Autobiography," 91.

24. "Population by Subdivisions of Counties," *The Seventh Census of the United States: 1850*, 101.

25. Wellman, "Crossing Over Cross," 159. See also Cross, *The Burned-Over District*; and Sernett, *North Star Country*, particularly chapters 1 and 2.

26. Painter, *Sojourner Truth*, 26, 31 42; Washington, *Sojourner Truth's America*, 84–86.

27. Johnson, *A Shopkeeper's Millennium*, 95; Hewitt, *Women's Activism and Social Change*, 74–76; Stowe, *Charles G. Finney and the Spirit of American Evangelicalism*; Cross, *The Burned-Over District*, 151–156.

28. Johnson, *A Shopkeeper's Millennium*, 95; Stowe, *Charles G. Finney and the Spirit of American Evangelicalism*; Cross, *The Burned-Over District*, 151–156.

29. Cross, *The Burned-Over District*, 3.

30. *History of Monroe County*, 161–163; Andrews, *Images of America around Brockport*, 90–94. Brockport public life followed a similar path as that of Rochester, particularly in the development of missionary societies, Bible study classes, and antislavery societies. See Hewitt, *Women's Activism and Social Change*, 79–96.

31. The original First Baptist Church, which was established in 1828, dissolved and was resurrected in 1841 as Second Baptist Church. The name was changed back to First Baptist in 1879. See Williams, *Historical Sketch of the First Baptist Church*, 3 and 14–15.

32. Harris, *In the Shadow of Slavery*, 268. For a discussion of the limits to black freedom before 1840, see also chapters 4 through 6.

33. Gellman and Quigley, *Jim Crow New York*, 253.

34. Ibid., 255.

35. Ibid., 256.

36. Ibid., 258.

37. See Bay, *The White Image in the Black Mind*, 42–43.

38. Gellman and Quigley, *Jim Crow New York*, 251.

39. Ibid., 259; Sernett, *North Star Country*, 9.

40. McFeely, *Frederick Douglass*, 146–162; Sernett, *North Star Country*, 179–184.

41. "The Colored Convention," *The North Star*, December 3, 1847, 1. See also Harris, *In the Shadow of Slavery*.

42. *History of Monroe County*, 158.

43. There are discrepancies about when Harriet Prince was born and where her mother and father were born. The 1850 Census lists her age as eighteen, which suggests that she was born in 1832. The 1860 Census lists her age as twenty-seven, suggesting that she was born in 1833. The 1880 census lists her birth year as 1836 and the birthplace of her mother and father as Vermont. The record of her death lists her birth year as 1835, Philantha Macy's birthplace as Connecticut, and Noah Prince's birthplace as Chenango, New York. Harriet Prince: Schedule I: Free Inhabitants of Town of Sweden, Monroe County, New York, 89, federal manuscript census for 1850; Harriet Prince, Schedule 1: Free Inhabitants of Sweden, Monroe County, New York, 91, federal manuscript census for 1860; Harriet Prince, Schedule 1: Inhabitants of Brockport, Town of Sweden, Monroe County, New York, 28, federal manuscript census for 1880, all available at Ancestry.com; see also Records of Deaths, County of Monroe Office of Vital Records, Rochester, New York. Noah Prince: Schedule of the Whole Number of Persons within the Division Allotted by the Marshall of the District, Elmira, Chemung County, New York, federal manuscript census for 1830; Schedule I: Free Inhabitants of Town of Sherburne, Chenango County, New York, federal manuscript census for 1850; Schedule I: Inhabitants of Sherburne, Chenango County, New York, federal manuscript census for 1870, all available at Ancestry.com. Harriet Prince Barrier: Schedule1: Inhabitants of Town of Sweden, Monroe County, New York, 103, federal manuscript census for 1870, available at Ancestry.com. For the education of Fannie Barrier's parents, see Williams, "A Northern Negro's Autobiography," 91.

44. "Married," *The North Star*, April 20, 1949, 3.

45. Williams, *Historical Sketch of the First Baptist Church*, 7.

46. See the newspaper article "Respected by His Race" (January 29, 1907) in the Miscellaneous File of William Andrews, Historian Emeritus, Brockport, New York. The names of Ella and Fannie have been recorded in several different ways; Ella is often listed as Ellen and Fannie is often listed as Fanny or Frances. But Fannie Barrier Williams always signed her name with the spelling "Fannie." The birth years of Ella, George, and Fannie have also been difficult to ascertain. The 1850 census, which was

taken in August, lists George as two and a half years old, which would make his birth year sometime in 1847. But the 1860 census, which was taken in June, lists George's age as eleven, suggesting that he was born in 1849. In the 1860 census, Ella (who is called Ellen) as recorded as age nine, suggesting that she was born in 1851, and Fannie is recorded as age six, suggesting that she was born in 1854. But the 1870 census lists George's age as twenty, suggesting that he was born in 1850; Ella's age as eighteen, suggesting that she was born in 1852; and Fannie's age as sixteen, suggesting that she was born in 1854. Fannie's gravesite headstone, however, states that she was born in 1855. Harriet Prince: Schedule I: Free Inhabitants of Town of Sweden, Monroe County, New York, 89, federal manuscript census for 1850; Schedule 1: Free Inhabitants of Sweden, Monroe County, New York, 91, federal manuscript census for 1860, both available at Ancestry.com. See also Harriet Prince Barrier, Schedule 1: Inhabitants of Town of Sweden, Monroe County, New York, 103, federal manuscript census for 1870, available at Ancestry.com.

47. Williams, *Historical Sketch of the First Baptist Church*, 12; Index of Deeds, Liber 88, 495, Monroe County Clerk's Office. The Index of Deeds also records a transaction by "Anthony A. Barrier of Brockport in the County of Monroe," who purchased $150 worth of property on Fayette Street in the village on September 2, 1844; Liber 66, 89. It is unclear who this was, since Anthony J. Barrier did not list any real estate holdings in the 1850 federal census. In all other property transactions, he is listed as Anthony J. Barrier, not Anthony A. Barrier. I am assuming that they are not the same person.

48. Index of Deeds, Liber 103, 257, Monroe County Clerk's Office; *Catalogue of the Officers and Students of the Brockport Collegiate Institute, Brockport, N.Y., for the Year Ending June 30, 1865* (Rochester: Benton & Andrews, Printers, 1865), Catalogs and Circulars, Brockport Collegiate Institute, 1842–1866, RG 11/9/2, SUNY Brockport College Archives, Drake Memorial Library, Brockport, New York.

49. Index of Deeds, Liber 232, 105, Monroe County Clerk's Office; Anthony J. Barrier, in Schedule 1: Inhabitants of the Town of Sweden, Monroe County, New York, 91, federal manuscript census for 1860, available at Ancestry.com; *History of Monroe County*, 160.

50. Williams, "A Northern Negro's Autobiography," 91.

51. Ibid.

52. "The Brockport Fire," *Rochester Daily Democrat*, February 8, 1853, 2. For evidence of Anthony's business later in the decade, see "Business Cards," *The Brockport Republic*, July 7, 1859, 1.

53. Philantha Prince, in Schedule 1: Free Inhabitants of Sherburne, in the County of Chenango, New York, 87, federal manuscript census for 1860; Schedule 1: Free Inhabitants of Sherburne, in the County of Chenango, New York, 103, federal manuscript census for 1870, both available at Ancestry.com. See also Philantha Prince, in Schedule 1: Free Inhabitants of Sherburne, in the County of Chenango, New York, 15, federal manuscript census for 1850, where a fourteen-year-old girl with a similar name is listed in the Prince household.

54. Williams, "A Northern Negro's Autobiography," 91; Williams, *Historical Sketch of the First Baptist Church*, 24.

55. Williams, "A Northern Negro's Autobiography," 91.

56. Williams, *Historical Sketch of the First Baptist Church*, 26–27.

57. Williams, "A Northern Negro's Autobiography, 91.

58. Index of Deeds, Liber 232, 105, Monroe County Clerk's Office.

59. See Index of Deeds 1876, Liber 296, 342; and Index of Deeds 1882, Liber 360, 52, both at Monroe County Clerk's Office.

60. See Second Baptist Church Minutes, April 18, 1864, January 6, 1868, January 3, 1870, First Baptist Church Records, Brockport, New York; Williams, *Historical Sketch of the First Baptist Church*, 9; Martin, *The Story of Brockport for One-Hundred Years, 1829–1929*, 9, 21.

61. Williams, *Historical Sketch of the First Baptist Church*, 4, 26.

62. Second Baptist Church Minutes, April 18, 1864, April 15, 1867, January 6, 1868, and January 3, 1870, First Baptist Church Records, Brockport, New York; Williams, *Historical Sketch of the First Baptist Church*, 4.

63. Second Baptist Church Minutes, January 6, 1872, First Baptist Church Records, Brockport, New York.

64. "Douglass Lecture," *The Brockport Republic*, January 2, 1857, 1; Washington, *Frederick Douglass*, 159–161.

65. "Douglass Lecture."

66. Williams, "A Northern Negro's Autobiography," 91.

67. Dedman, *Cherishing This Heritage*, 61–62.

68. *Brockport History Articles: Brockport Republic Supplement, Brockport History* (Brockport, N.Y.: Brockport Republic, 1913), collection of newspaper clippings, Drake Memorial Library, State University of New York, Brockport, New York.

69. See Buckler, *Daniel Hale Williams*, 71; Sernett, *North Star Country*, 260.

70. Another prominent African American who lived in Brockport was William L. Page. He arrived after the Civil War and in many ways highlights the continuation of black success in the village. Born in 1834 in Key West, Florida, Page escaped the limitations of black life in the South by the using the Underground Railroad. According to one account, he lived with a Quaker family in a town near Rochester, was educated in the local public schools, and attended the University of Rochester. In 1867, shortly after he arrived in Brockport, he purchased a piece of property for $800 on which he built a permanent residence on Gordon Street. He married Katherine Burns and the couple had three children, two girls and a boy. For a short time in the 1870s, Anthony Barrier and William Page operated a coal business in the village. (Anthony's obituary in *The Brockport Republic* states that the business lasted only one to two years; "Mortuary," *The Brockport Republic*, August 28, 1890.) See Emily L. Knapp, "Personalities: Glimpses of a Few People Who Once Called Brockport Home," unpublished paper, Miscellaneous File of William G. Andrews, January 14, 1988; Martin, *The Story of Brockport for One-Hundred Years*, 21, 38–39.

71. *Catalogue of the Officers and Students of the Brockport Collegiate Institute, Brockport, N.Y., for the Year Ending July 1st, 1864*, 21–22, 24, 26, 33.

72. Ibid., 29–30, 33; "Register of the Collegiate Institute, Fall 1864–Spring 1866," 1, Material Relating to the Collegiate Institute, RG 30/1, SUNY Brockport College Archives; Dedman, *Cherishing This Heritage*, 34.

73. See for example Ada J. McVicar, James H. McVicar, Emma Rich, and Oscar Parker in Schedule 1—Free Inhabitants in the town of Sweden in the Country of Monroe,

manuscript census for 1860, Ancestry.com; *Catalogue of the Officers and Students of the Brockport Collegiate Institute, Brockport, N.Y., for the Year Ending July 1st, 1864.*

74. These included principal Malcolm McVicar, associate principal Oliver Morehouse, and Albert W. Morehouse, a teacher in preparatory studies. *Catalogue of the Officers and Students of the Brockport Collegiate Institute, Brockport, N.Y., for the Year Ending July 1st, 1864,* 3, 5. See also Williams, *Historical Sketch of the First Baptist Church,* 7, 25; and Dedman, *Cherishing This Heritage,* 18–19.

75. *Catalogue of the Officers and Students of the Brockport Collegiate Institute, Brockport, N.Y., for the Year Ending July 1st, 1864,* 29–30.

76. Ibid., 29–30, 33; Dedman, *Cherishing This Heritage,* 34.

77. Field, *The Politics of Race in New York,* 34; Litwack, *North of Slavery,* 132–137.

78. "The Colored Convention."

79. Litwack, *North of Slavery,* 136.

80. See Strane, *A Whole-Souled Woman.*

81. *Brockport State Normal School Semicentennial;* "Dr. McVicar Talks," *Richmond Planet* (Richmond, Virginia), May 22, 1897.

82. *Catalogue of the Officers and Students of the Brockport Collegiate Institute, Brockport, N.Y., for the Year Ending July 1st, 1864,* 5, 22, 24, 26, 29–30, 33; "Register of the Collegiate Institute, Fall 1864–Spring 1866," 1; Dedman, *Cherishing This Heritage,* 34.

83. *Catalogue of the Officers and Students of the Brockport Collegiate Institute, Brockport, N.Y., for the Year Ending July 1st, 1864,* 24.

84. "Register of the Collegiate Institute, Fall 1864–Spring 1866."

85. *Catalogue of the Officers and Students of the Brockport Collegiate Institute, Brockport, N.Y., for the Year Ending July 1st, 1864,* 21–22, 24, 30, 33; "Register of the Collegiate Institute, Fall 1864–Spring 1866."

86. *Catalogue of the Officers and Students of the Brockport Collegiate Institute, Brockport, N.Y., for the Year Ending July 1st, 1864,* 22, 24, 26.

87. "Register of the Collegiate Institute, Fall 1864–Spring 1866."

88. *Catalogue of the Officers and Students of the Brockport Collegiate Institute, Brockport, N.Y., for the Year Ending July 1st, 1864,* 28.

89. Ibid., 29–30, 33.

90. Ibid., 29.

91. Ibid., 31–32.

92. *Brockport Collegiate Institute,* undated pamphlet showing course of study, Catalogs and Circulars, Brockport Collegiate Institute, 1842–1866, RG 11/9/2, SUNY Brockport College Archives; Dedman, *Cherishing This Heritage,* 18–19, 39, 44, 68–69.

93. Dedman, *Cherishing This Heritage,* 68–90.

94. "State Normal and Training School, Brockport, N.Y.," 1868 flyer, Catalogs and Circulars, Brockport Collegiate Institute, 1842–1866, RG 11/9/2, SUNY Brockport College Archives; *Catalogue of the Officers and Students of the Brockport Collegiate Institute, Brockport, N.Y., for the Year Ending July 1st, 1864,* 25–26.

95. "State Normal and Training School, Brockport, N.Y."

96. Brockport Collegiate Institute Academic Department, "Report of the Spring Term Commencing February 5, 1868 and ending June 23, 1868"; and "Report of the Spring

Term Commencing February 16, 1870 and ending July 1, 1870," both in RG 30/1, Material Relating to the Collegiate Institute, SUNY Brockport College Archives.

97. "Closing Exercises of the Brockport State Normal School," *The Brockport Republic*, June 25, 1868, 3; "Register of the Collegiate Institute, Fall 1864–Spring 1866"; "State Normal and Training School, Brockport, N.Y."; *Brockport State Normal School Semicentennial*, 38. Both Ella and George re-enrolled at some point. Ella graduated in 1871 under the Elementary English program, and George was a student during the 1870–1871 school year. But unlike Fannie and Ella, George does not appear to have graduated from the school.

98. "Register of the Collegiate Institute, Fall 1864–Spring 1866"; "State Normal and Training School, Brockport, N.Y."

99. "Register of the Collegiate Institute, Fall 1864–Spring 1866"; "Register of the Collegiate Institute, February 16, 1870–July 1, 1870," RG 30/1, SUNY Brockport College Archives; "State Normal and Training School at Brockport, N.Y."; *Brockport State Normal School Semicentennial*, 38; "Graduating Exercises," *The Brockport Republic*, July 7, 1870, 3.

100. "State Normal and Training School, Brockport, N.Y." 17–23.

101. *Brockport State Normal School Semicentennial*, 37–38; "Graduating Exercises."

102. Williams, "A Northern Negro's Autobiography," 91.

103. *Brockport State Normal School Semicentennial*, 37–38; Williams, "A Northern Negro's Autobiography," 91.

Chapter 2. *"Completely Surrounded by Screens": A Raced Identity*

1. Greene, Kremer, and Holland, *Missouri's Black Heritage*, 27–28, 88–103.

2. Ibid., 91–93; Powers, "The Development of Public Education in Hannibal, Missouri," 21–23. For a history of redemption in southern states, see McMillen, *Dark Journey*, 3–5; Ayers, *The Promise of the New South*, 8; and Tindall, *South Carolina Negroes*, 7–14.

3. Greene, Kremer, and Holland, *Missouri's Black Heritage*, 99–102, 107; Holcombe, *History of Marion County, Missouri*, 984. For discussions of the development of the school system for blacks in Hannibal and the Douglass School, see Powers, "The Development of Public Education in Hannibal, Missouri," 15–19, 26–30; and Hagood and Hagood, *Hannibal Yesterdays*, 73–74. Sources also refer to the school as both the Douglas School and the Douglasville School.

4. Powers, "The Development of Public Education in Hannibal, Missouri," 19, 30; Hagood and Hagood, *Hannibal Yesterdays*, 74–75; Hagood and Hagood, *The Story of Hannibal*, 69. Pelham first hired black schoolteachers in 1874; they were Ella Gordon and Jenny Golden. The next year, according to Hagood and Hagood, he hired Barrier and Marry Hubbard. But according to Powers, Barrier replaced Hubbard, who vacated the position. I am assuming that the woman Hagood and Hagood's list refers to as "Fannie Benier" is Fannie Barrier. See "Partial List of Douglass Teachers 1874–1959," in Hagood and Hagood, *Hannibal Yesterdays*, 80. For George Barrier's marriage, see "Married," *The Brockport Republic*, May 28, 1874, 2.

5. Powers, "The Development of Public Education in Hannibal, Missouri," 17–19, 29–30; Hagood and Hagood, *Hannibal Yesterdays*, 73.

6. Williams, "A Northern Negro's Autobiography," 91.

7. Ibid.

8. Ibid.

9. Ibid., 91–92.

10. Fannie A. Barrier to Frederick Douglass, March 19, 1877, Box 28–5, Folder 105, Frederick Douglass Papers, Frederick Douglass Collection, Moorland-Spingarn Research Center, Howard University, Washington, D.C.

11. *The Woman's Era*, February 1896, 13.

12. "Special Meeting," August 31, 1875, Minutes of the Board of Trustees, Public Schools of the District of Columbia, August 10, 1874, to July 8, 1879, 11, DC Public School Records, Charles Sumner School Museum & Archives, Washington, DC (hereafter DC Public School Records); *Brockport State Normal School Semicentennial*; *The Brockport Republic*, September 9, 1875, 3.

13. Gatewood, *Aristocrats of Color*, 38; Moore, *Leading the Race*, 9.

14. Gatewood, *Aristocrats of Color*, 38–39, 276; Moore, *Leading the Race*, 11, 14.

15. See Rhodes, *Mary Ann Shadd Cary*; Bearden and Butler, *Shadd*; "Teachers Assignment: 'One by One the Roses Fall,'" *The Washington Bee*, September 20, 1884, 2.

16. For a history of Greener's life, see Mounter, "Richard Theodore Greener." See also Weiss, "An African American Teacher in Washington, D.C.," 194.

17. See Stevenson, *The Journals of Charlotte Forten Grimké*.

18. Ibid., 51–55.

19. See Gatewood, *Aristocrats of Color*, chapters 6, 7 and 8; and Moore, *Leading the Race*, chapter 1.

20. "Literary Societies of Our People," *The People's Advocate*, July 5, 1879, 2.

21. "Monday Night Club," *The Evening Critic* (Washington, D. C.), November 28, 1882; "The Monday Night Literary Club," *The People's Advocate*, November 24, 1883, 3; "A Testimonial to Rev. Dr. Grimke," *The Evening Star* (Washington, D.C.), October 27, 1885.

22. "Monday Night Literary Society," *The Washington Bee*, June 2, 1883, 2.

23. Cromwell, *History of the Bethel Literary and Historical Association*, 3–4, 26.

24. See "Local," *The Washington Bee*, December 23, 1882, 3.

25. Cromwell, *History of the Bethel Literary and Historical Association*, 3–4.

26. Ibid., 3–11, 26.

27. Ibid., 18.

28. "Bethel Literary," *The People's Advocate*, February 2, 1884, 3.

29. "Bethel Literary," *The People's Advocate*, March 29, 1884, 3.

30. Cromwell, *History of the Bethel Literary and Historical Association*, 22.

31. Moore, *Leading the Race*, 16; Gatewood, *Aristocrats of Color*, 290.

32. See, for example, the interview in "Cultured Negro Ladies," *Chicago Tribune*, October 28, 1888, 26. For a discussion of clubwomen's views of emotionalism and black ministers, see White, *Too Heavy a Load*, 72–73.

33. Moore, *Leading the Race*, 16; Gatewood, *Aristocrats of Color*, 33, 290.

34. "Interesting Exercises," *The Evening Critic* (Washington, D.C.), January 8, 1883; Moore, *Leading the Race*, 73; Gatewood, *Aristocrats of Color*, 296.

35. "Receptions New Year's Day," *The People's Advocate*, January 10, 1880, 3; Gatewood, *Aristocrats of Color*, 118–119.

36. "Receptions New Year's Day."

37. Ibid.

38. "Washington Dots," *The People's Advocate*, August 26, 1876, 3; "Local," *The People's Advocate*, June 28, 1879, 3; "Summer Notes," *The People's Advocate*, July 17, 1880, 3; "Personals," *The Washington Bee*, June 24, 1882, 3.

39. Moore, *Leading the Race*, 26.

40. Quoted in ibid., 27.

41. Ibid., 24; Gatewood, *Aristocrats of Color*, 39. While the hotel catered to black elites, it also provided accommodations for white guests.

42. Green, *The Secret City*, 134–136; Moore, *Leading the Race*, 86–87.

43. "Regular Meeting," October 9, 1877, Minutes of the Board of Trustees, Public Schools of the District of Columbia, August 10, 1874, to July 8, 1879, 35, DC Public School Records; Green, *The Secret City*, 134–135.

44. Moore, *Leading the Race*, 87.

45. Weiss, "An African American Teacher in Washington, D.C.," 193–198; "Our Public Schools," *The Washington Bee*, October 4, 1884, 2; *Official Register of the United States Containing a List of Officers and Employees in the Civil, Military, and Naval Service*, 1:667.

46. "Regular Meeting," October 9, 1877, Minutes of the Board of Trustees, Public Schools of the District of Columbia, 35.

47. "Regular Meeting," November 11, 1879, Minutes of the Board of Trustees, Public Schools of the District of Columbia, August 12, 1879, to June 24, 1884, 45–46, DC Public School Records. For descriptions of teachers, see "Our Public Schools," *The Washington Bee*, October 4, 1884, 2. For the role of the Miner school in supplying teachers, see Moore, *Leading the Race*, 22.

48. "Regular Meeting," November 13, 1877, Minutes of the Board of Trustees, Public Schools of the District of Columbia, August 10, 1874, to July 8, 1879, 39–40, DC Public School Records.

49. *Official Register of the United States Containing a List of Officers and Employees in the Civil, Military, and Naval Service*, 1:667; "Regular Meeting," October 9, 1877, Minutes of the Board of Trustees, Public Schools of the District of Columbia, August 10, 1874, to July 8, 1879, 1877, 37, DC Public School Records. Barrier and Ella boarded with Henry S. Tilghman, a caterer; his wife, Margaret, who did not work outside the home; and their two daughters, Jerusha and Amelia. See Ella Barrier, in Schedule 1: Inhabitants in Washington, Washington County, District of Columbia, 32, federal manuscript census for 1880, available at Ancestry.com.

50. Weiss, "An African American Teacher in Washington, D.C.," 201–203; "Regular Meeting," October 9, 1877, Minutes of the Board of Trustees, Public Schools of the District of Columbia, 37; and "Regular Meeting," November 13, 1877, 43, DC Public School Records.

51. "Regular Meeting," June 24, 1879, Minutes of the Board of Trustees, Public Schools of the District of Columbia, August 10,1874, to July 8, 1879, 92; "Regular Meeting," June 29, 1880, Minutes of the Board of Trustees of Public Schools of the District of Columbia, August 12, 1879, to June 24, 1884, 95; "Regular Meeting," August 8, 1882, Minutes of the Board of Trustees, Public Schools of the District of Columbia, August 10,1874, to July 8, 1879, 17; "Regular Meeting," June 30, 1885, Minutes of the Board of Trustees of Public

Schools of the District of Columbia, August 12, 1884, to June 11, 1889, 119; July 13, 1886, Minutes of the Board of Trustees of Public Schools of the District of Columbia, August 12, 1884, to June 11, 1889, 15, all in DC Public School Records.

52. "Regular Meeting," August 8, 1882, Minutes of the Board of Trustees, Public Schools of the District of Columbia, August 12, 1879 to June 24, 1884, 17, DC Public School Records.

53. "Our Public Schools," *The Washington Bee*, October 25, 1884, 2.

54. Ibid.

55. See "Our Public Schools," *The Washington Bee*, September 20, 1884, 2; and "Our Public Schools," *The Washington Bee*, October 4, 1884, 2.

56. "Our Public Schools," *The Washington Bee*, October 4, 1884, 2.

57. Marsh, "Washington's First Art Academy," 23–25, 53–55.

58. "The Industrial Exhibition," *The Washington Bee*, October 23, 1886, 4. For Harriette Gibbs, the black graduate of Oberlin who opened a conservatory in Washington, D.C., see Woodson, "The Gibbs Family," 6; and Terrell, "The Washington Conservatory of Music for Colored People, and Its Teachers." Fannie Barrier apparently did not attend this conservatory.

59. Williams, "A Northern Negro's Autobiography," 92. It is unclear exactly where or when Barrier took the art class. She does not identify the city or state where she took the class or even the name of the art teacher. She does, however, clearly locate the ordeal she endured in the South. It is possible that the incident occurred in Hannibal, Missouri. Several sources report that Barrier attended a School of Fine Arts in Washington. To date, I have been unable to locate that school.

60. Williams, "A Northern Negro's Autobiography," 92.

61. Ibid.

62. "Our Public Schools," *The Washington Bee*, October 4, 1884, 2.

63. McPherson and Klein, *Measure by Measure*, 18, 20.

64. Ibid., 17, 37.

65. Academic Catalog, 1882–1883, 37–39, New England Conservatory of Music Archives, Spaulding Library, Boston, Massachusetts.

66. Student card for Fannie A. Barrier, 1884, New England Conservatory of Music Archives.

67. "Local News," *The Brockport Republic*, May 15, 1884, 3; "Local News," *The Brockport Republic*, August 28, 1884, 3.

68. Richardson, *The Death of Reconstruction*, 192.

69. Williams, "A Northern Negro's Autobiography," 92.

70. William Andrews, "Black Families Prospered in Early Centuries," *The Brockport Post*, February 19, 1998, Eunice Chesnut File, Morgan Manning House, Brockport, New York.

71. McFeely, *Frederick Douglass*, 310–323.

72. "Must We Intermarry?," *The People's Advocate*, February 9, 1884, 2.

73. Ibid.

74. Ibid.

75. "Some Opinions: What Our Contemporaries Think of the Douglass Marriage, Pro and Con," *The People's Advocate*, February 9, 1884, 2.

76. Ibid.

77. "Frederick Douglass and White Wife," *The Washington Bee*, June 13, 1885, 2.

78. See for example Fannie Barrier Williams to Frederick Douglass, January 14, 1893, Reel 6, Frederick Douglass Papers, Library of Congress (hereafter Frederick Douglass Papers).See also Barrier Williams's story about a mixed-raced woman engaged to be married to northern white man: Williams, "After Many Days: A Christmas Story."

79. There is some uncertainty about when S. Laing Williams was born. He is listed in the 1880 federal census as being twenty-five years old, which would mean that he was born in 1855. On the Necrology Report Blank for the University of Michigan at the Bentley Historical Library, Barrier Williams listed his birth year as 1857. Frank Mather listed his birth year as 1863; see Mather, *Who's Who of the Colored Race*, 1:286. In the manuscript census for 1870, he is listed as sixteen years old, suggesting that he was born in 1854. See S. Laing Williams in Schedule I: Free Inhabitants of Village of Columbiaville, Lapeer County, Michigan, 1, federal manuscript census for 1880, and in Schedule 1: Free Inhabitants of Fifth Ward, Chicago, Cook County, Illinois, 236, federal manuscript census for 1870, both available at Ancestry.com.

80. United States, Department of the Interior, Census Office, "Population, by Race and By Counties: 1880, 1870, 1860 Michigan," in *Statistics of the Population of the United States at the Tenth Census (June 1, 1880)*, 395.

81. Blue, *Footsteps into the Past*, 10–11, 54, 123; David Laing and household in Schedule 1: Inhabitants in Village of Columbiaville, in the County of Lapeer, State of Michigan, 1, federal manuscript census for 1880, available at Ancestry.com. There are discrepancies in the ages of David and Ann (which is sometimes spelled Anne). They are listed as sixty-two and sixty, respectively, in the 1870 federal manuscript census, but their ages were recorded as seventy-four and seventy-two, respectively, in the 1880 federal manuscript census.

82. Miscellaneous clipping, Necrology File, Office of Alumni Records, Bentley Historical Library, University of Michigan, Ann Arbor.

83. "The Colored Bar of Chicago," 391; Sisk, "Negro Education in the Alabama Black Belt, 1875–1900," 133; Samuel Williams, in Schedule 1: Inhabitants in Village of Columbiaville, in the County of Lapeer, State of Michigan, 1, federal manuscript census for 1880, available at Ancestry.com.

84. S. Laing Williams to Charles B. Sornborger, May 12, 1913, Applications and Endorsement, 1901–1933, General Records of the Department of Justice, RG 60, National Archives and Records Administration, Washington, D.C. See also *Catalogue of the Officers and Students of the Columbian University for the Academic Year 1883–84* (Washington, D.C.: Rufus H. Darby, 1884), 13, George Washington University Archives; Law School Commencement Program, June 3, 1884, Box 9, Folder 1884, George Washington University Archives; *The George Washington University Bulletin* 16, no 1 (March 1917): 178, George Washington University Archives; *The George Washington University Law Alumni Directory. 1866–1952*, 144, George Washington University Archives; "In and About the City," *Lapeer Democrat*, July 2, 1881; Untitled clipping, *Lapeer Democrat*, August 23, 1882; "Colored Bar of Chicago," 391; Gibson and Crogman, *The Colored American from Slavery to Honorable Citizenship*, 573. Thanks to Alton Hart of the Lapeer County Genealogical Society in Lapeer, Michigan, for the *Lapeer Democrat* clippings.

85. "Colored Bar of Chicago," 391; Gibson and Crogman, *The Colored American from Slavery to Honorable Citizenship*, 573.

86. "Chicago, Ill.," *The Cleveland Gazette*, July 17, 1886.

87. "Regular Meeting," April 12, 1887, Minutes of the Board of Trustees, Public Schools of the District of Columbia, August 12, 1884 to June 11, 1889, 89, DC Public School Records.

88. "Williams-Barrier," *The Brockport Republic*, April 21, 1887, 3; Williams, *Historical Sketch of the First Baptist Church, Brockport, New York*, 7.

89. "Williams-Barrier"; "Brockport," *The Union Advertiser* (Rochester, New York), April 22, 1887, 6.

90. "Williams-Barrier."

91. Williams, "A Northern Negro's Autobiography," 92.

92. Ibid.

93. "They Threatened to Leave the College," *Cleveland Gazette*, April 30, 1887.

94. "Williams-Barrier"; "Brockport."

Chapter 3. Creating Community in the Midwest: Chicago

1. "Knots & Tours: Matrimonial Linkings and Spring Migration of Prominent People," *Western Appeal* (St. Paul and Minneapolis, Minn.), April 23, 1887, 1; Spear, *Black Chicago*, 80; Reed, *"All the World Is Here!,"* 82.

2. See Drake and Cayton, *Black Metropolis*, 1:47–51, for a discussion of class stratification in Chicago's black community. The authors argue that before 1894 there were "three broad social groups," which they characterize as the "respectables," the "refined," and the "riffraff," or "sinners." Barrier Williams belonged to what Drake and Cayton call the "refined" group, which they characterize as "people, who, because of their education and breeding, could not sanction the less decorous behavior of their racial brothers." This group, I argue, was also divided between those who came before the Great Fire that destroyed much of Chicago in 1871 and those who arrived in the late 1870s and the decade of the 1880s.

3. United States, Department of the Interior, Bureau of the Census, "Population, by Race, of Cities and Towns, Etc.: 1880 and 1870, Illinois," and "Population, as Native and Foreign-Born, of Cities, Etc.: 1880 and 1870, Illinois," both in *Statistics of the Population of the United States at the Tenth Census (June 1, 1880)*, 417, 448, respectively.

4. Richard Junger, "'God and man helped those who helped themselves,'" 115–116, 121–123; Gosnell, *Negro Politicians*, 81–82; Fannie Barrier Williams: "Illinois: "A Word of Tribute to John Brown," *The Woman's Era*, December 1894, 15.

5. Junger, "'God and man helped those who helped themselves,'" 114–118; Gosnell, *Negro Politicians*, 81–82; Charles Branham, "Black Chicago," 219–221; Gatewood, *Aristocrats of Color*, 122.

6. Junger, "'God and man helped those who helped themselves,'" 114–118, 126–129; Branham, "Black Chicago," 219–223; Gatewood, *Aristocrats of Color*, 122.

7. Drake and Cayton, *Black Metropolis*, 50–51; Gosnell, *Negro Politicians*, 375.

8. Quoted in Reed, *"All the World Is Here!,"* 15.

9. Pierce, *A History of Chicago*, 3:20–21.

10. Ibid., 64–233.

11. Spear, *Black Chicago*, 12.

12. United States, Department of the Interior, Bureau of the Census, "Population, by Race, of Cities and Towns, Etc.: 1880 and 1870, Illinois"; and "Population, as Native and Foreign-Born, of Cities, Etc.: 1880 and 1870, Illinois." See also United States, Department of the Interior, Census Office, "Population by Sex, General Nativity, and Color, Of Places Having 2,560 Inhabitants or More: 1890," in *Report on Population of the Census of the United States at the Eleventh Census: 1890*, 454.

13. "The Garden City," *The Appeal*, December 28, 1889, 1; Spear, *Black Chicago*, 52–53.

14. Drake and Cayton, *Black Metropolis*, 51.

15. "Chicago," *Western Appeal*, February 11, 1888, 1. For a discussion of the black elite in the early twentieth century, see also Gaines, *Uplifting the Race*, chapter 3; and Gatewood, *Aristocrats of Color*.

16. For the "black 400," see *Chicago Daily News*, May 4, 1896, 4 in Reed, *"All the World Is Here!,"* 82.

17. Bradwell, "The Colored Bar of Chicago," 387; Giddings, *Ida: A Sword among Lions*, 345–345; Schechter, *Ida B. Wells-Barnett and American Reform*, 177; Gosnell, *Negro Politicians*, 85. Sources conflict about Ferdinand Barnett's biography. Some state that he was born in 1859 and that he attended the Chicago College of Law, now Northwestern University.

18. Bradwell, "The Colored Bar of Chicago," 387; Schechter, *Ida B. Wells-Barnett and American Reform*, 177; "Chicago," *Western Appeal*, February 11, 1888, 1; Giddings, *Ida: A Sword among Lions*, 346, 355–356. The Bradwell article places Mary Barnett's death in 1890, while Schechter places it in 1888.

19. Bradwell, "The Colored Bar of Chicago," 385–386; Buckler, *Daniel Hale Williams*, 26; Spear, *Black Chicago*, 66; "Chicago Colored People," *Chicago Daily Tribune*, May 4, 1890, 33; Reed, *"All the World Is Here!,"* 86. Bradwell and Reed claim that Sarah Wheeler was John Jones's niece, while Buckler and Spear write that she was his adopted daughter. I refer to her as the niece based on Bradwell's 1896 assertion.

20. Spear, *Black Chicago*, 57–58; Robb, *Intercollegian Wonder Book*, 1:113; Buckler, *Daniel Hale Williams*, 55.

21. Buckler, *Daniel Hale Williams*, 3–4, 55, 102; Robb, *Intercollegian Wonder Book*, 1:112–113.

22. "Chicago Colored People," *Chicago Daily Tribune*, May 4, 1890, 33; Gamble, *Making a Place for Ourselves*, 16; Spear, *Black Chicago*, 56–57; Gatewood, *Aristocrats of Color*, 120.

23. See, for example, "Chicago," *Western Appeal*, February 18, 1888, 1; "Normal Notes," *Western Appeal*, July 20, 1889, 1; and Gosnell, *Negro Politicians*, 214.

24. Barrier Williams displayed two oil paintings—*Gypsy Head* and *Swiss Scene*—at an industrial exhibition held at Bethel Hall in Washington in 1886. See "Industrial Exhibition," *The Washington Bee*, October 23, 1886; and "Chicago," *Western Appeal*, March 17, 1888, 1. Unfortunately, I have not been able to locate any of her art. Upon her death in 1944, Williams willed her "hand painted oil paintings" to her niece, Harriet Barrier of Detroit, who died in 1948.

25. "Chicago," *Western Appeal*, March 17, 1888, 1.

26. *The Washington Bee*, January 22, 1887; "The Windy City," *Western Appeal*, January 7, 1888, 1; "Chicago," *Western Appeal*, March 3, 1888, 1; "Chicago," *Western Appeal*, March

10, 1888, 1; "Chicago," *Western Appeal*, March 17, 1888, 1; "Prof. Adams' Novel Class," *Western Appeal*, March 24, 1888, 1.

27. Williams, "A Northern Negro's Autobiography," 91; S. Laing Williams in Necrology File, Office of Alumni Records, Bentley Historical Library, University of Michigan; "The Monday Night Literary Society," *Washington Bee*, June 2, 1883, 2.

28. According to the *Western Appeal*, the club was established in late 1887; see "The Windy City," *Western Appeal*, January 7, 1888, 1. But according to an interview with Barrier Williams, the club was formed in 1885; see "Cultured Negro Ladies," *Chicago Tribune*, October 28, 1888, 26. It is possible that the *Tribune* reporter mistakenly substituted years for months.

29. "Cultured Negro Ladies," *Chicago Tribune*, October 28, 1888, 26.

30. McHenry, *Forgotten Readers*, 188.

31. "The Windy City," *Western Appeal*, January 7, 1888, 1; "Special Appeal," *Western Appeal*, July 20, 1889, 1; "Cultured Negro Ladies," *Chicago Tribune*, October 28, 1888, 26.

32. "The Windy City," *Western Appeal*, January 7, 1888, 1; "Cultured Negro Ladies," *Chicago Tribune*, October 28, 1888, 26; Gosnell, *Negro Politicians*, 375.

33. "Cultured Negro Ladies," *Chicago Tribune*, October 28, 1888, 26.

34. Ibid.

35. "The Windy City," *Western Appeal*, January 7, 1888, 1; Flanagan, *Seeing with Their Hearts*, 39; "Cultured Negro Ladies," *Chicago Tribune*, October 28, 1888, 26.

36. "The Windy City," *Western Appeal*, January, 7, 1888, 1; "Chicago," *Western Appeal*, May 26, 1888, 1.

37. "Cultured Negro Ladies," *Chicago Tribune*, October 28, 1888, 26.

38. Ibid.

39. Ibid.

40. Ibid.

41. *Fifth Annual of All Souls Church*, 38; *Ninth Annual, 1892*, 99, 111–112; *Tenth Annual: All Souls Church* (Chicago: Press of Metcalf Stationery Company, 1893), 82, Unitarian Universalist Association of Congregations, Boston Massachusetts; Buckler, *Daniel Hale Williams*, 12.

42. "Chicago," *Western Appeal*, May 26, 1888, 1.

43. "Cultured Negro Ladies," *Chicago Tribune*, October 28, 1888, 26.

44. Ibid.

45. Ibid.; Pierce, *A History of Chicago*, 3:487.

46. "Cultured Negro Ladies," *Chicago Tribune*, October 28, 1888, 26.

47. Ibid.

48. Ibid.

49. Wheeler, *The Roads They Made*, 61.

50. "Cultured Negro Ladies," *Chicago Tribune*, October 28, 1888, 26.

51. Buhle, *Women and American Socialism*, 72.

52. *First Annual Report of the Illinois Woman's Alliance*, 3–4, 9; Buhle, *Women and American Socialism*, 71–72; Pierce, *A History of Chicago*, 3:487; Flanagan, *Seeing with Their Hearts*, 37.

53. *First Annual Report of the Illinois Woman's Alliance*, 5.

54. "Women Down on Judge Shepard," *Chicago Tribune*, November 2, 1889, 6.

55. "The Illinois Women's Alliance," *Chicago Tribune*, July 6, 1889, 8.

56. *First Annual Report of the Illinois Woman's Alliance*, 4; Flanagan, *Seeing with Their Hearts*, 39. Viola Bentley was probably Traviata Bentley, Charles Bentley's wife.

57. "Women Down on Judge Shepard," *Chicago Tribune*, November 2, 1889, 6; Flanagan, *Seeing with Their Hearts*, 39, 42–43; Wheeler, *The Roads They Made*, 85.

58. "The Illinois Women's Alliance," *Chicago Tribune*, July 6, 1889, 8, col. 2; "Women Down on Judge Shepard," *Chicago Tribune*, November 2, 1889, 6.

59. Flanagan, *Seeing with Their Hearts*, 39, 42–43.

60. Ibid., 41.

61. "Personal," *Brockport Republic*, August 21, 1890, 3; "Mortuary," *Brockport Republic*, August 28, 1890, 3. As the only male left in the immediate family, George began assisting his mother and was listed in the New York census of 1892 as a resident of Brockport and Detroit. See Harriet Prince Barrier, in Enumeration of the Inhabitants Living in the Third Election District of the Town of Sweden, Monroe County, New York, 6, New York State manuscript census for 1892, available at Ancestry.com.

62. "Chicago," *Western Appeal*, February 14, 1891, 1.

63. See Hine, *Black Women in White*; Gamble, *Making a Place for Ourselves*; and Rice and Jones, *Public Policy and the Black Hospital*.

64. Gamble, *Making a Place for Ourselves*, 14–19; Hine, *Black Women in White*, 12–14, 26–29.

65. Bradwell, "The Colored Bar of Chicago," 390–391; Spear, *Black Chicago*.

66. Spear, *Black Chicago*, 52–53, 62.

67. "Mr. Jones Protests," *Western Appeal*, April 18, 1891, 1.

68. Ibid.

69. Ibid.

70. Quoted in Buckler, *Daniel Hale Williams*, 71; Spear, *Black Chicago*, 62.

71. Quoted in Buckler, *Daniel Hale Williams*, 71.

72. Ibid.

73. Quoted in ibid.

74. Buckler, *Daniel Hale Williams*, 66–68; Hine, *Black Women in White*, Chapters 1 and 2.

75. Quoted in Buckler, *Daniel Hale Williams*, 75.

76. Quoted in ibid., 76.

77. Ibid., 73; Gamble, *Making a Place for Ourselves*, 15.

78. Buckler, *Daniel Hale Williams*, 72–74; Pierce, *A History of Chicago*, 3:112–116; Gamble, *Making a Place for Ourselves*, 17.

79. "Hospital for Colored People," *Chicago Tribune*, May 5, 1891, 3.

80. Ibid.

81. Ibid.

Chapter 4. Crossing the Border of Race: The Unitarians, the World's Fair, and the Chicago Woman's Club

1. "Notes from the Field," *Unity: Freedom, Fellowship and Character in Religion* 25 (June 26, 1890): 146.

2. See Susan Strane, *A Whole-Souled Woman*.

3. Lyttle, *Freedom Moves West*, 69–87.

4. Ibid., 117–119, 127.

5. Ibid., 127–130.

6. Ibid., xiv, xvii, 73–93.

7. Ibid., 137, 161. See also Thompson, "The First Unitarian Society of Chicago," 75.

8. Lyttle, *Freedom Moves West*, 158–161; Siry, "Frank Lloyd Wright's Unity Temple," 257–258.

9. Quoted in Lyttle, *Freedom Moves West*, 158–159.

10. Ibid., 159.

11. *Fifth Annual of All Souls Church* (Chicago: Rand, McNally & Co., 1888), 3, Unitarian and Universalist Papers, Manuscripts and Archives, Andover-Harvard Theological Library, Harvard Divinity School, Cambridge, Massachusetts; Siry, "Frank Lloyd Wright's Unity Temple," 258.

12. Siry, "Frank Lloyd Wright's Unity Temple," 257–260.

13. *Fifth Annual of All Souls Church*, 1, 41–51.

14. Siry, "Frank Lloyd Wright's Unity Temple," 259; All Souls Church, *Ninth Annual* (Chicago: All Souls Church, 1892), 89, Unitarian Universalist Association of Congregations, Boston, Massachusetts; Lee-Forman, "The Simple Love of Truth," 92–93.

15. Lee-Forman, "The Simple Love of Truth," 268.

16. *Fifth Annual of All Souls Church*, 6, 38, 40; All Souls Church, *Eighth Annual, 1891* (Chicago: All Souls Church, 1891), 82, Unitarian Universalist Association of Congregations, Boston, Massachusetts. Copies of the 1889 and 1890 church membership lists were not available at the Unitarian Universalist Association or at the Andover-Harvard Theological Library, so the first membership list I have seen that includes Fannie Barrier Williams and S. Laing Williams is the one for 1891; see All Souls Church, *Ninth Annual*, 89. See also Siry, "Frank Lloyd Wright's Unity Temple," 259; and Lee-Forman, "The Simple Love of Truth," 92–93. Buckler notes that Daniel Hale Williams often played the bass fiddle for Sunday services, but he does not appear on the membership list for All Souls; see Buckler, *Daniel Hale Williams Negro Surgeon*, 12 and 62.

17. "Chicago," *Western Appeal*, May 26, 1888, 1.

18. For Washington's visit to Unitarian headquarters in Boston, see J. F. B. Marshall to Eliza Brewer, June 13, 1887, Box 1, Folder 1, Booker T. Washington Papers, Archives and Museums, Tuskegee University (hereafter Booker T. Washington Papers); Booker T. Washington to Warren Logan, April 15, 1889, Box 1, Folder 3, Booker T. Washington Papers; and Booker T. Washington to Warren Logan, April 16, 1889, Box 1, Folder 3, Booker T. Washington Papers.

19. Washington, "The Tuskegee Normal School," 551.

20. Chaney, "How to Help the South," 530–531.

21. "A School for Industrial Education in the South," 27–28.

22. Quoted in "An Article in *Unity*," in *The Booker T. Washington Papers*, 3:16–17.

23. S. Laing Williams to Booker T. Washington, March 24, 1892, Box 1, Folder 8, Booker T. Washington Papers.

24. Flanagan, *Seeing with Their Hearts*, 41.

25. "Mrs. Celia Parker Woolley," *New York Times*, August 5, 1894, 18; Lee-Forman, "The Simple Love of Truth," 19–22, 24–30.

26. Lee-Forman, "The Simple Love of Truth," 72–77; Tucker, *Prophetic Sisterhood*, 75.

27. "Mrs. Celia Parker Woolley"; Lee-Forman, "The Simple Love of Truth," 79, 91, 94–96.

28. Lee-Forman, "The Simple Love of Truth," 100–101; Houde, *Reaching Out*, 54; *16th Annual Announcement of the Chicago Women's Club 1892–93*, 47, 53, 54.

29. Lee-Forman, "The Simple Love of Truth," 91–93, 119; Tucker, *Prophetic Sisterhood*, 121.

30. See, for example, "Notes from the Field," *Unity: Freedom, Fellowship and Character in Religion*, 25 (June 26, 1890): 1; "Notes from the Field," *Unity: Freedom, Fellowship and Character in Religion* 31 (May 25 and June 1, 1893): 132; "Mrs. Celia Parker Woolley."

31. Koby Lee-Forman, "The Simple Love of Truth," 124–131.

32. Truman, *History of the World's Fair*, 24; Gilbert, *Perfect Cities*, 2.

33. For a breakdown of attendance from the opening in May until the closing in October, see Truman, *History of the World's Fair*, 599.

34. "Chicago Colored People," *Chicago Daily Tribune*, May 4, 1890, 33

35. See Bontemps and Conroy, *Anyplace but Here*, 88–93; Christopher Robert Reed, *"All the World Is Here!"*; Rudwick and Meier, "Black Man in the 'White City,'" 354; Paddon and Turner, "African Americans and the World's Columbian Exposition"; Truman, *History of the World's Fair*, 107; Hendricks, *Gender, Race, and Politics in the Midwest*, 1–2.

36. Hendricks, *Gender, Race, and Politics in the Midwest*, 2.

37. Truman, *History of the World's Fair*, 163–164; Gullett, "'Our great opportunity,'" 270–272; Hendricks, *Gender, Race, and Politics in the Midwest*, 1–3. Only one black woman, Joan Imogene Howard of New York, was selected to serve on a state board.

38. "They Are Disappointed," *Chicago Daily Tribune*, November 26, 1890, 7. See also Weinman, *The Fair Women*; Hendricks, *Gender, Race, and Politics in the Midwest*, 3.

39. See Hendricks, *Gender, Race, and Politics in the Midwest*, 3.

40. "They Are Disappointed"; "Board of Lady Managers, Worl[d]'s Columbian Commission," *The State Capital*, October 17, 1891, 1; Truman, *History of the World's Fair*, 172; Reed, *"All the World Is Here!,"* 26–28.

41. Barnett, "The Reason Why," 68–69.

42. Gullett, "'Our great opportunity,'" 261–262.

43. "Board of Lady Managers, Worl[d]'s Columbian Commission."

44. Ibid.

45. Ibid.

46. Ibid.

47. "World's Fair Doings," *The Woman's Journal*, December 12, 1891, 410; Truman, *History of the World's Fair*, 53–58.

48. "Mrs. Fannie Barrier Williams," *The New York Age*, January 23, 1892, 1; Fannie Barrier Williams to Frederick Douglass, January 14, 1893, Reel 6, Frederick Douglass Papers, Library of Congress (hereafter Frederick Douglass Papers).

49. Barnett, "The Reason Why," 75; Reed, *"All the World Is Here!,"* 30; "Hospital for Colored People," *Chicago Tribune*, May 5, 1891, 3; "Boom-De-Ra," *Cleveland Gazette*, March 18, 1893, 2. According to Vanessa Northington Gamble, Mrs. A. M. Curtis was Nanahyoke Sockum Curtis. See Gamble, *Making a Place for Ourselves*, 15.

50. "Chicago," *Western Appeal*, April 16, 1892, 1; "The World's Fair," *Cleveland Gazette*, April 16, 1892, 2.

51. "Chicago."

52. "Anti-Slavery Men Are Honored," *Chicago Daily Tribune*, January 2, 1893, 9; Truman, *History of the World's Fair*, 508; McFeely, *Frederick Douglass*, 366.

53. Fannie Barrier Williams to Frederick Douglass, January 14, 1893, Reel 6, Frederick Douglass Papers; McFeely, *Frederick Douglass*, 366.

54. For Wells's visit with Mrs. L. Reynolds on Dearborn Street, see "Chicago," *Western Appeal*, September 7, 1889, 2. For Wells's August visit, see "Chicago," *Western Appeal*, August 27, 1892, 1. See also "Progress of Colored Brothers," *Chicago Daily Tribune*, September 3, 1893, 8; and *The Reason Why The Colored American Is Not in the World's Columbian Exposition*.

55. *Minutes of the Meeting of the Council of Administration of the World's Columbian Exposition*, 14–15; Barnett, "The Reason Why," 75.

56. Gullett, "'Our great opportunity,'" 268–269.

57. "On Work of Women," *Chicago Daily Tribune*, May 15, 1893, 1–2; Gullett, "'Our great opportunity,'" 263. David A. Johnson argues that there were many Unitarian and Universalist women who were involved in planning for and participating in the Columbian Exposition and the World's Parliament of Religions. See Johnson, *The Fair Women: Women at the 1893 World Parliament of Religions*.

58. "On Work of Women," *Chicago Daily Tribune*, May 15, 1893, 2; Sewall, *The World's Congress of Representative Women*, 433–437, 696–729.

59. "On Work of Women," *Chicago Daily Tribune*, May 15, 1893, 2; Sewall, *The World's Congress of Representative Women*, 433–437, 696–729.

60. Sewall, *The World's Congress of Representative Women*, 696.

61. Ibid., 698–700.

62. Ibid., 705.

63. Ibid., 709.

64. Barrows, *The World's Parliament of Religions*, 1:3–17, 18, 178, 1268–1269; Barrows, *The World's Parliament of Religions*, 2:1394–1396, 1434–1436; Jones, *A Chorus of Faith*, 11–22; Lyttle, *Freedom Moves West*, 205–208.

65. Barrows, *The World's Parliament of Religions*, 1:140–141; Barrows, *The World's Parliament of Religions*, 2:1114; Jones, *A Chorus of Faith*, 258–260.

66. Barrows, *The World's Parliament of Religions*, 2:1115; Jones, *A Chorus of Faith*, 258–260.

67. Fannie Barrier Williams to Frederick Douglass, January 14, 1893 [likely January 14, 1894], Reel 6, Frederick Douglass Papers; Jones, *A Chorus of Faith*, 258–260; Barrows, *The World's Parliament of Religions*, 2:1147.

68. Fannie Barrier Williams to Frederick Douglass, April 17, 1894, Reel 8, Frederick Douglass Papers. Caroline Bartlett, a Unitarian minister in Kalamazoo, Michigan, invited Barrier Williams "to deliver both my addresses read before the Congresses in her church on the 16th and also to give a parlor reading before the 20th Century Club connected with her church." Bartlett seems to have also become her agent. See Fannie Barrier Williams to Frederick Douglass, January 14, 1893, Reel 6, Frederick Douglass

Papers; and Johnson, *The Fair Women*, 5. For a discussion of the commercialization of the lyceum, see Tetrault, "The Incorporation of American Feminism." Tetrault argues, I believe incorrectly, that in general black women had a difficult time with the business of lecturing. That was probably true for many, but Barrier Williams seems to have done quite well. Whether her salary equaled that of white women, whose earnings could go as high as $40,000 annually, isn't clear. As of yet, I have not uncovered the information about the fees she earned, but she spoke to many more white audiences than black audiences. See also the pamphlet *Popular Lectures by Mrs. Fannie Barrier Williams* (Chicago: The Slayton Lyceum Bureau, ca. 1895). Many thanks to Williams Andrews, historian emeritus of Brockport, New York, for sharing this pamphlet with me.

69. Fannie Barrier Williams to Frederick Douglass, January 14, 1893, Reel 6, Frederick Douglass Papers.

70. Ibid.

71. "Notes from the Field," *Unity: Freedom, Fellowship and Character in Religion* 32 (February 15, 1894): 381; "News from the Field," *The Unitarian: A Magazine of Liberal Christianity* 9 (March 1894): 141.

72. Fannie Barrier Williams to Frederick Douglass, April 17, 1894, Reel 8, Frederick Douglass Papers.

73. "Notes from the Field," *Unity: Freedom, Fellowship and Character in Religion* 33 (May 3, 1894): 116; Fannie Barrier Williams to Frederick Douglass, April 17, 1894.

74. Fannie Barrier Williams to Frederick Douglass, April 17, 1984.

75. *14th Annual Announcement of the Chicago Women's Club 1890–91*, 10; *16th Annual Announcement of the Chicago Women's Club 1892–93*, 35; *18th Annual Announcement of the Chicago Women's Club 1894–95*, 78; "Mrs. Celia Parker Woolley."

76. *19th Annual Announcement Of The Chicago Woman's Club 1895–96*, 78; Houde, *The Clubwoman*, 16. The membership of the club ranges from 600 to 800, depending on the source.

77. Frank and Jerome, *Annals of the Chicago Woman's Club for the First Forty Years*, 145; *18th Annual Announcement of the Chicago Women's Club, 1894–95*, 38. See also Lee, *Friendship across the Color Line*; Lee-Forman, "The Simple Love of Truth," 192–205; "Color Line in a Club," *Chicago Daily Tribune*, November 14, 1894, 2; Houde, *Reaching Out*, 68–69.

78. Williams, "The Club Movement among Negro Women," 217; Williams, "A Northern Negro's Autobiography," 94.

79. "Color Line in a Club."

80. Ibid.

81. Ibid.

82. *Annals of the Chicago Woman's Club for the First Forty Years*, 145–146.

83. Williams, "The Club Movement among Negro Women," 217–218.

84. Williams, "A Northern Negro's Autobiography," 94.

85. Ibid.

86. Ibid.

87. Ibid.; "Notes And Comments," *The Woman's Era*, December 1894, 1, "The Chicago Woman's Club Reject Mrs. Williams," *The Woman's Era*, December 1894, 20; "Position of National W.C.T.U. in Relation to Colored People," *The Woman's Era*, July 1895, 6; *19th*

Annual Announcement of the Chicago Woman's Club, 1895–96, 73; Giddings, *When and Where I Enter*, 90–92.

88. "To Hear Mrs. Fannie B. Williams," *Chicago Daily Tribune*, December 17, 1894, 8.

89. *Popular Lectures by Mrs. Fannie Barrier Williams*.

90. "Plea for Her Race," *Chicago Tribune*, August 26, 1895, 9.

91. "Notes and Comments," *The Woman's Era*, April 1895, 1.

92. "In Honor of Mrs. E. C. Stanton," *New York Times*, November 12, 1895, 4; "Notes from Gotham," *Washington Bee*, November 23, 1895, 3; "Was Honored by All," *The San Francisco Call*, November 13, 1895.

93. *Annals of the Chicago Woman's Club for the First Forty Years*, 145; *18th Annual Announcement of the Chicago Women's Club, 1894–95*, 13; *19th Annual Announcement of the Chicago Woman's Club 1895–96*, 11; Lee, *Friendship across the Color Line*; "Personal," *The Brockport Republic*, February 28, 1895, 3.

94. "The Color Line in Chicago," *Unity: Freedom, Fellowship and Character in Religion* 34 (January 31, 1895): 649–650.

95. *18th Annual Announcement of the Chicago Women's Club, 1894–95*, 53; *Chicago Daily Tribune*, May 21, 1895, 8.

96. *20th Annual Announcement of the Chicago Woman's Club, 1896–97*, 81; "Breaking Down the Color Line," *Chicago Tribune*, January 24, 1896, 6.

97. *19th Annual Announcement of the Chicago Woman's Club, 1895–96*, 78; *20th Annual Announcement of the Chicago Woman's Club, 1896–97*, 76.

98. "Breaking Down the Color Line."

99. "The Women's Club and the Color Line," *Chicago Times-Herald*, January 24, 1896, 6.

100. "A Colored Woman Wins," *San Francisco Chronicle*, January 24, 1896, 2.

101. No title, *The Globe-Republican* (Dodge City, Kansas), January 30, 1896.

Chapter 5. A Distinctive Generation: "The Colored Woman's Era"

1. "Woman and the West," *Evening Star*, January 5, 1893, 7; Cromwell, *History of the Bethel Literary*, 21–23.

2. Cromwell, *History of Bethel Literary Association*, 21–23; "The Bethel Literary Society," *Evening Star*, January 10, 1893, 10.

3. "The Bethel Literary Society."

4. Ibid.

5. Wesley, *The History of the National Association of Colored Women's Clubs*, 25; Gatewood, *Aristocrats of Color*, 38–39, 249; "Discussion of the Same Subject by Mrs. A. J. Cooper of Washington, D.C.," 714; Shaw, "Black Club Women and the Creation of the National Association of Colored Women," 433.

6. Gibson and Crogman, *The Colored American from Slavery to Honorable Citizenship*, 204, 207; Moore, *Leading the Race*, 163, 165.

7. Gibson and Crogman, *The Colored American from Slavery to Honorable Citizenship*, 207; Moore, *Leading the Race*, 165.

8. "Colored Society Ablaze," *Washington Bee*, September 7, 1891, 1; Gibson and Crogman, *The Colored American from Slavery to Honorable Citizenship*, 207.

9. Cromwell, *History of the Bethel Literary*, 20–21; Gibson and Crogman, *The Colored American from Slavery to Honorable Citizenship*, 207.

10. Duster, *Crusade for Justice*, 77–79, 121; Wesley, *The History of the National Association of Colored Women's Clubs*, 26; Giddings, *Ida: A Sword among Lions*, 236–238; Hicks, *Talk with You Like a Woman*, 83.

11. *The Woman's Era*, May 1, 1894, 1; Wesley, *The History of the National Association of Colored Women's Clubs*, 26. For a recent discussion of black women and reform in New York, see Hicks, *Talk with You Like a Woman*, particularly 95–103 on Matthews.

12. "Shall We Have a Convention of the Colored Women's Clubs, Leagues and Societies?," *The Woman's Era*, June 1, 1894, 5.

13. "New Departments," *The Woman's Era*, November 1894, 1; "Women in Politics," *The Woman's Era*, November 1894, 12.

14. Wesley, *The History of the National Association of Colored Women's Clubs*, 27; "The Woman's Era," *The Woman's Era*, November 1894, 1; and "Advertise in the Woman's Era," *The Woman's Era*, November 1894, 8.

15. Ida B. Wells refers to the club as the Women's Club, but Rosie Moore refers to it as the Woman's Club. See Duster, *Crusade for Justice*, 122; "Chicago Letter," *The Woman's Era*, May 1, 1894, 2.

16. Duster, *Crusade for Justice*, 121–124; Giddings, *Ida: A Sword among Lions*, 281–282.

17. "Chicago Letter," *The Woman's Era*, May 1, 1894, 2; "Chicago," *The Woman's Era*, July 1894, 1; Duster, *Crusade for Justice*, 121–124; Giddings, *Ida: A Sword among Lions*, 281–282. According to Moore, the first meeting of the women on Ladies Day was in December 1893. She writes that fifty women met again on December 21, when W. T. Snead, a British minister, presented "Friendship between the Sexes"; Ida B. Wells presented a paper on December 28.

18. "Chicago Letter," *The Woman's Era*, May 1, 1894, 2; Duster, *Crusade for Justice*, 121–124.

19. Duster, *Crusade for Justice*, 123–124.

20. Ibid., 122–124; "Chicago Letter," *The Woman's Era*, May 1, 1894, 2.

21. "Chicago Letter," *The Woman's Era*, May 1, 1894, 2.

22. Williams, "The Awakening of Women," 392–393. These quotes refer to the Citizen's League of Chicago and its "effective resistance to all the social and political evils of the municipality." Barrier Williams also refers to Jane Addams as an example of a woman "sensitive to every form of human suffering about her, and always sisterly, motherly or friendly, as requirements demand" (394).

23. "Women's Council," *Evening Star*, February 21, 1895, 3.

24. "Need of Co-operation of Men and Women in Correctional Work," *The Woman's Era*, May 1895, 4.

25. Ibid.

26. See Hine, *Black Women In White*.

27. "Illinois," *The Woman's Era*, February 1896, 14.

28. "Will Play for Charity," *Chicago Tribune*, May 10, 1896, 16. For the history and development of the hospital and the nursing program and information about white benefactors, see Fannie Barrier Williams, "Chicago's Provident Hospital and Training School—Social Matters," *The Woman's Era*, October and November 1896, 13–14.

29. *First Annual Report of the Illinois Woman's Alliance for the Year Ending November*

1, 1889, 4; Wheeler and Wortman, *The Roads They Made*, 106; Materson, *For the Freedom of Her Race*, 20. For a discussion of the national scope of black women's involvement in suffrage and politics, see Terborg-Penn, *African American Women in the Struggle for the Vote*; and "Women in Politics," *The Woman's Era*, November 1894, 13.

30. "Women in Politics," 13.

31. Ibid.

32. Materson, *For the Freedom of Her Race*, 20.

33. "Women in Politics," 12–13.

34. Elizabeth Piper Ensley, "What Equal Suffrage Has Done for Colorado," *The Woman's Era*, November 1894, 13.

35. "Women in Politics," 13.

36. Materson, *For the Freedom of Her Race*, 28.

37. "Women in Politics," 13.

38. *Annals of the Chicago Woman's Club for the First Forty Years of Its Organization*, 135–136; *14th Annual Announcement of the Chicago Women's Club, 1890–1891; 18th Annual Announcement of the Chicago Women's Club, 1894–95*, 47, 64; Materson, *For the Freedom of Her Race*, 26.

39. Wheeler and Wortman, *The Roads They Made*, 106–107.

40. "Women in Politics," 13.

41. See, for example, McMillen, *Dark Journey*, 35–48.

42. Philpott, *The Slum and the Ghetto*, 120–121.

43. "Not So Many Coming North as Were a Few Years Ago," *Reno Evening Gazette*, November 28, 1899, 4, reprint of a *Times Herald* article by Barrier Williams.

44. Williams, "The Awakening of Women," 392.

45. Ibid., 396–397; White, *Too Heavy a Load*, 58. Four years earlier, at the World's Congress of Representative Women at the Chicago Exposition, Frances Ellen Watkins Harper had said that "to-day we stand on the threshold of the woman's era"; see Harper, "Woman's Political Future," 433–434.

46. See, for example, Shaw, "Black Club Women," 434.

47. "Shall We Have a Convention of the Colored Women's Clubs, Leagues and Societies?," *The Woman's Era*, May 1, 1894, 3.

48. Ibid., 4.

49. Ibid.

50. Ibid.

51. "Shall We Have a Convention of the Colored Women's Clubs, Leagues and Societies?," *The Woman's Era*, June 1, 1894, 5.

52. Ibid.

53. Ibid., 9.

54. "The National Council of Women," *The Woman's Era*, November 1894, 8; "The Work of Correction," *New York Times*, February 22, 1895, 2; Duster, *Crusade for Justice*, 231–232.

55. Fannie B. Williams to Frederick Douglass, April 17, 1894, Reel 7, Frederick Douglass Papers.

56. Ibid.

57. "Illinois," *The Woman's Era*, April 1895, 4.

58. Wesley, *The History of the National Association of Colored Women's Clubs*, 28–32; Duster, *Crusade for Justice*, 242; Giddings, *Ida: A Sword among Lions*, 348; White, *Too Heavy a Load*, chapter 1.

59. "Conference Notes," *The Woman's Era*, July 1895, 2.

60. Ibid., 1–2; "National Conference of Colored Women Held in Berkeley Hall, Boston, Mass., July 29, 30, 31, 1895," *The Woman's Era*, August 1895, 1–3, 13; Gibson and Crogman, *The Colored American from Slavery to Honorable Citizenship*, 209; Greener, "The First Congress of Colored Women," 23–26.

61. "National Conference of Colored Women Held in Berkeley Hall, Boston, Mass, July 29, 30, 31, 1895," *The Woman's Era*, August 1895, 1.

62. Ibid., 1, 3.

63. Ibid. See also Salem, *To Better Our World*, 21–23.

64. "Minutes of the First National Conference of Colored Women," *The Woman's Era*, August 1895, 3; "Will Increase Its Scope," *The Morning Times* (Washington, D.C.), August 2, 1895.

65. "The National Federation of Afro-American Woman," *The Langston City Herald* (Langston City, Oklahoma), October 26, 1895.

66. No title, *The Washington Bee*, August 17, 1895.

67. Williams, "The Club Movement among Colored Women in America," 396–397; Hendricks, *Gender, Race, and Politics in the Midwest*, 18–19.

68. Ida. B. Wells Woman's Club to Women's Conference, Care of Mrs. Josephine Ruffin, Berkeley, July 29, 1895, in *The Records of the National Association of Colored Women's Clubs, 1895–1992*, Part 1: Minutes of National Conventions, Publications, and President's Office Correspondence, reel 1, frame 29; "Illinois," *The Woman's Era*, August 1895, 22; Duster, *Crusade for Justice*, 242.

69. "The Atlanta Exposition," *The Washington Bee*, December 7, 1895, 1; "The Negro Congress," *The Constitution* (Atlanta, Ga.), December 28, 1895, 8.

70. "The National Colored Woman's Congress," *The Woman's Era*, January 1896, 7.

71. "The Negro Congress," *The Constitution* (Atlanta, Ga.), December 28, 1895, 8.

72. "The National Colored Woman's Congress," *The Woman's Era*, January 1896, 2.

73. "Illinois," *The Woman's Era*, February 1896, 13.

74. Black women had a long history of articulating their anger about the Jim Crow rail cars. See, for example, Coleman, "Black Women and Segregated Public Transportation: Ninety Years of Resistance," 295–302.

75. "The National Colored Woman's Congress," *The Woman's Era*, January 1896, 3.

76. Duster, *Crusade for Justice*, 18–20.

77. Margaret James Murray Washington to Ednah Dow Littlehale Cheney, November 23, 1896, in *The Booker T. Washington Papers*, 4:237–239.

78. Ibid., 238.

79. "Illinois," *The Woman's Era*, February 1896, 13.

80. Williams, "A Northern Negro's Autobiography," 95–96. Barrier Williams never stated the location of this encounter, but it was probably in Texas while she was on a lecture tour.

81. Ibid., 95.

82. White, *Too Heavy a Load*, 93–95.

83. Williams, "Perils of the White Negro," *The Colored American Magazine* 13, no. 6 (December 1907): 421–423. See Higginbotham, "African-American Women's History and the Metalanguage of Race."

84. Williams, "A Northern Negro's Autobiography," 95.

85. Ibid., 95–96.

86. "Mrs. Fannie Barrier Williams in Boston," *The Woman's Era*, June 1896, 3; "Anniversary Week and Visitors," *The Woman's Era*, June 1896, 3.

87. Cooper, "Discussion of the Same Subject by Mrs. A. J. Cooper of Washington, D.C.," 714; "The National Colored Woman's Congress," *The Woman's Era*, January 1896, 3; Shaw, "Black Club Women and the Creation of the National Association of Colored Women," 433.

88. "The Afro-American Women," *The Washington Bee*, July 25, 1896, 4; Williams, "The Awakening of Women," 393–394. See also Greener, "The First Congress of Colored Women," 29.

89. Hendricks, *Gender, Race, and Politics in the Midwest*, 20–21.

90. "Chicago," *The Appeal*, November 26, 1898; "An Appeal to the Afro American Women of Illinois," *The Appeal*, February 11, 1899, 4.

91. "An Appeal to the Afro American Women of Chicago," *The Appeal*, February 11, 1899. Only four clubs were included in the Federation: Phyllis Wheatley Club, the Woman's Civic League, the Ideal Social Club, and the Woman's Conference.

92. Ibid.; "Our Churches," *Baltimore Afro-American*, March 18, 1899, 1; "Mrs. Fannie B. Williams to Lecture," *The Washington Post*, March 28, 1899, 2; "Lecture by Mrs. Fannie Barrier Williams," *The Washington Post*, April 9, 1899, 24.

93. *Minutes of the Second Convention of the National Association of Colored Women: Held at Quinn Chapel, 24th Street and Wabash Avenue, Chicago, Ill., August 14th, 15th, and 16th, 1899* (Chicago: The Association, 1899) in Williams, *Records of the National Association of Colored Women's Clubs*, reel 1, frame 0253.

94. *The National Association Notes*, June 1899, Mary Church Terrell Papers, Library of Congress, container #41, reel 29; Hendricks, *Gender, Race, and Politics in the Midwest*, 21; *National Association Notes* announced that the meeting would be held over a five-day period from August 13 to 17, but the minutes of the Chicago convention recorded that the conference was held on August 14–16, 1899; see *Second Convention of the National Association of Colored Women held at Quinn Chapel*. See also Giddings, *Ida: A Sword among Lions*, 417–418; "The Women: The National Association of Afro-American Women," *The Appeal*, August 19, 1899, 1.

95. "The National Association of Colored Women," *The Broad Ax*, August 12, 1899, 1.

96. Ibid.; "Society Notes," *The Broad Ax*, August 26, 1899, 1; *Minutes of the Second Convention of the National Association of Colored Women*, 9.

97. Wesley, *The History of the National Association of Colored Women's Clubs*, 45–46; *Minutes of the Second Convention of the National Association of Colored Women*.

98. Houde, *Reaching Out*, 68, 80, 455–456; *Minutes of the Second Convention of the National Association of Colored Women*.

99. *Board of Directors Minutes 1890–1894*, 1:59, General Federation of Women's Clubs Papers, Women's History and Resource Center, General Federation of Women's Clubs, Washington, D.C. See also Houde, *Reaching Out*, 41–65.

100. Giddings, *Ida: A Sword among Lions*, 417; Flanagan, *Seeing with Their Hearts*, 49–50;Wesley, *The History of the National Association of Colored Women's Clubs*, 45–46.

101. "Personals," *The Club Woman* 5, no. 1 (October 1899): 32. Stoutenborough noted Henrotin's presence as "the only white woman on the platform the first evening" and commented on several of the women present, including Terrell, Washington, and Josephine Bruce. While she seemed genuinely impressed with the conference, she paid particular interest to Bruce's complexion and argued that she "would pass anywhere for a white woman."

102. Duster, *Crusade for Justice*, 258–260. Wells-Barnett's autobiography fails to recognize Barrier Williams's leadership or the local arrangement committee, which had been planning the conference for some time. According to her recollection, she was not consulted about local preparations. Mary Church Terrell, she noted, revealed to her when she arrived in Chicago "that the reason she had not put me on the program or asked my assistance in making local arrangements was because she had received letters from women in Chicago declaring that they would not aid in entertaining the National Association if this was done." So she stayed away for much of the conference and only attended to deliver the invitations. See also Giddings, *Ida: A Sword among Lions*, 418.

103. "The National Afro-American Council," *The Broad Ax*, July 29, 1899, 1.

104. Wesley, *The History of the National Association of Colored Women's Clubs*, 45.

105. For a discussion of the long-term relationship between religious women and the NACW, see Collier-Thomas, *Jesus, Jobs, and Justice*, 263–271. Collier-Thomas argues that church women were part of the first conference of black women held in Boston in 1895 and continued to be a part of the NACW for many years.

106. "Take Up Negro's Rights," *The Chicago Tribune*, August 14, 1899, 9; "Society Items," *The Broad Ax*, August 12, 1899, 4; Wesley, *The History of the National Association of Colored Women's Clubs*, 46–47.

107. "Has Become a Part of History," *The Broad Ax*, August, 26, 1899, 1, col. 1.

108. "The Women: The National Association of Afro-American Women," 2; *Minutes of the Second Convention of the National Association of Colored Women*, 16.

109. See Hendricks, *Gender, Race, and Politics in the Midwest*, 23–26; Flanagan, *Seeing with Their Hearts*, 48.

Chapter 6. The New Century: North and South Meet

1. "Mrs. Fannie B. Williams to Lecture," *Washington Post*, March 28, 1899, 2.

2. See, for example, Williams, "The Colored Woman of To-Day," 28–32.

3. See Fortune, "Industrial Education: Will It Solve the Negro Problem?," 13.

4. Fannie Barrier Williams quoted in Ella E. Lane Bowes, "Illinois," *The Club Woman* 5, no. 1 (October 1899): 24–26.

5. Ibid., 25.

6. Ibid.

7. Ibid., 24–26.

8. Minutes of the Board of Directors [of the General Federation of Women's Clubs], Milwaukee, Wisconsin, June 4, 1900, 2:247–253, General Federation of Women's Clubs Papers, Women's History and Resource Center, General Federation of Women's Clubs, Washington, D.C.

9. Williams, "Club Movement among Negro Women," 221.

10. Minutes of the Board of Directors [of the General Federation of Women's Clubs], Milwaukee, Wisconsin, June 4, 1900, 2:247; *General Federation of Women's Clubs, Sixth Biennial Convention: Official Proceedings* (Detroit, Michigan: John Bornman & Son, 1902), 25, Women's History and Resource Center, General Federation of Women's Clubs of the General Federation of Women's Clubs, Washington, D.C.; Houde, *Reaching Out*, 456. Unless otherwise noted, all of the official proceedings of the GFWC were consulted at the GFWC archive.

11. Minutes of the Board of Directors [of the General Federation of Women's Clubs], Milwaukee, Wisconsin, June 4, 1900, 2:254–255.

12. Ibid., 2:259; Houde, *Reaching Out*, 71, 88, 455–456. The sentiment of the southern delegations commanded so much attention in part because of Lowe's background; she was a resident of Georgia and the wife of a former Confederate officer. She rose through the ranks of the federation quickly and in 1895, she was elected the first president of the Atlanta Woman's Club, which was founded that same year. One year later, she became the first president of the newly formed Georgia Federation, which was founded shortly after a group met at the Cotton States Exposition in Atlanta. In 1898, she became the first southerner to lead the GFWC since its establishment in 1890. Her presidency seemed designed to encourage support from southern women and increase their engagement with the federation.

13. "Woman Astonished: Afro-American Women's Clubs Will Not Be Represented at the General Federation," *The Appeal*, May 26, 1900, 4.

14. "Women Astonished," *The Appeal*, May 26, 1900, 4.

15. "The Color Question—America's 'Old Man of the Sea,'" *The Colored American* 8 (June 16, 1900): 8.

16. "The Story of the Fifth Biennial," *The Club Woman* 6, no. 4 (July 1900): 132.

17. Etta A. Glidden, "The Medford Club Episode," *The Club Woman* 7, no. 4 (January 1901): 125–126.

18. Helen A. Whitter, "The Position of Massachusetts," *The Club Woman* 7, no. 6 (March 1901): 181.

19. Annie E. Johnson, "A Word from Georgia," *The Club Woman* 7, no. 6 (March 1901): 182–183.

20. Annie Hungerford White, "Letter to the Editor," *The Club Woman* 7, no. 6 (March 1901): 183.

21. Houde, *Reaching Out*, 97–98; Kraditor, *The Ideas of the Woman Suffrage Movement*, 169–173. For a discussion of black women and suffrage, see Terborg-Penn, *African American Women in the Struggle for the Vote*, 112. The GFWC debacle occurred on the heels of the public rejection of another white women's organization of black women as members. The National American Woman Suffrage Association (NAWSA), the organization that Barrier Williams's colleagues Elizabeth Cady Stanton and Susan B. Anthony had helped build, launched its own strategy to increase southern white women's support for suffrage. In 1895, NAWSA held its convention in Atlanta, the first to be held outside Washington in nearly thirty years. Susan B. Anthony even asked woman's suffrage advocate Frederick Douglass not to attend the meeting for fear of offending southern women. By the time NAWSA members convened in Grand Rapids, Michigan, in 1899,

southern suffragists had been courted and offered the chance to play a significant role in shaping organizational policy. The best example of their power was when Lottie Wilson Jackson, a black representative from Michigan, called on members to pass a resolution condemning the Jim Crow cars that black women were forced to travel in throughout the South. Southern white women strenuously objected to the request, arguing that it interfered with states' rights. Some even suggested that conditions were not as difficult for black women as Jackson had claimed. But for longtime activists such as Susan B. Anthony, fears of dividing the national coalition took precedence over elite black women's concerns and any attempt to assist black southerners. In her response, Anthony blamed the railroad companies, not regional laws. She told the audience: "We women are a helpless disfranchised class. Our hands are tied. While we are in this condition, it is not for us to go passing resolutions against railroad corporations or anybody else." The pronouncement effectively ended discussion of the issue and signaled an accommodation to white southern racial policies. See Wheeler, *New Women of the New South*, chapters 4 and 5; and Aileen S. Kraditor, *The Ideas of the Woman Suffrage Movement*, 169–173.

22. Williams, "A Northern Negro's Autobiography," 96.

23. "Woman's Column," *The Broad Ax*, December 1, 1900, 1.

24. "Chips," *The Broad Ax*, February 2, 1901, 1.

25. Ibid.

26. *Annals of the Chicago Woman's Club for the First Forty Years of Its Organization*, 368–378.

27. Ibid., 239.

28. *The Club Record*, December 1908, 5.

29. *Annals of the Chicago Woman's Club for the First Forty Years of Its Organization*, 232.

30. Ibid., 371. Tuskegee was not the only educational institution of interest to members. The Philosophy and Science Department donated $50 to an industrial school for black children in Georgia for the purchase of tools. See ibid., 222.

31. Williams, "A Growing Negro Center," *The Colored American* 9, no. 26 (October 18, 1902): 11; Williams, "Social Bonds in the 'Black Belt' of Chicago," 117; Spear, *Black Chicago*, 12–19. Spear adds Virginia and Georgia to the list.

32. "'Charities' to Discuss the Negro," *New York Tribune*, September 15, 1905, 14; Williams, "Social Bonds in the 'Black Belt' of Chicago," 117–124; Spear, *Black Chicago*, 12–19.

33. Williams, "Social Bonds in the 'Black Belt' of Chicago," 117–124.

34. "Fifty Year History of the Chicago and Northern District Association of Colored Women, Inc.," 7, Illinois Association of Club Women and Girls, Inc. Papers, Illinois State Historical Library, Springfield, Illinois; Davis, *The Story of the Illinois Federation of Colored Women's Clubs*, 32–33; Bethea, *The Colored People's Blue Book of Chicago*, 17–18.

35. "Fifty Year History of the Chicago and Northern District Association of Colored Women, Inc.," 7; Bethea, *The Colored People's Blue Book of Chicago*, 17. In 1921, the name changed to the Chicago and Northern District Association of Colored Women, Inc.

36. Williams, "The Colored Woman of To-Day," 29. Barrier Williams argued that the new generation of black women had access to increased opportunities in nearly every region of the country. Glenda Elizabeth Gilmore poses a similar argument for southern black women in *Gender and Jim Crow*. But there were clear regional differences. The limitations, constraints, and boundaries imposed in the Jim Crow South stymied the

ability of southern black women to make wholesale changes and engage in activities with white women. Black women in Chicago did not face these obstacles.

37. Bradwell, "The Colored Bar of Chicago," 397; Williams, "The Colored Woman of To-Day," 30; Bethea, *The Colored People's Blue Book of Chicago*, 48–50.

38. Bethea, *The Colored People's Blue Book of Chicago*, 12. Other black female probation officers in 1906 included Elizabeth McDonald, Hattie R. Jarvis, Gertrude B. Smith, Mrs. M. B. Anderson, and Joana C. Snowden; Alberta Moore-Smith, "Women's Development in Business," *Proceedings of the National Negro Business League: Its First Meeting, Held in Boston, Massachusetts, August 23 and 24, 1900* (Boston: J. R. Hamm, 1901), 131–141, in Hamilton, *Records of the National Negro Business League*, reel 1, frame 0089; Alberta Moore Smith, "Negro Women's Business Clubs: A Factor in the Solution of the Vexed Problem," in *Report of the Second Annual Convention of the National Negro Business League, Chicago, Illinois, August 21–22–23, 1901* (Chicago: R. S. Abbott, 1901), 60–62, in Hamilton, *Records of the National Negro Business League*; Knupfer, *Toward a Tenderer Humanity and a Nobler Womanhood*, 152.

39. Davis, *The Story of the Illinois Federation of Colored Women's Clubs*, 65, 111; Knupfer, *Toward a Tenderer Humanity and a Nobler Womanhood*, 147.

40. Davis, *The Story of the Illinois Federation of Colored Women's Clubs*, 43, 111; "Letter of Thanks," *The Appeal*, April 25, 1903, 4; Knupfer, *Toward a Tenderer Humanity and a Nobler Womanhood*, 111–113.

41. Giddings, *Ida: A Sword among Lions*, 442. Bentley reported for the *Chicago Record-Herald* and the *Philadelphia Daily Ledger*, while Barrier Williams reported in the mid-1890s for the *Chicago Times-Herald*; see "The Negro Congress," *The Constitution* (Atlanta, Ga.), December 28, 1895, 8; "Chips," *The Broad Ax*, February 11, 1905, 1; Buckler, *Daniel Hale Williams*, 189; and Bethea, *The Colored People's Blue Book of Chicago*, 26.

42. Duster, *Crusade for Justice*, 272–273; Giddings, *Ida: A Sword among Lions*, 411, 432, 439–440; "National Association of Colored Women Holds Biennial Meeting in Buffalo," *The Appeal*, July 20, 1901; "Letter of Thanks," *The Appeal*, April 25, 1903.

43. Elizabeth Lindsay Davis, *The Story of the Illinois Federation of Colored Women's Clubs*, 27, 95.

44. "Mrs. Elizabeth Lindsay Davis," *The Broad Ax*, November 12, 1921. See also "National Association of Colored Women Holds Biennial Meeting in Buffalo"; Davis, *Lifting as They Climb*; and Davis, *The Story of the Illinois Federation of Colored Women's Clubs*.

45. Bethea, *The Colored People's Blue Book and Business Directory of Chicago*, 140; "Afro-Americans Defended," *The Seattle Republican*, February 26, 1904, 5.

46. Williams, "After Many Days: A Christmas Story," 158–159.

47. Williams, "Do We Need Another Name?," 33–36.

48. Quoted in Brown, *Pauline Elizabeth Hopkins*, 270.

49. Williams, "The Negro and Public Opinion," 31; "Voice of the Negro," *American Baptist* (Louisville, Ken.), January 8, 1904, 1.

50. "Afro-Americans Defended," *The Seattle Republican* (Seattle, Wash.), February 26, 1904, 5.

51. See Fortune, "Industrial Education; Will It Solve the Negro Problem?"; Bruce, "Industrial Education; Will It Solve the Negro Problem?"; Washington, "Industrial Education; Will It Solve the Negro Problem[?]"; Miller, "Industrial Education—Will It Solve the Negro

Problem[?]"; Burroughs, "Industrial Education—Will It Solve the Negro Problem[?]"; Garrison, "Industrial Education—Will It Solve the Negro Problem[?]"; Du Bois, "Industrial Education—Will It Solve the Negro Problem[?]"; Horton, "Industrial Education; Will It Solve the Negro Problem?"; Williams, "Industrial Education—Will It Solve the Negro Problem[?]"

52. Booker T. Washington to Samuel Laing Williams, February 15, 1895, in *The Booker T. Washington Papers*, 3:518; S. Laing Williams to Booker T. Washington, May 4, 1895, Box 2, Folder 10, Booker T. Washington Papers; "At Tuskegee," *Western Appeal*, June 1, 1895, 1–2.

53. S. Laing Williams to Booker T. Washington, September 19, 1895, in *The Booker T. Washington Papers*, 4:19.

54. Haley, *Afro-American Encyclopedia*, 151.

55. Fannie Barrier Williams, "Women and Business Occupations," in *Report of the Third Annual Convention of the National Negro Business League, Richmond, Virginia, August 25–26–27, 1902* (Chicago: R. S. Abbott Publishing Company, n.d.), 89–90, in *Records of the National Negro Business League*, reel 1, frame 0277.

56. Giddings, *Ida: A Sword among Lions*, 370. For example, S. Laing had invested financially in The United Brotherhood, a fraternal insurance association, with J. C. Napier of Tennessee, John Davis of Louisiana, and Daniel Hale Williams, David Weir, J. S. Madden, J. R. Taylor, J. D. Smith, and A. Perry of Chicago. See Williams, "A Growing Negro Center." S. Laing was also on the Board of Directors of the Black Diamond Development Company in 1906, which invested in an oil field in Kansas. The company issued stock for a stake in the oil field and promised riches. See Bethea, *The Colored People's Blue Book of Chicago*, 78.

57. Fannie Barrier Williams, "The Woman's Part in a Man's Business," in *Report of the Fifth Annual Convention, National Negro Business League Held at Indianapolis, Indiana, August 31, September 1st and 2d, 1904* (Pensacola, Fla.: M. M. Lewey, n.d.), 69, 78, in *Records of the National Negro Business League*, reel 1, frame 0405.

58. Williams, "Industrial Education—Will It Solve the Negro Problem[?]," 492–493.

59. "Negro Problems from the Negro Standpoint," *New York Times*, July 19, 1903, 11; Williams, "The Problem of Employment for Negro Women," 432–437.

60. Williams, "Industrial Education—Will It Solve The Negro Problem[?]," 494.

61. See "In Dixie Land," 2, where Burroughs included Barrier Williams in a distinguished list that included Frederick Douglass, Blanche K. Bruce, Phyllis Wheatley, John M. Langston, Booker T. Washington, W. E. B. Du Bois, Francis Ellen Harper, and Mary Church Terrell. See also Higginbotham, *Righteous Discontent*; Barnett, "Nannie Burroughs and the Education of Black Women," 97–108; Williams, "An Extension of the Conference Spirit," 300–302; and *Annals of the Chicago Woman's Club for the First Forty Years of Its Organization*, 373. Also see "Domestic Science," *Chicago Tribune*, October 13, 1903, 13, for Williams's essay "Field for Colored Women," which was Lesson 70 in a series published in the paper for the School of Domestic Arts and Science of Chicago.

62. Stone, "The Economic Future of the Negro," 256.

63. "Not So Many Coming North as There Were a Few Years Ago," *Reno Evening Gazette* (Reno, Nev.), November 28, 1899, 4 (reprinted from the *Chicago Times Herald*).

64. Stone, "The Economic Future of the Negro," 250; "Menial Jobs Lost, We Go Higher," *New York Age*, June 15, 1905, 2.

65. "Menial Jobs Lost, We Go Higher."

66. Let Us Stand By Servant Girls," *New York Age*, September 28, 1905, 7.

67. "Menial Jobs Lost, We Go Higher."

68. Spear, *Black Chicago*, 36–41.

69. Williams, "A Growing Negro Center"; "Rising Higher Than Opportunities," *The Seattle Republican*, May 17, 1907.

70. Williams, "A Growing Negro Center"; "Rising Higher Than Opportunities."

71. "Let Us Stand By Servant Girls."

72. "Learning How to Work," *The St. Paul Globe*, July 11, 1902, 10.

73. Williams, "Dr. Booker T. Washington in Chicago," *The Colored American* 10, no. 38 (April 16, 1904): 4.

74. "Learning How to Work."

75. Williams, "The Council at St. Paul."

76. "Meeting of the Afro-American Council," *The Broad Ax*, July 11, 1903, 1.

77. Bradwell, "The Colored Bar of Chicago," 388–389; Gosnell, *Negro Politicians*, 66, 375; Spear, *Black Chicago*, 62–63.

78. Giddings, *Ida: A Sword among Lions*, 426, 437–438, 447–449.

79. Lewis, *W. E. B. Du Bois*, 277.

80. Lee-Forman, "The Simple Love of Truth," 238–241; The University of Chicago attracted a number of black students, including Monroe Nathan Work, who enrolled in the school during the last years of the nineteenth century to study theology but then switched to sociology. He later worked with Du Bois and moved to Alabama to join Booker T. Washington at Tuskegee in the Department of Records and Research. See McMurry, *Recorder of the Black Experience*, 17–23, 238–239.

81. Lee-Forman, "The Simple Love of Truth," 238–241. Also see "Chicago," *The Appeal*, September 2, 1899, 4.

82. "For Social Settlements," *Baltimore Afro-American*, May 28, 1904, 1.

83. See, for example, the $135 contribution from the club in *Annals of the Chicago Woman's Club for the First Forty Years of Its Organization*, 369; Lee-Forman, "The Simple Love of Truth," 280–281.

84. Woolley, "The Frederick Douglass Center, Chicago," 328.

85. Williams, "The Frederick Douglass Center," 334; Lee-Forman, "The Simple Love of Truth," 247.

86. Lee-Forman, "The Simple Love of Truth," 246. Plummer was director of Mary Thompson Hospital for Women and Children and a member of the CWC.

87. Williams, "The Frederick Douglass Center," 334.

88. Ibid., 334–336.

89. Williams, "A New Method of Dealing with the Race Problem," 503–504. She refers to it as the Educational Department on the list but then refers to it as the Education Department later on.

90. Williams, "The Frederick Douglas Center," 601–602.

91. *The Broad Ax*, June 23, 1906, quoted in Spear, *Black Chicago*, 105.

92. Woolley, "The Frederick Douglass Center, Chicago," 328–329.

93. Duster, *Crusade for Justice*, 280–282.

94. Ibid., 283. Wells-Barnett would eventually become president; see Bethea, *The Colored People's Blue Book of Chicago*, 18.

95. Duster, *Crusade for Justice*, 258–259, 272–273; Giddings, *Ida: A Sword among Lions*, 410–420, 432, 439–440; White, *Too Heavy a Load*, 106.

96. "Chips," *The Broad Ax*, October 17, 1903, 1.

97. "Chips," *The Broad Ax*, June 6, 1903, 1; Williams, "The New Negro," *Record-Herald*, October 9, 1904, quoted in Spear, *Black Chicago*, 70. See also White, *Too Heavy a Load*, chapter 2; White, "The Cost of Club Work, the Price of Black Feminism," 247–269; Gaines, *Uplifting the Race*, chapter 5.

98. Advertisement for *A New Negro for a New Century*, *The Colored American*, 9 no. 9 (June 1, 1901): 16.

99. Williams, "Club Movement among Negro Women," 197–232.

100. See for example, Samuel Laing Williams to Emmett Jay Scott, July 10, 1905, in *The Booker T. Washington Papers*, 8:324–325; Spear, *Black Chicago*, 66–70.

101. Emmett Jay Scott to Booker T. Washington, December 15, 1905, in *The Booker T. Washington Papers*, 8:465; Booker T. Washington to Samuel Laing Williams, January 22, 1906, in *The Booker T. Washington Papers*, 8:507–508; Spear, *Black Chicago*, 68.

102. Booker T. Washington to Theodore Roosevelt, November 15, 1905, in *The Booker T. Washington Papers*, 8:439; Booker T. Washington to Samuel Laing Williams, January 22, 1906, and Booker T. Washington to Elihu Root, February 23, 1906, in *The Booker T. Washington Papers*, 8:532–533.

103. Attorney General to S. Laing Williams, March 28, 1908, and Attorney General to S. Laing Williams, April 1, 1908, Department of Justice, Appointment Letter Books, 1884–1934, vol. 108, 422–423 and 446, respectively, General Records of the Department of Justice, RG 60, National Archives and Records Administration, College Park, Maryland.

104. Fannie Barrier Williams to Booker T. Washington, August 10, 1905, in *The Booker T. Washington Papers*, 8:341. See also Harlan, "The Secret Life of Booker T. Washington," 393–416.

105. S. Laing Williams to Booker T. Washington, January 20, 1905, in Part I, Special Correspondence, Williams, Samuel Laing, Booker T. Washington Papers, Library of Congress, reel 89; Washington, *Frederick Douglass*, 5–6.

106. "Chips," *The Broad Ax*, February 2, 1901, 1; "Mrs. Fannie Barrier Booker T. Washington Williams Slops Over on the Negro Question," *The Broad Ax*, October 15, 1904, 1.

107. "Our Chicago Letter," *The New Age* (Portland, Ore.), September 24, 1904, 5.

108. "It Is Not True," *The Broad Ax*, January 18, 1908, 1.

109. Lewis, *W. E. B. Du Bois*, 315–317.

110. See Harlan, "Booker T. Washington and the *Voice of the Negro*," 45–62; Lewis, *W. E. B. Du Bois*, 319.

111. George Barrier, in Schedule 1—Population, City of Detroit, Wayne County, Michigan, 91, federal manuscript census for 1900, available at Ancestry.com; newspaper clipping dated January 29, 1907, from William Andrews, historian emeritus, Brockport, New York; *Detroit City Directory 1890*, 242; No title, *The Washington Bee*, February 9,

1907, 5; Warren, *Michigan Manual of Freedmen's Progress*, 93–94, 275–276; Gatewood, *Aristocrats of Color*, 127–129.

112. November Meeting, 1909, *Proceedings of the Board of Regents (1906–1910), University of Michigan* (Ann Arbor, University of Michigan), 568, Bentley Library, University of Michigan, Ann Arbor; "In Memoriam," *The Michigan Technic* 23 (January 1910).

113. Richard Junger, "'God and man helped those who helped themselves,'" 130.

114. See Senechal, *The Sociogenesis of a Race Riot*; and Hendricks, *Gender, Race, and Politics in the Midwest*, 62–66.

115. "A Southern Easter Celebration," *The Chicago Defender*, April 2, 1910, 1.

Chapter 7. A New Era: Duty, Responsibility, and Tension

1. August 26, 1908, *Minutes of the Fifth Biennial Meeting or Sixth Convention of the National Association of Colored Women* (New Bedford, Mass.: New Bedford Printing Co., 1909), 4–5, in Williams, *Records of the National Association of Colored Women's Clubs*, Part 1: Minutes of National Conventions, Publications, and President's Office Correspondence, reel 1; Williams, "Work Attempted and Missed in Organized Club Work," 282; White, "The Cost of Club Work, the Price of Black Feminism," 261–262.

2. Williams, "Work Attempted and Missed in Organized Club Work," 281–282.

3. Ibid., 282.

4. Williams, "The Colored Girl," 401–403.

5. Williams, "The Need of Organized Womanhood," 652.

6. Gaines, *Uplifting the Race*, 80.

7. Ibid., 80–83; Williams, "The Need of Organized Womanhood," 653.

8. Williams, "The Need of Organized Womanhood," 652–653.

9. Williams, "Colored Women of Chicago," 565.

10. Davis, *The Story of the Illinois Federation Of Colored Women's Clubs*, 16.

11. Ibid., 7, 87–88; Knupfer, *Toward a Tenderer Humanity and a Nobler Womanhood*, 83. Knupfer argues that the Phyllis Wheatley Home "may have functioned largely as an employment agency, especially given the large number of women who secured employment through the home." It is likely that many of the women and girls who were housed at the home were referred there by the court system.

12. Williams, "Colored Women of Chicago," 565; Spear, *Black Chicago*, 155.

13. Davis, *The Story of the Illinois Federation of Colored Women's Clubs*, 16; "The Aims and Objects of the Phyllis Wheatley Home," *The Broad Ax*, February 26, 1916, 1, 5.

14. Knupfer, *Toward a Tenderer Humanity and a Nobler Womanhood*, 35–36, 157.

15. "The Thanksgiving Matinee at the Perkin Theatre for the Benefit of the Phyllis Wheatley Home Was a Grand Success," *The Broad Ax*, December 2, 1911; "Phyllis Wheatley Club Notes," *The Broad Ax*, January 8, 1916, 4; "Phyllis Wheatley Home," *The Broad Ax*, July 2, 1921, 3.

16. *Annals of the Chicago Woman's Club for the First Forty Years of Its Organization*, 373, 378; "Phyllis Wheatley Notes," *The Broad Ax*, November 14, 1908, 2; "Phyllis Wheatley Club Notes," *The Broad Ax*, March 14, 1914, 2; "Phyllis Wheatley Club Notes"; "Phyllis Wheatley Club," *Chicago Defender*, May 20, 1911, 7.

17. Davis, *The Story of the Illinois Federation of Colored Women's Clubs*, 16–17; Materson, *For the Freedom of Her Race*, 55, 74–77, 82–83; "Girls Plan Big Benefit: Phyllis Wheatley

Girls to Aid Famous Home—Miss Jennie Lawrence Leader," *The Broad Ax*, September 6, 1913, 2; "The Aims and Objects of the Phyllis Wheatly Home," *The Broad Ax*, February 26, 1916, 1, 5.

18. Giddings, *Ida: A Sword among Lions*, 492.

19. Williams, "A Northern Negro's Autobiography," 92–93; Williams, "The Intellectual Progress of the Colored Women of the United States," 706.

20. Williams, "The Colored Woman of To-Day," 28; Fine, *The Souls of the Skyscraper*, 33, 173–174.

21. Fine, *The Souls of the Skyscraper*, 81.

22. Ibid., 33. See also Spear, *Black Chicago*, 154.

23. "Frederick Douglass Center," *Chicago Defender*, May 24, 1913, 5.

24. Quoted in Flanagan, *Seeing with Their Hearts*, 168; Lee-Forman, "The Simple Love of Truth," 274–275.

25. "Afro-American Cullings," *The Kansas City Sun*, August 29, 1914, 7.

26. Williams, "Colored Women of Chicago," 564.

27. Ibid., 564–565.

28. Ibid., 564.

29. *Annals of the Chicago Woman's Club for the First Forty Years of Its Organization*, 242–243, 370, 375.

30. Flanagan, *Seeing with Their Hearts*, 73.

31. Ibid., 126.

32. "News of the Women's Clubs," *The Chicago Sunday Tribune*, December 7, 1913, V3; Flanagan, *Seeing with Their Hearts*, 96.

33. Flanagan, *Seeing with Their Hearts*, 74, 77.

34. "Frederick Douglass Center," *The Chicago Defender*, June 27, 1914, 5; Knupfer, *Toward a Tenderer Humanity and a Nobler Womanhood*, 51.

35. "Frederick Douglass Center."

36. Davis, *The Story of the Illinois Federation of Colored Women's Clubs*, 125.

37. See Hendricks, *Gender, Race, and Politics in the Midwest*, 89–91; and Hendricks, "'Vote for the advantage of ourselves and our race,'" 172.

38. "Chicago Women Join Suffragettes," *The Afro-American Ledger* (Baltimore), January 11, 1913, 1; "The Alpha Suffrage Club to Give a Banquet," *The Broad Ax*, November 15, 1913, 2; Hendricks, "'Vote for the advantage of ourselves and our race.'"

39. "Clubs and Societies," *The Chicago Defender*, February 21, 1914, 1.

40. Quoted in Flanagan, *Seeing with Their Hearts*, 126; Williams, "Colored Women of Chicago," 566.

41. Flanagan, *Seeing with Their Hearts*, 135, 168; Giddings, *Ida: A Sword among Lions*, 538.

42. See Hendricks, "'Vote for the advantage of ourselves and our race,'" 171–180; Materson, *For the Freedom of Her Race*, 85–95.

43. "Mrs. Fannie Barrier Williams before the Progressive League," *The Broad Ax*, November 7, 1914, 2.

44. Ibid.

45. Ibid.

46. Ibid.

47. Davis, *The Story of the Illinois Federation of Colored Women's Clubs*, 126.

48. Gosnell, *Negro Politicians*, 83, 108, 163–172.

49. "Hon. Oscar DePriest Launched His Aldermanic Boom for Alderman of the Second Ward at Second Baptist Church," *The Broad Ax*, January 30, 1915; Hendricks "'Vote for the advantage of ourselves and our race,'" 182–184; Gosnell, *Negro Politicians*, 170–171.

50. Spear, *Black Chicago*, 190–191; "Morris Demands Rights for Race," *Chicago Defender*, July 10, 1920, 1.

51. "Colored Women's Hughes Republican Headquarters, Western Branch," *The Broad Ax*, October 7, 1916. Barrier Williams's name in the paper is misspelled as "Mrs. Fanny Barrin Williams." See also Materson, *For the Freedom of Her Race*, 102.

52. "Dr. Washington Tours Arkansas," *Afro-American* (Baltimore), September 2, 1911, 3; S. Laing Williams to [Attorney General] George W. Wickersham, May 1, 1909, Applications and Endorsements, 1901–1933, General Records of the Department of Justice, RG 60, National Archives and Records Administration, College Park, Maryland.

53. James H. Wilkerson to the Attorney General [George W. Wickersham], October 4, 1911, Applications and Endorsements, 1901–1933, General Records of the Department of Justice, RG 60.

54. Charles Nagel to George W. Wickersham, October 12, 1911, Applications and Endorsements, 1901–1933, General Records of the Department of Justice, RG 60.

55. George W. Wickersham to James H. Wilkerson, October 19, 1911, Applications and Endorsements, 1901–1933, General Records of the Department of Justice, RG 60. See also George W. Wickersham to Charles Nagel, October 19, 1911, in the same collection. Wickersham wrote, "I am sorry that you have no opening for him in your Department, but I entirely understand the situation as you describe it."

56. Booker T. Washington to Samuel Laing Williams, January 20, 1913, in Harlan, *The Booker T. Washington Papers*, 12:105.

57. Booker T. Washington to William Henry Lewis, January 20, 1913, in ibid., 105–106.

58. S. Laing Williams to the President of the United States, February 1, 1913, Applications and Endorsements, 1901–1933, General Records of the Department of Justice, RG 60.

59. S. Laing Williams to the Attorney General of the United States, April 20, 1913, Applications and Endorsements, 1901–1933, General Records of the Department of Justice, RG 60; S. Laing Williams to Charles Sornborger, Appointment Clerk, Department of Justice, May 12, 1913, Applications and Endorsements, 1901–1933, General Records of the Department of Justice, RG 60.

60. "Ex-U. S. Attorney S. Laing Williams Stricken on Street," *Chicago Defender*, November 22, 1913, 1; "The Sick List," *Chicago Defender*, December 13, 1913, 2; "Ex U. S. Attorney S. Laing Williams Recovered," *Chicago Defender*, December 27, 1913, 3; "Two Prominent Men Improve," *The Broad Ax*, November 29, 1913, 1.

61. Spear, *Black Chicago*, 68–69; Reed, *The Chicago NAACP and the Rise of Black Professional Leadership*, 37.

62. "Emancipation Day Marked by Chicago Organizations," *Chicago Tribune*, February 12, 1913, 13.

63. *The World's Most Unique Exposition*, 1–5, Illinois State Historical Library, Springfield, Illinois.

64. Ibid., 12–13, 21; Davis, *The Story of the Illinois Federation of Colored Women's Clubs*, 46, 114–115.

65. *The World's Most Unique Exposition*, 12, 21; Davis, *The Story of the Illinois Federation of Colored Women's Clubs*, 62–63.

66. *The World's Most Unique Exposition*, 12; Knupfer, *Toward a Tenderer Humanity and a Nobler Womanhood*, 24, 150; Davis, *The Story of the Illinois Federation of Colored Women's Clubs*, 89–90.

67. *The World's Most Unique Exposition*, 4.

68. Ibid., 5–7.

69. Ibid., 5.

70. "The Lincoln Jubilee and Fifty Years of Freedom Celebration Is Running at Full Blast in the Coliseum," *The Broad Ax*, August 28, 1915, 1.

71. Warren, *Michigan Manual of Freedmen's Progress*, 275–276.

72. See Grossman, *Land of Hope*; Baldwin, *Chicago's New Negroes*; Philpott, *The Slum and the Ghetto*, chapter 5; Spear, *Black Chicago*, 12. For a broad discussion of the Great Migration, see Carole Marks, *Farewell—We're Good and Gone*; and Wilkerson, *The Warmth of Other Suns*.

73. Marks, *Farewell—We're Good and Gone*, 94.

74. Grossman, *Land of Hope*, 156.

75. Davis, *The Story of the Illinois Federation of Colored Women's Clubs 1900–1922*, 26; Knupfer, *Toward a Tenderer Humanity and a Nobler Womanhood*, 139–143.

76. Strickland, *History of the Chicago Urban League*, 29–30; Davis, *The Story of the Illinois Federation of Colored Women's Clubs*, 26.

77. Grossman, *Land of Hope*, 140.

78. Ibid., 145–150.

79. "Douglass Neighborhood Association," *Chicago Defender*, October 23, 1915, 6; Grossman, *Land of Hope*, chapter 5.

80. See Philpott, *The Slum and the Ghetto*, 155–157.

81. Tuttle, *Race Riot*; Tuttle, "Contested Neighborhoods and Racial Violence," 273–275.

82. "Douglass Neighborhood Association"; Tuttle, "Contested Neighborhoods and Racial Violence," 273–274, 276–277; Grossman, *Land of Hope*, chapter 5.

83. "Chicago Protective League," *The Broad Ax*, August 18, 1917, 4. Barrier Williams was the third vice-president and Ida B. Wells-Barnett was the organizer for the league in 1917. A number of other prominent citizens held offices, including Oscar DePriest. The Legislative Committee was headed by Ferdinand Barnett, the Civil Rights Committee by attorney A. L Williams, the Labor and Industry Committee by Prof. A. J. Bowling, the Federal Relations Committee by J. A. Scott, the Vital Statistics Committee by Dr. Roscoe C. Giles, and the Memorial Committee by Prof. Richard T. Greener.

84. Tuttle, *Race Riot*; Tuttle, "Contested Neighborhoods and Racial Violence," 279. For a discussion of the race riot in East St. Louis in 1917 that left forty blacks dead and was a precursor to the Chicago riot, see Rudwick, *Race Riot at East St. Louis*.

85. Tuttle, *Race Riot*. See also Wilkerson, *The Warmth of Other Suns*, 271–275; and Chicago Commission on Race Relations, *The Negro in Chicago*, 1–52.

86. Entry for Harriet A. Barrier, Record of Deaths, Monroe County Office of Vital Records, Rochester, New York; "Mrs. Harriet A. Barrier Dead," *The Washington Herald*,

April 18, 1915, 5. The obituary incorrectly stated that her body would be taken to Sherburne.

87. "The Tuskegee Club," *The Chicago Defender*, May 23, 1914, 5.

88. "Death Notices," *Chicago Tribune*, March 11, 1918, 15; Deegan, *The New Woman of Color*, 138.

89. Deegan, *The New Woman of Color*, 139.

90. Strickland, *History of the Chicago Urban League*, 38–41. See also Armfield, *Eugene Kinkle Jones*, chapter two.

91. "Death Takes Lloyd Jones, Noted Pastor," *The Chicago Daily Tribune*, September 13, 1918, 11; "Rev. Jenkin Lloyd Jones," *New York Times*, September 13, 1918, 11.

92. Necrology file for Samuel Laing Williams, Office of Alumni Records, Bentley Historical Library, The University of Michigan, Ann Arbor, Michigan.

93. "The Late S. Laing Williams," *The Broad Ax*, January 21, 1922, 2; *Chicago Defender*, December 31, 1921, 4; necrology file for Samuel Laing Williams.

94. "Meetings," *The Broad Ax*, April 2, 1921, 2; Reed, *The Rise of Chicago's Black Metropolis*, 156.

Conclusion

1. Fannie B. Williams to Francis Grimké, January 3, 1927, Box 40–5, Folder 249, Francis Grimké Papers, Moorland-Spingarn Research Center, Howard University, Washington, DC.

2. Ibid.

3. "The Week in Society," *The Washington Bee*, August 20, 1910, 5, col. 1; "Phyllis Wheatley Club Notes," *The Broad Ax*, July 19, 1919, 5; "Phyllis Wheatley Home," *The Broad Ax*, August 6, 1921, 3; "Society," *The Chicago Defender*, July 17, 1920, 10; "Another New School for Colored Pupils," *The Evening Times* (Washington, D.C.), November 14, 1902; "Colored Americans Dine," *The Colored American*, August 25, 1900, 3; "Chicago," *The Appeal*, August 13, 1904; Williams, "Work Attempted and Missed in Organized Club Work," 281; Ella D. Barrier Passport Application, June 21, 1900, Ancestry.com.

4. "Additional Personals," *The Brockport Republic*, August 31, 1911, 1.

5. "The Broad Ax Hall of Fame," *The Broad Ax*, October 2, 1920, 2; Minutes of the Eleventh Biennial Convention of the Association of Colored Women, 80, reel 16, Mary Church Terrell Papers, Library of Congress; Schwieder, Hraba, and Schwieder, *Buxton: Work and Racial Equality in a Coal Mining Community*, 156.

6. "Poem Read by Mrs. Frances Barrier Williams of Chicago at the Alumni Exercises June 22," *The Brockport Republic*, July 7, 1898, 3; "W.C.T.U.," *The Brockport Republic*, July 14, 1898, 3; "W.C.T.U.," *The Brockport Republic*, July 21, 1898, 3.

7. "Brevities," *The Brockport Republic*, April 7, 1932, 5.

8. Fannie Barrier Williams, Last Will and Testament, Monroe County Surrogate Court, Rochester, New York. The will was signed on January 25, 1937.

9. Ella died the following year and was buried next to Fannie. See Ella D. Barrier, Last Will and Testament, Monroe County Surrogate Court, Rochester, New York.

10. "Negro Leader Dies At Local Residence," *Brockport Republic*, March 9, 1944, 4. There were mistakes in the obituary. It stated that her father was Geo. A. Barrier rather than Anthony J. Barrier; that she was a life member of the Women's City Club, which

probably should have been the Chicago Woman's Club, and that her husband S. Laing was the first black to be admitted to the Chicago Bar Association, which was not correct. Lloyd Wheeler was the first black admitted to the Illinois (not Chicago) Bar, in 1869.

11. "Obituaries," *New York Times*, March 8, 1944; "Death Notices: Mrs. Fannie Barrier Williams," *Chicago Daily Tribune*, March 8, 1944, 23.

12. "Fannie Williams, Former Resident, Succumbs in East," *The Chicago Defender*, March 18, 1944, 1, 5.

13. Woodson, "Honor to Booker T. Washington," 126.

Bibliography

Archival Collections

Andover-Harvard Theological Library, Harvard Divinity School, Cambridge, Massachusetts
    Fifth Annual of All Souls Church. Chicago: Rand, McNally & Co., 1888.
Andrews, William G., Historian Emeritus, Brockport, New York
    Miscellaneous Files
Bentley Historical Library, University of Michigan, Ann Arbor
    Necrology File, Office of Alumni Records
Charles Sumner School Museum & Archives, Washington, D.C.
    DC Public School Records
First Baptist Church, Brockport, New York
    First Baptist Church Records, Brockport, New York
    First Baptist Church Minutes
    Membership List
    Second Baptist Church Minutes
George Washington University, Special Collections Research Center, Gelman Library, Washington, D.C.
    Catalogue of the Officers and Students of the Columbian University, for the Academic Year 1883–1884. Washington, D.C.: Rufus H. Darby, Printer, 1884.
    The George Washington University Alumni Directory, 1824–1937. Washington, D.C.: The George Washington University, 1938.
    The George Washington University Bulletin 16, no 1 (March 1917).
    The George Washington University Law Alumni Directory, 1866–1952. Washington, D.C.: The George Washington University, 1953.
    Records of the University Marshal
Illinois State Historical Library, Springfield, Illinois
    Papers of the Illinois Association of Club Women and Girls, Inc.

The World's Most Unique Exposition, Coliseum, Chicago, Illinois, August, 1915, Illinois Commission (National) Half-Century Anniversary of Negro Freedom. [Chicago]: n.p., 1915.

Library of Congress, Washington, D.C.
    Frederick Douglass Papers
    Mary Church Terrell Papers
    Booker T. Washington Papers, 1853–1946
Monroe County Clerk's Office, Rochester, New York
    Index of Deeds
Moorland-Spingarn Research Center, Howard University, Washington, D.C.
    Frederick Douglass Collection
    Francis Grimké Papers
National Archives and Records Administration, College Park, Maryland
    General Records of the Department of Justice, RG 60
New England Conservatory of Music Archives, Spaulding Library, Boston, Massachusetts
    Academic Catalog, 1882–1883
    Barrier, Fannie A. Student card, 1884
Office of Vital Records, Monroe County, New York, Rochester, New York
    Record of Deaths
SUNY Brockport College Archives, Drake Memorial Library, Brockport, New York
    Brockport History Articles: Brockport Republic Supplement, Brockport History. Brockport, N.Y.: Brockport Republic, 1913.
    Catalogs and Circulars, Brockport Collegiate Institute, 1842–1866, RG 11/9/2
    Material Relating to the Collegiate Institute, RG 30/1
    Brockport Collegiate Institute Semi-Centennial, 1917, RG 30/4
    Fannie Barrier Williams Miscellaneous File
Surrogate Court, Monroe County, New York, Rochester, New York
    Surrogate Court Records
Tuskegee University, Archives and Museums
    Papers of Booker T. Washington
Unitarian Universalist Association of Congregations, Boston, Massachusetts
    Eighth Annual, 1891. Chicago: All Souls Church, 1891.
    Ninth Annual, 1892. Chicago: All Souls Church, 1892.
    Tenth Annual: All Souls Church. Chicago: Press of Metcalf Stationery Company, 1893.
University of Illinois at Chicago Special Collections
    Caroline Alden Huling Papers
Western Monroe Historical Society, Morgan Manning House, Brockport, New York
    Eunice Chestnut File Collection
    Fannie Barrier Williams (1855–1944)
Women's History and Resource Center, General Federation of Women's Clubs, Washington, D.C.
    General Federation of Women's Clubs Papers

Newspapers

The Afro-American Ledger (Baltimore)
American Baptist (Louisville, Kentucky)
The Appeal (Saint Paul, Minn.)
The Atlanta Constitution
Baltimore Afro-American
Broad Ax
The Brockport Post
Brockport Republic
Chicago Daily News
Chicago Daily Tribune
Chicago Defender
Chicago Record-Herald
The Chicago Sunday Tribune
Chicago Times-Herald
Chicago Tribune
The Cleveland Gazette (Ohio)
The Club Record
The Club Woman
The Colored American
The Constitution (Atlanta, Ga.)
Daily Public Ledger (Maysville, Ken.)
The Evening Critic (Washington, D.C.)
Evening Star (Washington, D.C.)
The Evening Times (Washington, D.C.)
Globe-Republican (Dodge City, Kansas)
The Kansas City Sun
The Langston City Herald (Langston City, Okla.)
Lapeer Democrat
The Minneapolis Journal
The Morning Call (San Francisco)
The Morning Times (Washington, D.C.)
National Republican (Washington, D.C.)
The New Age (Portland, Ore.)
The New York Age
New York Times
The Norfolk Weekly News-Journal
The North Star
The People's Advocate
Philadelphia Daily Ledger
Reno Evening Gazette (Reno, Nev.)
Richmond Planet (Richmond, Va.)
Rochester Daily Democrat
The San Francisco Call

San Francisco Chronicle
The Seattle Republican
The St. Paul Globe
The State Capital
The Washington Bee
The Washington Herald
Western Appeal (St. Paul and Minneapolis, Minn.)
The Woman's Era

Microfilm

Hamilton, Kenneth, ed. *Records of the National Negro Business League.* Part I. Bethesda, Md.: University Publications of America, 1995.

Williams, Lillian Serece, ed. *Records of the National Association of Colored Women's Clubs, 1895–1992.* Part 1, *Minutes of National Conventions, Publications, and President's Office Correspondence.* Bethesda, Md.: University Publications of America, 1993.

Books, Articles, Theses, and Dissertations

Anderson, James D. *The Education of Blacks in the South, 1860–1935.* Chapel Hill: University of North Carolina Press, 1988.

Andrews, William G. *Images of America around Brockport.* Charleston, S.C.: Arcadia Publishing, 2002.

Armfield, Felix L. *Eugene Kinckle Jones: The National Urban League and Black Social Work, 1910–1940.* Urbana: University of Illinois Press, 2012.

Ayers, Edward L. *The Promise of the New South: Life After Reconstruction.* New York: Oxford University Press, 1992.

Baldwin, Davarian L. *Chicago's New Negroes: Modernity, the Great Migration, and Black Urban Life.* Chapel Hill, N.C.: University of North Carolina Press, 2007.

Barnett, Evelyn Brooks. "Nannie Burroughs and the Education of Black Women." In *The Afro-American Woman Struggles and Images*, ed. Sharon Harley and Rosalyn Terborg-Penn, 97–108. Baltimore, Maryland: Black Classic Press, 1997.

Barnett, Ferdinand L. "The Reason Why." In Ida B. Wells, et al., *The Reason Why the Colored American Is Not in the World's Columbian Exposition*, ed. Robert W. Rydell, 68–69. Urbana, Illinois: University of Illinois Press, 1999.

Barrows, John Henry, ed. *The World's Parliament of Religions.* 2 vols. Chicago: Parliament Publishing Company, 1893.

Bay, Mia. *The White Image in the Black Mind: African-American Ideas about White People, 1830–1925.* New York: Oxford University Press, 2000.

Bearden, Jim, and Linda Jean Butler. *Shadd: The Life and Times of Mary Shadd Cary.* Toronto: NC Press, 1977.

Bethea, D. A., comp. *Colored People's Blue Book and Business Directory of Chicago, 1905.* Chicago: Celebrity Printing, 1905.

Blue, Robert L. *Footsteps into the Past: A History of the Columbiaville, Michigan Area.* Michigan: Columbiaville Historical Society, 1985.

Bontemps, Arna, and Jack Conroy, *Anyplace but Here.* New York: Doubleday, Doran, 1945; reprint ed., New York: Hill and Wang, 1966.

Bradwell, James B. "The Colored Bar of Chicago." *Michigan Law Journal* 5 (1896): 385–398.

Branham, Charles. "Black Chicago: Accommodationist Politics before the Great Migration." In *The Ethnic Frontier: Essays in the History of Group Survival in Chicago and the Midwest*, ed. Melvin G. Holli and Peter d'A. Jones, 219–221. Grand Rapids, Mich.: Eerdmans, 1977.

Bristol, Douglas W., Jr. "From Outposts to Enclaves: A Social History of Black Barbers, 1750–1915." Ph.D. diss., University of Maryland, 2002.

Brown, Lois. *Pauline Elizabeth Hopkins: Black Daughter of the Revolution*. Chapel Hill: University of North Carolina Press, 2008.

Bruce, John Edward. "Industrial Education; Will It Solve the Negro Problem?" *The Colored American Magazine* 7, no. 1 (1904): 17–21.

Buckler, Helen. *Daniel Hale Williams: Negro Surgeon*. 1954. Reprint, New York: Pitman, 1968.

Buhle, Mari Jo. *Women and American Socialism, 1870–1920*. Urbana: University of Illinois Press, 1981.

Burroughs, Nannie H. "Industrial Education—Will It Solve the Negro Problem[?]" *The Colored American Magazine* 7, no. 3 (1904): 188–190.

Bush, Charles T. *Hiel Brockway: The Story of Hiel Brockway, Founder of Brockport: His Life, His Descendants, His Ancestry*. Brockport, N.Y.: Western Monroe Historical Society, 1976.

Chaney, George L. "How to Help the South." *The Unitarian: A Magazine of Liberal Christianity* 11, no. 11 (November 1891): 530–531.

Chicago Commission on Race Relations. *The Negro in Chicago: A Study of Race Relations and a Riot*. Chicago: University of Chicago Press, 1922.

Chicago Women's Club. *14th Annual Announcement of the Chicago Women's Club, 1890–91*. Chicago: n.p., n.d.

———. *16th Annual Announcement of the Chicago Women's Club, 1892–93*. Chicago: Craig Press, n.d.

———. *18th Annual Announcement of the Chicago Women's Club, 1894–95*. Chicago: Press of the Eight Hour Herald.

———. *19th Annual Announcement of the Chicago Woman's Club, 1895–96*. Chicago: Wm. C. Hollister & Bros. Printers.

———. *20th Annual Announcement of the Chicago Woman's Club, 1896–97*. Chicago: A. N. Murdoch, Printer.

Coleman, Willi. "Black Women and Segregated Public Transportation: Ninety Years of Resistance." In *Black Women in United States History*, ed. Darlene Clark Hine, 5:295–302. New York: Carlson Publishing, 1990.

Collier-Thomas, Bettye. *Jesus, Jobs, and Justice: African American Women and Religion*. New York: Alfred A. Knopf, 2010.

———, ed. *A Treasury of African-American Christmas Stories*. New York: Henry Holt and Company, 1997.

Cooper, Mrs. A. J. "Discussion of the Same Subject by Mrs. A. J. Cooper of Washington, D.C." In *The World's Congress of Representative Women*, ed. May Wright Sewall, 711–715. Chicago and New York: Rand, McNally & Company, 1894.

Cromwell, John W. *History of the Bethel Literary and Historical Association.* Washington: Press of R. L. Pendleton, 1896.

Cross, Whitney R. *The Burned-Over District: The Social and Intellectual History of Enthusiastic Religion in Western New York, 1880–1850.* Ithaca, N.Y.: Cornell University Press, 1950.

Davis, Elizabeth Lindsay. *Lifting as They Climb.* 1933. Reprint, New York: G. K. Hall, 1996.

———. *The Story of the Illinois Federation of Colored Women's Clubs, 1900–1922.* Chicago: n.p., 1922.

Dedman, W. Wayne. *Cherishing This Heritage: The Centennial History of the State University College at Brockport, New York.* New York: Appleton-Century-Crofts, 1969.

Deegan, Mary Jo, ed. *The New Woman of Color: The Collected Writings of Fannie Barrier Williams, 1893–1918.* DeKalb, Ill.: Northern Illinois University Press, 2002.

Department of the Interior, U.S. Census Office. *Statistics of the Population of the United States at the Tenth Census (June 1, 1880).* Washington: Government Printing Office, 1883.

Detroit City Directory, 1890. Detroit: R. L. Polk & Co., 1890.

Drake, St. Clair, and Horace R. Cayton, *Black Metropolis: A Study of Negro Life in a Northern City.* Vol. 1. New York: Harper& Row, 1962.

Du Bois, W. E. B. "Industrial Education—Will It Solve the Negro Problem[?]" *The Colored American Magazine* 7, no. 5 (1904): 333–339.

Duster, Alfreda M., ed. *Crusade for Justice: The Autobiography of Ida B. Wells.* Chicago: University of Chicago Press, 1970.

Ensley, Elizabeth Piper. "What Equal Suffrage Has Done for Colorado." *The Woman's Era* (November 1894):13–14.

"Experiences of the Race Problem." *The Independent,* 56, no. 2885 (March 17, 1904): 590–594.

Field, Phyllis F. *The Politics of Race in New York: The Struggle for Black Suffrage in The Civil War Era.* Ithaca, N.Y.: Cornell University Press, 1982.

Fine, Lisa M. *The Souls of the Skyscraper: Female Clerical Workers in Chicago, 1870–1930.* Philadelphia: Temple University Press, 1990.

First Annual Report of the Illinois Woman's Alliance for the Year Ending November 1, 1889. Chicago: Purdy, 1890.

Flanagan, Maureen A. *Seeing with Their Hearts: Chicago Women and the Vision of the Good City, 1871–1933.* Princeton, N.J.: Princeton University Press, 2002.

Fortune, T. Thomas. "Industrial Education; Will It Solve the Negro Problem?" *The Colored American Magazine* 7, no. 1 (1904): 13–17.

Frank, Henriette Greenbaum, and Amalie Hofer Jerome. *Annals of the Chicago Woman's Club for the First Forty Years of Its Organization, 1876–1916.* Chicago: Chicago Woman's Club, 1916.

Gaines, Kevin K. *Uplifting the Race: Black Leadership, Politics, and Culture in the Twentieth Century.* Chapel Hill: University of North Carolina Press, 1996.

Gamble, Vanessa Northington. *Making a Place for Ourselves: The Black Hospital Movement, 1920–1945.* New York: Oxford University Press, 1995.

Garrison, William Lloyd. "Industrial Education—Will It Solve the Negro Problem[?]" *The Colored American Magazine* 7, no. 4 (1904): 188–190.

Gatewood, Willard B. *Aristocrats of Color: The Black Elite, 1880–1920.* 1991. Reprint, Fayetteville, Arkansas: University of Arkansas Press, 2000.

Gellman, David N., and David Quigley. *Jim Crow New York: A Documentary History of Race and Citizenship, 1777–1877.* New York: New York University Press, 2003.

Gibson, J. W., and W. H. Crogman. *The Colored American from Slavery to Honorable Citizenship.* Atlanta, Georgia: J. L. Nichols & Co., 1903.

Giddings, Paula J. *Ida: A Sword among Lions.* New York: Amistad, 2008.

———. *When and Where I Enter: The Impact of Black Women on Race and Sex in America.* New York: William Morrow and Company, 1984.

Gilbert, James. *Perfect Cities: Chicago's Utopias of 1893.* Chicago, Ill.: The University of Chicago Press, 1991.

Gilmore, Glenda Elizabeth. *Gender and Jim Crow: Women and the Politics of White Supremacy in North Carolina, 1896–1920.* Chapel Hill: University of North Carolina Press, 1996.

Gosnell, Harold F. *Negro Politicians: The Rise of Negro Politics in Chicago.* 1935. Reprint, Chicago: University of Chicago Press, 1967.

Green, Constance McLaughlin. *The Secret City: A History of Race Relations in the Nation's Capital.* Princeton, N.J.: Princeton University Press, 1967.

Greene, Lorenzo J., Gary R. Kremer, and Antonio F. Holland. *Missouri's Black Heritage.* Rev. ed. Columbia, Mo.: University of Missouri Press, 1993.

Greener, Richard R. "The First Congress of Colored Women." *A.M.E. Church Review* 30 (July 1913): 23–26.

Grimké, Charlotte Forten. *The Journals of Charlotte Forten Grimké.* Edited by Brenda Stevenson. New York: Oxford University Press, 1988.

Grossman, James R. *Land of Hope: Chicago, Black Southerners, and the Great Migration.* Chicago: University of Chicago Press, 1989.

Gullett, Gayle. "'Our great opportunity': Organized Women Advance Women's Work at the World's Columbian Exposition of 1893." *Illinois Historical Journal* 87 (Winter 1994): 259–276.

Hagood, J. Hurley, and Roberta (Roland) Hagood. *Hannibal Yesterdays: Historic Stories of Events, People, Landmarks, and Happenings in and near Hannibal.* Marceline, Mo.: Jostens, 1992.

———. *The Story of Hannibal.* Hannibal, Mo.: Hannibal Bicentennial Commission, 1976.

Haley, James T., comp. *Afro-American Encyclopedia; or, The Thoughts, Doings, and Sayings of the Race.* Nashville, Tennessee: Haley & Florida, 1895.

Harlan, Louis R. "Booker T. Washington and the *Voice of the Negro,* 1904–1970." *Journal of Southern History* 45 (February 1979): 45–62.

———. "The Secret Life of Booker T. Washington." *Journal of Southern History* 37 (August 1971): 393–416.

———, ed. *The Booker T. Washington Papers.* Vol. 3, *1889–95.* Urbana: University of Illinois Press, 1974.

———, ed. *The Booker T. Washington Papers.* Vol. 12, *1912–14.* Urbana: University of Illinois Press, 1975.

Harlan, Louis R., and Raymond Smock, eds. *The Booker T. Washington Papers.* Vol. 4, *1895–98.* Urbana: University of Illinois Press, 1975.

———, eds. *The Booker T. Washington Papers*. Vol. 8, *1904–6*. Urbana: University of Illinois Press.

Harper, Frances E. W. "Woman's Political Future—Address by Frances E. W. Harper of Virginia." In *The World's Congress of Representative Women*, ed. May Wright Sewall, 433–437. Chicago and New York: Rand, McNally & Company, 1894.

Harris, Leslie M. *In The Shadow of Slavery: African Americans in New York City, 1626–1863*. Chicago: University of Chicago Press, 2003.

Hendricks, Wanda A. *Gender, Race, and Politics in the Midwest: Black Club Women in Illinois*. Bloomington: Indiana University Press, 1998.

———. "'Vote for the advantage of ourselves and our race': The Election of the First Black Alderman in Chicago." *Illinois Historical Journal* 87 (Autumn 1994): 171–184.

Hewitt, Nancy A. *Women's Activism and Social Change: Rochester, New York, 1822–1872*. Ithaca, N.Y.: Cornell University Press, 1984.

———, and Suzanne Lebsock, eds. *Visible Women: New Essays on American Activism*. Urbana: University of Illinois Press, 1993.

Hicks, Cheryl D. *Talk with You Like a Woman: African American Women, Justice, and Reform in New York, 1890–1935*. Chapel Hill: University of North Carolina Press, 2010.

Higginbotham, Evelyn Brooks. "African-American Women's History and the Metalanguage of Race." *Signs: Journal of Women in Culture and Society* 17 (1992): 251–274.

———. *Righteous Discontent: The Woman's Movement in the Black Baptist Church, 1880–1920*. Cambridge, Mass.: Harvard University Press, 1993.

Hine, Darlene Clark. *Black Women in White: Racial Conflict and Cooperation in the Nursing Profession, 1890–1950*. Bloomington: Indiana University Press, 1989.

History of Monroe County, New York; With Illustrations Descriptive of Its Scenery, Palatial Residences, Public Buildings, Fine Blocks and Important Manufactories. Philadelphia: J. B. Lippincott & Co., 1877.

Holcombe, R. I. *History of Marion County, Missouri*. 1884. Reprint, Hannibal, Mo.: Marion County Historical Society, 1979.

Holli, Melvin G., and Peter d'A. Jones, eds. *The Ethnic Frontier: Essays in the History of Group Survival in Chicago and the Midwest*. Grand Rapids, Mich.: Eerdmans, 1977.

Horton, Edward A. "Industrial Education; Will It Solve the Negro Problem?" *The Colored American Magazine* 7, no. 6 (1904): 437–439.

Houde, Mary Jean. *The Clubwoman: A Story of the Illinois Federation of Women's Clubs*. [Chicago]: Illinois Federation of Women's Clubs, 1970.

———. *Reaching Out: A Story of the General Federation of Women's Clubs*. Chicago: The Mobium Press, 1989.

"In Dixie Land." *The Colored American* 10, no. 31 (February 13, 1904): 2.

"In Memoriam." *The Michigan Technic* 23 (January 1910).

Johnson, David A. *The Fair Women: Women at the 1893 World Parliament of Religions*. Occasional Paper #18. Malden, Mass.: Unitarian Universalist Women's Heritage Society, 1998.

Johnson, Paul E. *A Shopkeeper's Millennium: Society and Revivals in Rochester, New York, 1815–1837*. New York: Hill and Wang, 2004.

Jones, Jenkin Lloyd. *A Chorus of Faith as Heard in the World Parliament of Religions.* Chicago: Unity Publishing Company, 1893.

Junger, Richard. "'God and man helped those who helped themselves': John and Mary Jones and the Culture of African American Self-Sufficiency in Mid-Nineteenth-Century Chicago." *Journal of Illinois History* 11 (Summer 2008): 111–132.

Knupfer, Anne Meis. *Toward a Tenderer Humanity and a Nobler Womanhood: African American Women's Clubs in Turn-of-the-Century Chicago.* New York: New York University Press, 1996.

Kraditor, Aileen S. *The Ideas of the Woman Suffrage Movement, 1890–1920.* New York: W. W. Norton & Company, 1981; Columbia University Press, 1965.

Lee, Koby. *Friendship across the Color Line: Celia Parker Woolley and Fannie Barrier Williams.* Occasional Paper #15. Malden, Mass.: Unitarian Universalist Women's Heritage Society, 1997.

Lee-Forman, Koby. "The Simple Love of Truth: The Racial Justice Activism of Celia Parker Woolley." Ph.D. diss., Northwestern University, 1995.

Lewis, David Levering. *W. E. B. Du Bois: Biography of a Race, 1868–1919.* New York: Henry Holt and Company, 1993.

Litwack, Leon F. *North of Slavery: The Negro in the Free States, 1790–1860.* Chicago: University of Chicago Press, 1961.

"Lynch Law and Riot in Ohio." *The Independent* 56, no. 2885 (March 17, 1904): 580.

Lyttle, Charles H. *Freedom Moves West: A History of the Western Unitarian Conference, 1852–1952.* Boston: Beacon Press, 1952.

Marks, Carole. *Farewell—We're Good and Gone: The Great Black Migration.* Bloomington: Indiana University Press, 1989.

Marsh, Allan Thomas. "Washington's First Art Academy, The Corcoran School of Art, 1875–1925." Ph.D. diss., University of Maryland, 1983.

Martin, Charlotte Elizabeth. *The Story of Brockport for One-Hundred Years, 1829–1929.* Brockport, New York: 1929.

Materson, Lisa G. *For the Freedom of Her Race: Black Women and Electoral Politics in Illinois, 1877–1932.* Chapel Hill: University of North Carolina Press, 2009.

Mather, Frank Lincoln, ed. *Who's Who of the Colored Race: A General Biographical Dictionary of Men and Women of African Descent.* Vol. 1. 1915. Reprint, Detroit: Gale Research Company, 1976.

McFeely, William S. *Frederick Douglass.* New York: W. W. Norton & Company, 1991.

McHenry, Elizabeth. *Forgotten Readers: Recovering the Lost History of African American Literary Societies.* Durham, N.D.: Duke University Press, 2002.

McMillen, Neil R. *Dark Journey: Black Mississippians in the Age of Jim Crow.* Urbana: University of Illinois Press, 1990.

McMurry, Linda O. *Recorder of the Black Experience: A Biography of Monroe Nathan Work.* Baton Rouge: Louisiana State University Press, 1985.

McPherson, Bruce, and James Klein. *Measure by Measure: A History of New England Conservatory from 1867.* Boston: Trustees of New England Conservatory of Music, 1995.

Miller, Kelley. "Industrial Education—Will It Solve the Negro Problem[?]" *The Colored American Magazine* 7, no. 3 (1904): 185–187.

Minutes of the Meeting of the Council of Administration of the World's Columbian Exposition Held at Jackson Park, Tuesday, April 18th, 1893, at 10:00 O'clock A.M. Chicago: Henson Bros., 1893.

Moore, Jacqueline M. *Leading the Race: The Transformation of the Black Elite in the Nation's Capital, 1880–1920.* Charlottesville: University Press of Virginia, 1999.

Mounter, Michael Robert. "Richard Theodore Greener: The Idealist, Statesman, Scholar and South Carolinian." Ph.D. diss., University of South Carolina, 2002.

"News from the Field." *The Unitarian: A Magazine of Liberal Christianity* 9, no. 3 (March 1894): 138–144.

"Observations of the Southern Race Feeling." *The Independent* 56, no. 2885 (March 17, 1904): 594–599.

Official Register of the United States Containing a List of Officers and Employees in the Civil, Military, and Naval Service on the First of July, 1883; Together with a List of Ships and Vessels Belonging to the United States. Vol. 1. Washington, D.C.: Government Printing Office, 1883.

Paddon, Anna R., and Sally Turner. "African Americans and the World's Columbian Exposition." *Illinois Historical Journal* 88 (Spring 1995): 19–36.

Painter, Nell Irvin. *Sojourner Truth: A Life, a Symbol.* New York: W. W. Norton & Company, 1996.

Philpott, Thomas Lee. *The Slum and the Ghetto: Immigrants, Blacks, and Reformers in Chicago, 1880–1930.* Belmont, California: Wadsworth Publishing Company, 1991.

Pierce, Bessie Louise. *A History of Chicago.* Vol. 3, *The Rise of a Modern City, 1871–1893.* New York: Alfred A. Knopf, 1957.

Powers, Marion Daniel. "The Development of Public Education in Hannibal, Missouri, with Special Emphasis on the Education of the Negro." MA thesis, Lincoln University, 1948.

Preston, E. Delorus, Jr. "William Syphax, a Pioneer in Negro Education in the District of Columbia." *Journal of Negro History* 20 (October 1935): 448–476.

"The Race Problem—An Autobiography." *The Independent* 56, no. 2885 (March 17, 1904): 586–589.

Reed, Christopher Robert. *"All the World Is Here!" The Black Presence at White City.* Bloomington: Indiana University Press, 2000.

———. *The Chicago NAACP and the Rise of Black Professional Leadership, 1910–1966.* Bloomington: Indiana University Press, 1997.

———. *The Rise of Chicago's Black Metropolis, 1920–1929.* Urbana: University of Illinois Press, 2011.

Rhodes, Jane. *Mary Ann Shadd Cary: The Black Press and Protest in the Nineteenth Century.* Bloomington, Indiana: Indiana University Press, 1998.

Rice, Mitchell F., and Woodrow Jones Jr. *Public Policy and the Black Hospital from Slavery to Segregation to Integration.* Westport, Conn.: Greenwood Press, 1994.

Richardson, Heather Cox. *The Death of Reconstruction: Race, Labor, and Politics in the Post-Civil War North, 1865–1901.* Cambridge, Mass.: Harvard University Press, 2001.

Robb, Frederic H., comp. *Intercollegian Wonder Book, or The Negro in Chicago, 1779–1927.* Vol. 1. Chicago: The Washington Intercollegiate Club of Chicago, 1927.

Rudwick, Elliott. *Race Riot at East St. Louis, July 2, 1917.* Urbana: University of Illinois Press, 1982.

Rudwick, Elliot M., and August Meier. "Black Man in the 'White City': Negroes and the Columbian Exposition, 1893." *Phylon* 26 (1965): 354–361.

Rydell, Robert W., ed. *The Reason Why the Colored American Is Not in the World's Columbian Exposition*. Urbana: University of Illinois Press, 1999.

Salem, Dorothy. *To Better Our World: Black Women in Organized Reform, 1890–1920*. Vol. 14 of *Black Women in United States History*, ed. Darlene Clark Hine. New York: Carlson, 1990.

Schechter, Patricia A. *Ida B. Wells-Barnett and American Reform, 1880–1930*. Chapel Hill: University of North Carolina Press, 2001.

"A School for Industrial Education in the South." *The Unitarian: A Magazine of Liberal Christianity* 1, no. 1 (January 1892): 27–28.

Schwieder, Dorothy, Joseph Hraba, and Elmer Schwieder. *Buxton: Work and Racial Equality in a Coal Mining Community*. Ames: Iowa State University Press, 1987.

Senechal, Roberta. *The Sociogenesis of a Race Riot: Springfield, Illinois, in 1908*. Urbana: University of Illinois Press, 1990.

Sernett, Milton C. *North Star Country: Upstate New York and the Crusade for African American Freedom*. New York: Syracuse University Press, 2002.

Sewall, May Wright, ed. *The World's Congress of Representative Women*. Chicago and New York: Rand, McNally, 1894.

Shaw, Stephanie. "Black Club Women and the Creation of the National Association of Colored Women." In *"We Specialize in the Wholly Impossible": A Reader in Black Women's History*, ed. Darlene Clark Hine, Wilma King, and Linda Reed, 433–447. New York: Carlson, 1995.

Siry, Joseph. "Frank Lloyd Wright's Unity Temple and Architecture for Liberal Religion in Chicago, 1885–1909." *The Art Bulletin* 73, no. 2 (June 1991): 257–282.

Sisk, Glenn N. "Negro Education in the Alabama Black Belt, 1875–1900." *The Journal of Negro Education* 22, no. 2 (Spring 1953): 126–135.

Smith, Mary E., and Shirley Cox Husted, eds. *We Remember Brockport: Reminiscences of 19th Century Village History*. Brockport, N.Y.: Monroe County Historians Office, 1979.

Somerville, James K. "Homesick in Upstate New York: The Saga of Sidney Roby, 1843–1847." *New York History* 72 (April 1991): 179–196.

Spear, Allan H. *Black Chicago: The Making of a Negro Ghetto, 1890–1920*. Chicago: University of Chicago Press, 1967.

Stone, Alfred Holt. "The Economic Future of the Negro: The Factor of White Competition." *American Economic Association Publications*, series 3, vol. 7 (February 1906): 243–294.

Stowe, Charles E. Hambrick. *Charles G. Finney and the Spirit of American Evangelicalism*. Grand Rapids, Mich.: Wm. B. Eerdmans Publishing, 1996.

Strane, Susan. *A Whole-Souled Woman: Prudence Crandall and the Education of Black Women*. New York: W. W. Norton & Company, 1990.

Strickland, Arvarh E. *History of the Chicago Urban League*. Urbana: University of Illinois Press, 1966.

Terborg-Penn, Rosalyn. *African American Women in the Struggle for the Vote, 1850–1920*. Bloomington: Indiana University Press, 1998.

Terrell, Mary Church. "The Washington Conservatory of Music for Colored People, and Its Teachers." *The Voice of the Negro* 1 (November 1904): 525–530.

Tetrault, Lisa. "The Incorporation of American Feminism: Suffragists and the Postbellum Lyceum." *Journal of American History* 96, no. 4 (2010): 1027–1056.

Thompson, Donald Alexander. "The First Unitarian Society of Chicago: Its Relation to a Changing Community." BD diss., Meadville Theological School, Chicago, 1933.

Tindall, George Brown. *South Carolina Negroes, 1877–1900.* Columbia: University of South Carolina Press, 1952.

Truman, Benjamin C. *History of the World's Fair Being a Complete and Authentic Description of the Columbia Exposition from Its Inception.* 1893. Reprint, New York: Arno Press, 1976.

Tucker, Cynthia Grant. *Prophetic Sisterhood: Liberal Women Ministers of the Frontier, 1880–1930.* Boston: Beacon Press, 1990.

Tuttle, Ray. *The Village of Brockport.* Brockport, New York: 1940.

Tuttle, William M., Jr., "Contested Neighborhoods and Racial Violence: Prelude to the Chicago Riot of 1919." *The Journal of Negro History* 55 (October 1970): 273–275.

———. *Race Riot: Chicago in the Red Summer of 1919.* New York: Atheneum, 1977.

United States. Bureau of the Census. *The Seventh Census of the United States: 1850. Embracing a Statistical View of Each of the States and Territories, Arranged by Counties, Towns, Etc.* Vol. 1. 1853. Reprint, New York: Norman Ross, 1990.

United States. Census Office. Department of State. *Sixth Census or Enumeration of the Inhabitants of the United States as Corrected at the Department of State in 1840.* Vol. 1. 1841. Reprint, New York: Norman Ross, 1990.

United States. Department of the Interior. Census Office. *Statistics of the Population of the United States at the Tenth Census (June 1, 1880).* Vol. 1. 1883. Reprint, New York: Norman Ross, 1990.

———. *Report on Population of the Census of the United States at the Eleventh Census: 1890.* Vol. 1. 1895. Reprint, New York: Norman Ross, 1990

United States. Department of State. *Fifth Census; or Enumeration of the Inhabitants of the United States, to Which Is Prefixed a Schedule of the Whole Number of Persons within Several Districts of the United States, Taken According to the Acts of 1790, 1800, 1810, 1820.* 1832. Reprint, New York: Norman Ross, 1990.

Walker, Francis Amasa. *The Statistics of the Population of the United States, Embracing the Tables of Race, Nationality, Sex, Selected Ages, and Occupations, to Which Are Added the Statistics of School Attendance and Illiteracy, of Schools, Libraries, Newspapers and Periodicals, Churches, Pauperism and Crime, and of Areas, Families, and Dwellings, Compiled from the Original Returns of the Ninth Census (June 1, 1870).* Vol. 1. 1872. Reprint, New York: Norman Ross, 1990.

Warren, Francis H. *Michigan Manual of Freedmen's Progress.* Detroit: J. M. Green, 1915.

Washington, Booker T. "Industrial Education; Will It Solve the Negro Problem[?]" *The Colored American Magazine* 7, no. 2 (1904): 87–92.

———. *Frederick Douglass.* 1906. Reprint, New York: Argosy-Antiquarian Ltd., 1969.

———. "The Tuskegee Normal School." *The Unitarian: A Magazine of Liberal Christianity* 1, no. 11 (November 1890): 551.

———, ed. *A New Negro for a New Century: An Accurate and Up-to-Date Record of the Upward Struggle of the Negro Race.* Chicago: American Publishing House, 1900.

Washington, Margaret. *Sojourner Truth's America*. Urbana: University of Illinois Press, 2009.

Weinman, Jeanne Madeline. *The Fair Women*. Chicago: Academy Chicago, 1981.

Weiss, Beverly J. "An African American Teacher in Washington, D.C.: Marion P. Shadd (1856–1943)." In *Lives of Women Public School Teachers: Scenes from American Educational History*, ed. Madelyn Holmes and Beverly Weiss, 191–218. New York: Garland Publishing, 1995.

Wellman, Judith. "Crossing Over Cross: Whitney Cross's Burned-Over District as Social History." *Reviews in American History* 17, no. 1 (1989): 159–174.

Wesley, Charles Harris. *The History of the National Association of Colored Women's Clubs: A Legacy of Service*. Washington, D.C.: Mercury Press, 1984.

Wheeler, Adade Mitchell, and Marlene Stein Wortman. *The Roads They Made: Women in Illinois History*. Chicago: Charles H. Kerr Publishing Company, 1977.

Wheeler, Marjorie Spruill. *New Women of the New South: The Leaders of the Woman Suffrage Movement in the Southern States*. New York: Oxford University Press, 1993.

White, Deborah Gray. "The Cost of Club Work, the Price of Black Feminism." In *Visible Women: New Essays on American Activism*, ed. Nancy A. Hewitt and Suzanne Lebsock, 247–269. Urbana: University of Illinois Press, 1993.

———. *Too Heavy a Load: Black Women in Defense of Themselves, 1894–1994*. New York: W. W. Norton & Company, 1999.

Wilkerson, Isabel. *The Warmth of Other Suns: The Epic Story of America's Great Migration*. New York: Random House, 2010.

Williams, Fannie Barrier. "After Many Days: A Christmas Story." In *A Treasury of African-American Christmas Stories*, ed. Bettye Collier-Thomas, 132–162. New York: Henry Holt and Company, 1997. Originally published in *The Colored American Magazine* 6, no. 2 (December 1902): 140–153.

———. "The Awakening of Women." *A.M.E. Church Review*, 13, no. 4 (Spring 1897): 392–398.

———. Chicago's Provident Hospital and Training School: Social Matters." *The Woman's Era* 3, no.4 (October and November 1896): 13–14.

———. "Club Movement among Negro Women." In J. W. Gibson and W. H. Crogman, *The Colored American from Slavery to Honorable Citizenship*, 197–232. Atlanta, Georgia: J. L. Nichols & Co., 1903.

———. "The Club Movement among Colored Women in America." In *A New Negro for a New Century: An Accurate and Up-to-Date Record of the Upward Struggle of the Negro Race*, ed. Booker T. Washington, 379–428. Chicago: American Publishing House, 1900.

———. "The Club Movement among the Colored Women," *The Voice of the Negro* 1, no. 3 (March 1904): 99–102.

———. "The Colored Girl." *The Voice of the Negro* 2, no. 6 (June 1905): 400–403.

———. "Colored Women of Chicago." *The Southern Workman* 43 (October 1914): 564–566.

———. "The Colored Woman of To-Day: Some Notable Types of the Present Generation in America." *Godey's Magazine* 135 (July 1897): 28–32.

———. "The Council at St. Paul." *The Colored American* 11, no. 16 (August 2, 1902): 5.

———. "Do We Need Another Name?" *The Southern Workman* 33, no. 1 (January 1904): 33–36.

——. "Dr. Booker T. Washington in Chicago." *The Colored American*, 10, no. 38 (April 16, 1904), 4–5.

——. "An Extension of the Conference Spirit." *The Voice of the Negro* 1, no. 7 (July 1904): 300–303.

——. "The Frederick Douglass Center." *The Southern Workman* 35, no. 6 (June 1906): 334–336.

——. "The Frederick Douglass Center" A Question of Social Betterment and Not Social Equality." *The Voice of the Negro* 1, no. 12 (December 1904): 601–604.

——. "Great Britain's Compliment to American Colored Women." *The Woman's Era* 1, no. 5 (August 1894): 1.

——. "A Growing Negro Center." *The Colored American* 9, no. 24 (October 4, 1902): 13.

——. "A Growing Negro Center." *The Colored American*, 9, no. 26 (October 18, 1902): 11.

——. "Industrial Education—Will It Solve The Negro Problem[?]" *The Colored American Magazine* 7, no. 7 (July 1904): 491–495.

——. "The Influence of Art on Home Life." *The Woman's Era* 2, no. 12 (May 1896): 13–14.

——. "The Intellectual Progress of the Colored Women of the United States since the Emancipation Proclamation—An Address by Fannie Barrier Williams of Illinois." In *The World's Congress of Representative Women*, ed. May Wright Sewall, 696–711. Chicago, 1893.

——. "Need of Co-Operation of Men and Women in Correctional Work." *The Woman's Era* 2, no. 2 (May 1895): 4–5.

——. "The Need of Organized Womanhood." *The Colored American Magazine* 15, no. 1 (January 1909): 652–653.

——. "The Need of Social Settlement Work for the City Negro." *Southern Workman* 33, no. 9 (September 1904): 501–506.

——. "The Negro and Public Opinion." *The Voice of the Negro* 1, no. 1 (January 1904): 31–32.

——. "A New Method of Dealing with the Race Problem." *The Voice of the Negro* 3, no. 7 (July 1906): 502–505.

——. "A Northern Negro's Autobiography." *The Independent* 57, no. 2902 (July 14, 1904): 91–96.

——. "Opportunities and Responsibilities of Colored Women." In *Afro-American Encyclopaedia; Or, The Thoughts, Doings, and Sayings of the Race*, compiled and arranged by James T. Haley, 146–161. Nashville, Tennessee: Haley & Florida, 1895.

——. "Perils of the White Negro." *The Colored American Magazine* 13, no. 6 (1907): 421–423.

——. "The Problem of Employment for Negro Women." *Southern Workman* 32, no. 9 (September 1903): 432–437.

——. "Refining Influence of Art." *The Voice of the Negro* 3, no. 3 (March 1906): 211–214.

——. "Smaller Economies." *The Voice of the Negro* 1, no. 5 (May 1904): 184–185.

——. "Social Bonds in the 'Black Belt' of Chicago." In *The Collected Writings of Fannie Barrier Williams 1893–1918*, ed. Mary J. Deegan, 117–124. DeKalb: Northern Illinois University Press, 2002.

——. "The Timely Message of the Simple Life." *The Voice of the Negro* 2, no. 3 (March 1905): 160–162.

———. "Vacation Values." *The Voice of the Negro* 2, no. 12 (December 1905): 863–866.

———. "What Can Religion Further Do to Advance the Condition of the Negro?" In *The World's Parliament of Religions, an Illustrated and Popular Story of the World's First Parliament of Religions, Held in Chicago in Connection with the Columbian Exposition of 1893*, vol. 2, ed. John Henry Barrows, 114–115. Chicago: Parliament Publishing Co., 1893.

———. "The Woman's Part in a Man's Business." *The Voice of the Negro* 1, no. 11 (November 1904): 543–547.

———. "Women in Politics." *The Woman's Era* 1, no. 8 (November 1894): 12–13.

———. "A Word of Tribute to John Brown." *The Woman's Era* 1, no. 9 (December 1894): 15–17.

———. "Work Attempted and Missed in Organized Club Work." *The Colored American Magazine* 14, no. 5 (1908): 282–285.

Williams, L. C. *Historical Sketch of the First Baptist Church Brockport, New York*. Rochester, New York: The Genesee Press, 1908.

Woodson, Carter G. "The Gibbs Family." *The Negro History Bulletin* 11, no. 1 (October 1947): 3–12, 22.

———. "Honor to Booker T. Washington." *The Negro History Bulletin* 10, no. 6 (March 1947): 123–129, 143.

———. "The Wormley Family." *The Negro History Bulletin* 11, no. 4 (January 1948): 75–84.

Woolley, Celia Parker. "The Frederick Douglass Center, Chicago." *The Commons: A Monthly Record Devoted to Aspects of Life and Labor from the Social Settlement Point of View* 9, no. 7 (July 1904): 328–329.

Index

WANDA A. HENDRICKS is an associate professor of history at the University of South Carolina and is the author of *Gender, Race, and Politics in the Midwest: Black Club Women in Illinois.*

The New Black Studies Series

Beyond Bondage: Free Women of Color in the Americas
  Edited by David Barry Gaspar and Darlene Clark Hine
The Early Black History Movement, Carter G. Woodson,
  and Lorenzo Johnston Greene   *Pero Gaglo Dagbovie*
"Baad Bitches" and Sassy Supermamas:
  Black Power Action Films   *Stephane Dunn*
Black Maverick: T. R. M. Howard's Fight for Civil Rights
  and Economic Power   *David T. Beito and Linda Royster Beito*
Beyond the Black Lady: Sexuality and the New African American
  Middle Class   *Lisa B. Thompson*
Extending the Diaspora: New Histories of Black People
  Dawne Y. Curry, Eric D. Duke, and Marshanda A. Smith
Activist Sentiments: Reading Black Women
  in the Nineteenth Century   *P. Gabrielle Foreman*
Black Europe and the African Diaspora   *Edited by Darlene Clark Hine,*
  Trica Danielle Keaton, and Stephen Small
Freeing Charles: The Struggle to Free a Slave on the Eve
  of the Civil War   *Scott Christianson*
African American History Reconsidered   *Pero Gaglo Dagbovie*
Freud Upside Down: African American Literature
  and Psychoanalytic Culture   *Badia Sahar Ahad*
A. Philip Randolph and the Struggle for Civil Rights   *Cornelius L. Bynum*
Queer Pollen: White Seduction, Black Male Homosexuality,
  and the Cinematic   *David A. Gerstner*
The Rise of Chicago's Black Metropolis, 1920–1929   *Christopher Robert Reed*
Living with Lynching: African American Lynching Plays,
  Performance, and Citizenship, 1890–1930   *Koritha Mitchell*
Africans to Spanish America: Expanding the Diaspora
  Edited by Sherwin K. Bryant, Rachel Sarah O'Toole, & Ben Vinson III
Rebels and Runaways: Slave Resistance
  in Nineteenth-Century Florida   *Larry Eugene Rivers*
The Black Chicago Renaissance   *Edited by Darlene Clark Hine*
  and John McCluskey Jr.
The Negro in Illinois: The WPA Papers   *Edited by Brian Dolinar*
Along the Streets of Bronzeville: Black Chicago's
  Literary Landscape   *Elizabeth Schlabach*
Gendered Resistance: Women, Slavery, and the Legacy
  of Margaret Garner   *Edited by Mary E. Fredrickson and Delores M. Walters*
Racial Blackness and the Discontinuity of Western Modernity   *Lindon Barrett,*
  edited by Justin A. Joyce, Dwight A. McBride, and John Carlos Rowe
Fannie Barrier Williams: Crossing the Borders
  of Region and Race   *Wanda A. Hendricks*

The University of Illinois Press
is a founding member of the
Association of American University Presses.

———————————————————————

Composed in 11/13 Adobe Minion Pro
by Lisa Connery
at the University of Illinois Press
Manufactured by Sheridan Books, Inc.

University of Illinois Press
1325 South Oak Street
Champaign, IL 61820-6903
www.press.uillinois.edu